Kentucky Hospitality

Illustrations by Miriam Woolfolk

Kentucky Hospitality
A 200-Year Tradition

Dorothea C. Cooper, Editor

With an Introduction by Jay Anderson
& Historical Essays by Various Hands

Kentucky Federation of Women's Clubs 1976

Contents

Preface

Kentucky is the oldest state west of the Allegheny Mountains. The people and their style of life reflect the traditions of Old Virginia and those of the many ethnic and religious groups who settled here. Enhanced by the beauty of the mountains in the east, the bluegrass in the central area, and the lakes and caves in the west, it is a colorful state with a style of hospitality all its own. This book, a Bicentennial project of the Kentucky Federation of Women's Clubs, attempts to bring you the essence of Kentucky in the essays, the illustrations, and the recipes.

Most of the recipes are from the twentieth century. Some are handed down from an earlier era. And a few are only intended to be read for enjoyment. Among the contributors are representatives of Kentucky's oldest families, as well as those of newcomers, and the noted eating places that have added to our heritage. The recipes, although not original, are largely the favorites of Federation members.

The Kentucky Federation of Women's Clubs wishes to express our appreciation to the University Press of Kentucky for their advice and cooperation in making this book possible; and to express a special tribute to those firms who assisted so generously in this Bicentennial effort: Magna-Graphic, Incorporated, Nationwide Paper Company, Courier-Journal Lithographing Company, and the C. J. Krehbiel Company. We also wish to thank those who wrote the historical essays for the book. Mrs. Damon Harrison, Kentucky Archivist, was extremely helpful in locating material.

We are grateful to the Federation members who contributed recipes, historical data, and personal interest stories and to the restaurants who permitted their recipes to be reproduced in this book. We regret that space limitations made it impossible to print all recipes and stories that were contributed.

Dorothea C. Cooper

An Introduction to Kentucky Foodways

Jay Anderson

The test of a regional cookbook is its success in reflecting the uniqueness of the foodways of a particular place. Does it acknowledge the importance of the people who call the region home and examine the ways in which their culture has shaped their choice of food and the way it is prepared and served? Does it balance this important human factor with the equally crucial physical or environmental influences which frequently define what potential foodstuffs are available and which create a seasonality of diet? And finally, does the book through its recipes offer a record of the variety of dishes which have been perfected and used throughout the region's history by a wide range of its inhabitants in all of its diverse locales?

Kentucky Hospitality: A 200–Year Tradition meets the test. It is a reminder to Kentuckians of their gastronomic heritage. Friends of Kentucky will also appreciate the wealth of historic material here and perhaps be surprised by the significance of Kentucky's contribution to American foodways. Brillat-Savarin once wrote that "the discovery of a new dish does more for the happiness of mankind than the discovery of a star." Kentucky "discovered" Bibb lettuce, mint juleps, bourbon, and burgoo (to cite four excellent examples), and mankind is obviously the happier for them. But there are many more dishes, and *Kentucky Hospitality* is a suitable guide to them and the traditions they represent.

The Kentucky tradition begins with people: the Indian hunters, gatherers, and farmers who settled the Commonwealth's mountains and plains thousands of years ago and the European settlers and their black slaves who followed in the late eighteenth and early nineteenth century. Each ethnic group which came brought its own foodways— ideas about what plants and animals are edible, how they should be procured, preserved, and prepared, when they should be eaten and by whom, and what the gastronomic effects would be. These ideas, as Gerald Alvey points out in his essay (pp. 11–19), are rooted in a society's cultural history and are extremely durable.

The first people to contribute to Kentucky's foodways were the Creek, Chickasaw, Cherokee, and Shawnee Indian tribes of the eastern American woodlands. Through centuries of experimentation they discovered what wild plants and animals were fit for human consumption. Many of the wild foods mentioned by Otis Rice in his essay (pp. 20–28) were staples in the Indian diet: bear, deer, elk, turkey, buffalo, nuts, fruits, and greens. Yet even more important to the Indians were the wild plants domesticated over thousands of years: corn, pumpkin, beans and squashes. These comprised the heart of their foodways complex. This hunting and agricultural economy provided most tribes with a varied yet balanced diet year round. Their success at survival was respected by the early Appalachian explorers and the Long Hunters, who borrowed the Indians' foods, hunting, and husbandry, and even their preservation and cooking skills. Elizabeth Helton's discussion of food preservation (pp. 286–93) cites some of these cultural borrowings, such as drying corn and pumpkins. And many of the recipes in this book are of Indian origin: burgoo, hoe cakes, jerusalem artichokes, poke sallet, and sassafras tea, to name a few. In short, the Indian contribution to Kentucky's and America's foodways is significant.

No less impressive is the impact of the Scotch-Irish. Over 250,000 of these Lowland Scotsmen emigrated to America from Presbyterian colonies in Ulster in the eighteenth century. Life in the Appalachian mountain wilderness with all its dangers they found preferable to the continuing misery of life in war-torn and poverty-ridden Ireland. Many settled in western Pennsylvania but a vanguard trekked southwestward down the valley trails of Virginia into the coves and hollows of the harsh Cumberlands, where they settled. For them, Kentucky was the best land for a poor man. Clannish and independent, the Scots dug in and evolved foodways that perfectly meshed Indian traditions, which they freely borrowed, with their own culinary heritage. The farming economy they established, with its emphasis on corn, garden vegetables, wild greens, and milk, laid the basis for Kentucky's folk foodways. The Scots' mastery of corn was total. Using the limited inventory of kitchen equipment described by Marcia Cebulska (pp. 29–35), they perfected a variety of porridges, pancakes, and hot breads ranging from green corn pudding to cornmeal batter cakes, hoe cakes, and cracklin' corn bread. Corn provided their staff of life. Augmenting this starch was a variety of vegetable dishes. Scots women were excellent kitchen gardeners and worked wonders with green beans, potatoes, and a variety of salads, such as dandelion greens. The Scots were also inordinately fond of milk products. They found Kentucky ideal for dairying and by 1800 their butter was being shipped downriver to New Orleans and the West Indies. The buttermilk stayed home, however, and was put into growing children and such dishes as baked hominy and soda biscuits.

But paramount among the Scots' contribution to Kentucky's heritage is corn whiskey, the "hosesome beverage" that Marie Campbell writes about so ably (pp. 132–38). In Scotland and Ireland, farmers had perfected techniques for the inexpensive home distillation of surplus grain, usually barley, into whiskey, an easily transportable and highly marketable product. In Pennsylvania, the Scots experimented with rye and later corn, creating beverages different from but no less worthy than their Old World malt whiskey. Desire for this product rose sharply during the American Revolution, when the supply of cheap rum from the West Indies was generally cut off. After the war, the demand increased and a lively trade developed between the frontier and the eastern seaboard. Western Pennsylvania farmers could not meet the growing need and when Kentucky opened up it quickly became a major whiskey producer. Kentucky's perfect corn-growing climate and soil, its limestone water, and seemingly endless hardwood forests all contributed to the quality of the beverage. A skilled

Kentucky farmer could produce eighty gallons of sour-mash whiskey from an acre of corn, and many did. Sometime early in the nineteenth century the tradition of aging whiskey in charred oak barrels developed and bourbon was born. It quickly became the standard by which all other American whiskeys were to be judged. The impact of the Kentucky Scots couldn't have been more complete.

Englishmen comprise the third major group to influence Kentucky's foodways. Unlike the Indians and Scots, English settlers came from a thousand-year tradition of successful family farming around small market towns. On the broad plains of the English Midlands and East Anglia (the regions from which most immigrants came) farmers maintained a balance between grain, meat, dairy products, and fruits and vegetables. Much food was preserved from seasons of plenty (summer and fall) for use in seasons of need (winter and spring). And generally enough food was raised to provide the household with both a good diet and a surplus to market. Cash earned in this way could then be invested in improved stock, especially horses, and luxury items such as wine, imported foods, and spices. This English tradition was transplanted to Virginia, Pennsylvania, and the Carolinas, and from there to Kentucky, particularly the Bluegrass region, where the standard of living for farm families soon surpassed that of most other states. As Mary Clay (pp. 36–42) and Burton Milward note (pp. 50–61), by 1800 Kentucky's larger towns possessed a style of living "nearly as fashionable as the urban areas of the East." This prosperity was a direct result of the successful transplantation of the English rural economic system.

Examples of English dishes which became traditional in Kentucky abound. Preserved foods such as country ham, pickles, fruit butters, marmalades, and preserves, and cured beef are English in origin. Add to them most of this book's pie and cake recipes and such entrées as roast goose, pheasant, pork sausage, fried chicken, and fried oysters, and the English legacy becomes monumental. Without it, Kentucky's foodways would be considerably diminished in quality and variety.

Other early settlers, such as the blacks brought in as slaves and the Germans, also made important contributions in dishes such as okra, shrimp creole, sour meat, and springerle. And the Frenchmen fleeing the unrest in their own land, as Burton Milward tells us, brought their own sophisticated cuisine. But the foundation of Kentucky's foodways was laid by the Indians, Scots, and English.

Another element besides ethnicity strongly influenced the development of Kentucky's foodways. Although we think today that the settlement of Kentucky was mainly by poor pioneers, in fact there were many "middle-class" settlers. The eastern states, and later Kentucky, offered immigrants bent on improving themselves economically the opportunity to do so. Land, the most important commodity, was plentiful, the climate was favorable in most places for a balanced mixture of European and American crops, and markets were developing as settlements grew. Most important, however, was the freedom and independence America offered. Individuals were not held back by a restricting feudal system which relegated them to the status in life into which they were born. America offered the opportunity to move up the economic ladder. An indentured servant could become a tenant farmer and even a yeoman freeholder if he worked and fought hard. Before the settlement of Kentucky, tens of thousands of immigrants had done just this and a strong rural middle class had developed in the seaboard states. Many of these yeoman farmers saw in Kentucky a second, more promising opportunity to model their lives on those of the Virginia planters. They had money enough or land grants to acquire large tracts of land and establish farms quickly. Many seized this opportunity, and Kentucky's prosperity and its foodways developed quickly as a result.

A second crucial factor in the shaping of Kentucky's foodways was geography. Simply put, Kentucky's natural environment is ideal for fostering a rich variety of foods. A good example is topography. The broad plains of central Kentucky are perfect for mixed farming on the grand English scale. This is "grass" country, excellent for corn and rye, clover, and timothy hay, as well as the famed bluegrass. No wonder, then, that it became one of the nation's finest livestock-producing regions, famous for its horses, cattle, and sheep. To the south, on the Cumberland Plateau, the landscape favors horticulture, and apples, peaches, cherries, and other fruits have been major crops. In the far west, the semitropical Jackson Purchase with its fertile plains, cypress swamps, and winding creeks is a virtual paradise for wild game and freshwater fish. Finally, the rich valleys of the Cumberland, Green, Kentucky, Licking, Big Sandy, and especially Ohio rivers offer bottomlands in their floodplains that will grow anything from sorghum to sweet potatoes. Add to this variety of landscapes an amenable climate with a long growing season, a frequently open winter, and adequate and well-distributed rainfall. The result was, in the pioneers' words, a "land flowing with milk and honey." Interestingly, the Knobs which arc around the Bluegrass region actually became a famous milk- and honey-producing area in the early nineteenth century.

If these regions had remained isolated and remote, there would never have been a Kentucky tradition, only a variety of regional foodway systems within the borders of the state. Fortunately, the creation of the Commonwealth of Kentucky, with all political roads leading to and from Frankfort, provided the means by which these traditions were diffused and cross-pollinated. The result was synergic —the whole of Kentucky's foodways is far greater than the sum of its parts. An old-fashioned Kentucky barbecue, such as that described on page 109, combines foods from every geographic region of the state and representing all of its basic ethnic traditions: country ham, barbecued mutton, burgoo, slaw, baked beans, potato salad, wheat breads, corn on the cob, cornmeal cakes, fried fish, watermelon, fried pies, and stack cakes. The result is a unique blend—pure Kentucky.

History is the third crucial factor that has shaped Kentucky's foodways. For two hundred years its tradition has been formed by the fusion of differing ethnic and regional economies and tastes within the commonwealth and by the ties Kentucky has established with other regions of the United States. The former came naturally. The Scots borrowed heavily from Indians out of need and then merged their "mountain" diet with that of the English settlers out of desire. The result was a symbiotic relationship: descendants of the English settlers grew fond of bourbon, butter, potatoes, and honey; descendants of the Scots developed a taste for sorghum, country ham, mutton, and wheat breads. The flowering of this fusion of folk foodways is described by Elizabeth Kremer in her essay on the Shakers (pp. 43–49). The Shakers rejected the pleasures of sex but embraced the joys of growing, processing, and eating good food. They became rural, folk Epicureans. The uniqueness of the Shakers' achievement is that they evolved their foodways from local food products using local recipes, with little outside influence, but their attitude toward the work of their hands resulted in a cuisine of the highest excellence, epitomizing the best of Kentucky's foodways in the nineteenth century.

Another, more worldly, tradition has been evident since Kentucky's beginnings. The state's unique geographical position helped foster a sophisticated, virtual *haute cuisine*. By early in the nineteenth century, Kentuckians found themselves at the very center of the growing nation, a crossroads for travel and trade routes that linked East and West, North and South. Kentucky cuisine reflected all these influences. The taverns, inns, and later spas described by Mary Clay were important centers for accumulating and disseminating culinary influences from outside the state. Merchants and other travelers from throughout the United States and later the world visited Kentucky to purchase tobacco, bourbon, horses, wool, and later timber and coal. They influenced and were influenced by Kentucky's foodways. Just as the traditional folk foods reached their highest development with the Shakers, so Kentucky's *haute cuisine* reached its height in the elegant banquets and Derby entertainments of the Bluegrass and other areas. Fortunately, as Burton Milward shows, a balance was struck between the two traditions. For example, when Alice Longworth, daughter of President Theodore Roosevelt, visited Lexington in 1907, she was served champagne and Queen Elizabeth salad instead of bourbon and poke, but the menu also included country ham, beaten biscuits, and barbecued mutton.

This tradition of combining various influences continues to today, as many of the recipes in this book indicate. Some of these dishes blend Kentucky foods with those from outside the state: Derby Spread, with its butter, Roquefort cheese, and bourbon, is a particularly good example. Cheese Thins, made with cheddar cheese and pecans is another. Sometimes the blend occurs not in a recipe but in a menu. Using *Kentucky Hospitality* as a guide, one could put together an eclectic meal consisting of dishes from varying traditions popular in Kentucky which go together quite well. The result might be something like this:

Mint Juleps
Beaten Biscuits with Derby Spread
Polk Sallet with Fried Salt Pork
Real Turtle Soup
Country Ham Stuffed with Wild Greens
Onions Viennese, Old South Asparagus, Marinated Carrots
Granny's Corn Relish
Spoon Bread
Cranberry Ice
Pralines, Anis Cookies, Marguerites
Coffee, Maxwell Place Spiced Tea

Any number of other suitable menu combinations drawing on old and new, Kentucky and foreign recipes, are possible and valid, for the history of Kentucky's foodways is a record of the mixing of adaptable cultural and regional economies, techniques, and tastes into one tradition. *Kentucky Hospitality* is not only a guide to this heritage but strong evidence that the Kentucky culinary tradition will continue for at least another two hundred years.

Our Heritage

Folk Beliefs about Food and Eating in Kentucky

R. Gerald Alvey

Of all mankind's common activities, those concerning food perhaps most reflect each cultural group's beliefs—beliefs surrounding not only food and how it is to be used, but many other aspects of the group's social composition, as well. I use the term belief in its broadest sense, including not only what we normally label superstition, but the entire array of social customs, rites, traditions, attitudes, taboos, preferences, and the like. Beliefs, though they exist only in the human mind, are expressed in social situations and one cannot begin to appreciate them, much less analyze them, apart from their social contexts. To provide a framework in which to view the beliefs of Kentuckians, past and present,[1] concerning specific foods and eating customs, a brief consideration of similar attitudes and beliefs among much of mankind seems in order.

[1] Some of the beliefs and practices I discuss here, such as the shivaree, are nearly forgotten in Kentucky. Others, such as various beliefs about tomatoes, still exist primarily in rural areas. A few are contemporary and exist throughout the state, such as beliefs surrounding the wedding cake. Remnants of most of these beliefs prevail in mutated contemporary forms, however. For example, the custom of tampering with the newlyweds' car in various ways is a transformation of the older shivaree. Because all folk beliefs and practices persist and undergo transformations as times change, and because older beliefs are often revived, it is difficult to say when a particular belief or practice is outdated and when it is contemporary.

Apparently from his beginnings, man has considered his three fundamental biological necessities—eating, sexual behavior, and excretory functions—to be more or less private activities. As man's social activities became more complex with the passage of time, and as populations expanded, eating, alone of these three activities, came to be more or less a communal affair, although still recognized as a private activity for those partaking of the meal. Many historical accounts of early Kentucky describe the traditional taboo, especially prevalent in rural or mountain areas, according to which women were not allowed to eat with the men, but served them as in ancient societies. Furthermore, females were, and still are, in certain areas, enjoined not to prepare certain foods during menstruation, to prevent "contamination" of the foods. Not only did men eat apart from women, but certain foods were and are designated, often tacitly, as properly "masculine" or "feminine." Meat and potatoes, pie, coffee, and alcoholic beverages usually have been considered "masculine," while dairy products, soups, vegetables, salads, eggs, puddings, and tea have often been regarded as properly "feminine" foods. In earlier periods, bread—usually corn bread, in some form—apparently represented an acceptable bisexual food; today, rye, whole wheat, and especially corn bread are often believed more properly "masculine," while rolls or white bread are considered "feminine."

In the seeming paradox of private yet communal eating can be seen several other age-old beliefs and customs. The preference for private eating may be associated with the ancient belief that evil spirits can enter the body through one's open mouth, which at the same time provides a passageway out of the body for one's own soul. Hence, in Kentucky we have many customs and beliefs, usually prohibitive, concerning sneezing, whistling, singing, or unnecessary chatter, especially at the meal table. Such beliefs may be imbedded in the ubiquitous admonition to children not to talk with full mouths.

Sinister forces, natural or supernatural, could easily contaminate food about to be consumed, and private dining afforded protection. The belief that containers of food should be covered (as they are today for sanitary or other practical reasons) may have begun as a means to prevent pollution by potentially malevolent forces; this custom was particularly followed among nobility. Today, the common and often unconscious custom of systematically picking up dropped particles of food from the table, particularly bread crumbs, probably stems from the ancient belief that one became vulnerable to sorcerers if they gleaned particles of the food one had eaten. The sorcerer thereby gained access to the eater, for he had the "same" food that was "in" the eater. To prevent bewitchment, the eater left no crumbs.

Some scholars contend that the envy of other people constitutes a further reason for secluded dining customs. Precautions about envy and the worldwide ancient but continuing belief in the evil eye even have Biblical precedent. Proverbs 23:6-8 warns:

> *Eat thou not the bread of him who hath an evil eye, neither*
>   *desire thou his dainty foods;*
> *For as he thinketh in his heart, so is he. Eat and drink, saith*
>   *he to thee; but his heart is not with thee.*
> *The morsel which thou hast eaten shalt thou vomit up, and lose*
>   *thy sweet words.*   [KJV]

In addition to the obvious function of offering thanks, some scholars see the custom of saying grace before meals, which also has several Biblical precedents, as an effort to elicit divine or supernatural protection from the potential dangers accompanying eating—whether from sinister sources or polluted food. Elaborate, often ritualistic, preparation of food, especially cooking, was believed to decontaminate potentially harmful food. Many religions still advise the ritualistic preparation of certain foodstuffs.

One way to assure that one's neighbor wishes him no harm and has not polluted one's food is to invite the neighbor to share the meal. Sharing food, of course, also satisfies other social customs and cultural beliefs. One does not readily eat with those of inferior or superior social rank, unless the superior orders such communal dining, or unless either the subordinate or the superior wishes to extend "hospitality." Hospitality has long been recognized as a Kentucky custom. Ancient, often subconscious, beliefs probably underlie and perpetuate it. Certainly, from a practical standpoint, the dangers of the sparsely populated frontier compelled everyone to afford shelter and food to friendly passersby, whether acquaintances or strangers. But such pragmatic necessity does not fully explain Kentucky hospitality. Many scholars note that much of mankind considers the stranger potentially sacred. The Bible, in fact, admonishes its readers to "be mindful of entertaining strangers, for thereby some have entertained angels unawares." Some societies carried hospitality to such a degree that wives were proffered in addition to shelter and food. (I know of no documented evidence of such practice in Kentucky.) If a stranger is, on the one hand, feared and, on the other, considered potentially sacred, then one way to certify his benevolence is to invite him to dine. Some scholars contend that, to some extent, both differences in social status and fear of strangers explain the taboo of interracial dining in the South.

Kentucky hospitality, whether in rural or in urban areas, has invariably included sumptuous feasts, often accompanied by such statements from the host as "if you don't mind eatin' a poor man's meal," "make out a meal for yourself," or "make yourself at [or to] home," and "help yourself." Nonetheless, gluttony has always been censured in Kentucky. Proverbs 23:21 warns us of the irony that "the glutton shall come to poverty." Consequently, one does not take the last morsel from the platter or bowl, and, indeed, one often leaves a morsel on his own plate to illustrate that he is not a glutton. Moderation is the ideal. However, in earlier and poorer days Kentuckians often insisted that every last bite be consumed, with no charge of gluttony, for they do not easily forget that their forbears' cyclical situation was often almost literally one of feast or famine. At ceremonial occasions, feasts and feasting are usually sanctioned, and such ritualistic festivities reflect perhaps some of the deeper beliefs surrounding Kentucky's communal eating customs.

That communal eating functions as a rite of integration or incorporation for the diners is generally agreed. Because communal dining in itself constitutes a symbolic union, it is often incorporated within a larger and more complex ceremony of symbolic union, such as a wedding with its attendant feasts. Grace, in addition to the functions mentioned above, also expresses the symbolic spiritual union of those about to eat. When one eats with others, each "becomes"—symbolically—a part of the other. Each takes the common food into himself. Therefore, the "same" food being "in" everyone, all become "one." This belief is epitomized in religious communion services, but the same concept functions in a predominantly secular context as well. In a similar vein, the sharing of beliefs or customs surrounding the acquisition, processing, and use of foods represents something of a shibboleth. The compilation of a set of recipes more or less common to a group—such as this book of Kentucky food—is itself an indication of the cohesiveness of the group. One is recognized as a member of the group by the food he keeps (and eats).

Special ceremonies common to most of mankind often become localized, taking on aspects of the particular culture, especially when communal eating is involved. Weddings and funerals are nearly universal human rites, but some customs and beliefs surrounding them may be considered uniquely Kentuckian. Similarly, widespread American holiday festivities, such as the Thanksgiving-Christmas-New Year's-Easter cycle, often involve food customs or beliefs recognized, whether overtly or tacitly, as Kentuckian. A few social activities involving food are often in some way identified as more or less peculiarly Kentuckian. They include hog-butcherings, family reunions, harvest gatherings, all-day singings or memorial services (with "dinner on the ground"), often church oriented, and barbecues, often in conjunction with religious or political interests, where burgoo, that uniquely Kentuckian dish, is usually served. (The term burgoo possibly derives from a folk etymological process combining 'barbecue' and 'goo'—the soupy mixture of barbecue remnants; thus, 'barbecue goo' became 'burgoo.')

To exemplify how beliefs and customs involving food permeate many traditional Kentucky celebrations, I will elaborate somewhat on romance, courtship, and wedding customs. Kentuckians have always adhered to innumerable beliefs and customs concerning the use of food for romantic divination. One of the more popular customs prescribed that a girl of marriageable age should sleep with a piece of wedding cake (someone else's, naturally) beneath her pillow, often for three successive nights, thereby invoking a dream of her intended. Such a custom in itself testifies to the symbolic and magical significance of the wedding cake. To attract courtship, a girl could wear a small container of dried tomato seeds around her neck, reflecting the seventeenth-century belief that the tomato, or "love-apple," as it was called, was an aphrodisiac. Indeed, until the early nineteenth century many Kentuckians believed tomatoes were poison and would not eat them, probably a moralistic way to proscribe the older, "sexy" tomato beliefs. Some Kentuckians still consider the tomato taboo.

Apples have been used in various ways to predict love, revealing the persistence of the ancient Roman veneration of Pomona, the romantic and fecund diety of fruit trees, and it is recalled that for a wedding gift Zeus gave an apple to his daughter. An apple a day not only keeps the doctor away, but can possibly bring lovers in sway. Kentucky youth have traditionally (especially at Halloween) peeled apples and tossed the peelings over their shoulders, where they are thought to fall in such a manner as to spell out the prospective lover's name or initials. Or one can hold the apple under his armpit until it is warmed, then eat it, thereby invoking special powers to enchant a loved one. If one is strong enough to break an apple in two, the desired loved one is then subject to the apple-breaker's whims. Apple seeds have been used to foretell love seemingly in as many ways as there have been imaginations to invent methods of prognostication.

Swallowing a thimbleful of salt before retiring assured a girl that her dreams would reveal her intended. If this failed, she could trust a snail to trace her future beau's name in a dish of cornmeal—the latter always readily available, being one of Kentucky's traditional foodstuffs. Taking the last portion of a food at the table can predict either good or ill fortune in love; therefore, prudence would seem to dictate leaving the morsel. Likewise, a girl's expertise, or lack thereof, at baking—especially breadstuffs—can portend respective ill or good fortune in acquiring a mate. If her corn bread is rough, so will be her husband's face. Such a belief exemplifies the magic dictum that like produces like. On a more practical level, it may prompt the girl to become an adept cook. One custom by which a youth can demonstrate readiness for marriage involves the ability to turn a hoe cake without breaking it. To eat beets or pickles (or to dream of pickles) indicates love is imminent. And to assure that one's intended will be handsome and wealthy a girl should eat the inside of a chicken gizzard or take the last piece of pie on a plate.

Kentucky youth have used so many food divination procedures that it is impossible even to list them all here. But one rather elaborate procedure deserves mention. It is variously called the "dumb supper," the "silent supper," the "deaf and dumb supper," or the "backward supper." Several girls, in absolute and total muteness, prepare a supper and perform all the necessary steps backwards—walking backwards, with hands behind them, and so on. Often two places at the table are set for each girl. Near the end of the preparations some supernatural sign will indicate which of the girls (usually only one) is to marry that year. The "sign" may be the actual appearance of one of the girl's "hopefuls," who may have been previously tipped off by some knowledgeable well-wisher. Some believers maintain, however, that truly supernatural portentous phenomena are likely to occur at the dumb supper.

Once courtship is undertaken, and after a length of time, the usual custom has been to invite each of the lovers to the home of their prospective parents-in-law for a symbolic meal. Here again the exchange of communal meals symbolizes potential union, not only of the couple but of the two families. Such meals also provide opportunity for the families to assess various characteristics and attributes of the prospective in-law, and vice versa, for one reveals much about himself while dining. Such meals are usually a prerequisite to engagement, and certainly to marriage.

That Kentucky weddings traditionally have involved feasts needs no documentation. The wedding feast symbolizes not only the union of the bride and groom and the new affinity of their families, but also the strengthening of the entire society by these new relationships.

Through the wedding, everybody is more closely united, and the communal dining that follows the actual ceremony expresses that fact. That the bride's parents provide the feast symbolizes age-old beliefs that economic advantages accompany the acquisition of a bride, and also that the girl's family gives her to perpetuate the society. Thus ancient rites and beliefs of both fertility and economics are symbolically imbedded in the wedding feast.

Immediately following the nuptials, the wedding cake is the center of activity. The modern wedding cake has evolved from very old wedding customs involving the use of wheat as a symbol of fertility. Wheat grains were thrown at or sprinkled around the bride (rice, in a similar function, has never been as widely used in Kentucky weddings as it has elsewhere). Later the bride's family provided small cakes made *from* wheat (as, of course, is the modern wedding cake) for favored guests, or distributed them to the poor. Then, guests themselves brought small cakes and either threw them at the bride or crumbled them over her. Eventually the cakes were merely stacked at the feet of the bridal pair. Tradition says that a Frenchman suggested icing the stack of individual cakes, thus creating one tiered, iced, wedding cake. In various sections of Kentucky, small individual cakes have traditionally been given to wedding attendants. Often, one cake contains a ring, and it is believed that whoever receives the ring will be the next to marry. Many modern Kentucky wedding cakes have had various good luck items baked in them, to be removed and saved by the bride and groom.

In Kentucky, as elsewhere, the typical modern wedding cake is round, symbolizing eternal happiness, union, and so on; it is usually tiered, with a replica of the bride and groom on the top tier, symbolizing the new "elevated," or more holy, state of the couple. The top tier (the one closest the heavens) is usually saved by the couple, to be eaten on their first wedding anniversary, signifying perpetuity of all symbolic blessings. The bride is admonished to administer the first cut in the cake herself, for should anyone else cut it first he "cuts into" the bride's happiness. She also must offer the first bite of cake to the groom, then he in turn offers her a bite. These actions symbolize the new intimate union, fertility, health, prosperity, and, because it is a communal eating display, that all present approve and share, to a lesser extent, similar benefits. Indeed, some societies believe that "sharing food" between two lovers in itself constitutes matrimony.

Often the Kentucky wedding feast has been at the house of the bride, further underscoring the belief that the bride's parents are symbolically "nurturing" the entire community. Beginning with the wedding feast and lasting at least through the wedding night shivaree, young male Kentuckians have customarily freely passed the "Brown Betty" (or "Black Betty"), the liquor jug, which reflects remnants of the ancient Celtic custom of celebrants drinking honey wine for one month after a wedding—constituting a "honeymoon."

Following the wedding night, and providing they survive the shivaree, the Kentucky bride and groom have often been expected to attend another feast, prepared by the groom's parents and eaten at their house, called the "infare." The infare meal at the groom's home symbolizes that the bride is now a member of the groom's family, in the patriarchal lineage, also especially symbolized, of course, in the name change. The infare celebration, coming the "morning after," is intended to illustrate for the benefit of the entire community that the marriage has indeed been consummated and that the groom's family affirms and receives the bride as a new member of the family, thereby strengthening the family's social position and assuring that the family name, and consequently the community itself, will be perpetuated.

During the romance-courtship-wedding sequence, the general symbolic significance of beliefs and customs surrounding communal dining are thus all operable, but are expanded to symbolize and intensify more specific beliefs and functions pertaining particularly to the courtship and wedding.

It would be possible to analyze in a similar manner the beliefs and customs surrounding any of the various social activities in Kentucky where food is eaten, and certainly there are innumerable traditional beliefs and customs involving specific foods—the planting and growing of them, their preparation, and the eating of them. Indeed, a lengthy volume could be written on nothing but Kentucky beliefs and customs involving foods used for cures or as preventive medicine. In this brief space I hope I have demonstrated that there is more to Kentuckians and their use of food than can be savored in one bite.

SOURCES

Arnow, Hariette Simpson. *Seedtime on the Cumberland.* New York: Macmillan, 1960.

Botkin, B. A. *A Treasury of Southern Folklore.* New York: Crown Publishers, 1949.

Clark, Thomas D. *The Kentucky.* New York: Rinehart and Company, 1942.

Thomas, Daniel L., and Thomas, Lucy B. *Kentucky Superstitions.* Princeton: Princeton University Press, 1920.

Thompson, Lawrence S. "Hogs in Ohio Valley Superstition." *Kentucky Folklore Record* 10 (October–December 1964):59–61.

————. *Kentucky Tradition.* Hamden, Conn.: Shoe String Press, 1956.

The Foods of Pioneer Kentucky

Otis K. Rice

When Felix Walker, who accompanied Daniel Boone to Kentucky in 1775, beheld the Bluegrass region, he was so struck by its beauty and abundance that, like Columbus upon reaching the shores of the Bahamas after many weary and uncertain weeks at sea, he was moved to kiss the earth beneath him. Although most of those who first saw Kentucky as fur traders, captives of the Indians, explorers, Long Hunters, and finally as settlers, were less demonstrative than Walker, they too sensed that this was no ordinary land. They could describe it only in superlatives, as an Elysium, or in such Biblical phrases as "the Promised Land" or "the land of Goshen."

The Kentucky pioneer might envision a land flowing with milk and honey once he had set his hand to the plow and had begun to build his herds and flocks, but he knew from generations of westward migration that for sustenance he must first rely upon the bounties of the land. Fortunately, bear, deer, elk, wild turkeys, and smaller game filled the forests which covered much of Kentucky. Extensive grasslands attracted vast herds of buffalo and a profusion of rabbits, and the streams were filled with fish. In such an environment hunting, at least for a time, assumed a crucial place in the life of the pioneer family.

The first Kentuckians were well prepared to take advantage of their environment. Most of them migrated from the Holston Valley and its tributaries, the Valley of Virginia, and other parts of the back-country of Virginia, Pennsylvania, Maryland, and North Carolina. On these older frontiers they had become skilled in the use of the Kentucky, or Pennsylvania, rifle and had learned to regard it as a prized possession. Hunting, in fact, had already become an integral part of their lives, and it persisted in isolated sections of Kentucky into the twentieth century. As Joseph Doddridge, the noted historian of trans-Appalachian frontier society, observed, even after hunting was no longer a necessity many men continued to experience a great restlessness, particularly in the autumn, and could find peace only after a successful hunting expedition.

Hunters and settlers who reached Kentucky by way of the Cumberland Gap and the Wilderness Road or by floating down the majestic Ohio River encountered great herds of buffalo, an animal seen but infrequently in the mountain valleys. As later happened on the Great Plains, they launched a massive assault upon the unfortunate creature. They considered the tongue one of the most delectable parts. In its preparation they first scorched it and peeled off the outside coating, then left it to roast overnight in a bed of embers. They often placed the tongue on spits made of spicewood, which flavored it and made it "delicious eating." Other favorite parts were the hump and the marrow bones. To prepare the marrow for eating, large leg bones were boiled or roasted in embers until well done, then cracked open with an ax. Smoked and dried buffalo meat, or jerk, also proved useful in times of food shortages and on extended journeys.

Of greater importance to the pioneer diet were the bear and the deer. Fresh bear meat, particularly that of cubs, was considered by many to be tastier than that of any other wild game. The spareribs and sides of young bears could be cured by salting and smoking, and the oil, made clear with slippery elm bark, was commonly used as a shortening. Venison was probably less common, but fresh venison steaks were regarded by many Kentucky families as a delicacy, as they are today.

Flocks of wild turkeys numbering in the hundreds were not at all unusual. If the turkey was to be roasted whole, small incisions might be made in its skin and bits of bear fat and seasoning inserted. Turkey breasts and venison often served as "bread" during long expeditions or whenever flour, corn, and meal were in short supply, but in this form they could become monotonous fare indeed.

Many pioneers considered the tail of the beaver a rare delight. In its preparation they first wrapped the tail in oak leaves and covered it in a bed of embers overnight. Before eating it, they removed the skin, which peeled off easily, and added salt. Beaver tails also formed one of the principal ingredients of a soup held in high esteem by many early settlers. Like the buffalo, however, the beaver was rapidly depleted, and beaver dishes had but a short life among the earliest residents of Kentucky.

Sometimes a great variety of game animals found their way into the same kettle. A popular stew included choice bits of buffalo, deer, elk, bear, and turkey. This mixture was seasoned, usually with sage and red pepper, to suit the taste, and vegetables of whatever kinds were available were added. Those who partook of the stew sought out whichever meats and vegetables they preferred. The stew always had something of a mystery about it, since almost anything edible might turn up in the pot. It enjoyed great popularity, however, at social gatherings, particularly in the mountainous areas, and has come down to us as burgoo.

The larger game of Kentucky rapidly disappeared or became scarce, but small animals and fowl remained plentiful for many years, especially in the hill country. Recipes for squirrel, rabbit, opossum, and other wild meats varied considerably, with frying, stewing, and roasting determined by individual preference and by the availability of other necessary ingredients. Throughout much of Kentucky, partridges and pheasants could be found, and residents living along the water courses had numerous opportunities to add wild geese and ducks to their tables. Many streams continued to provide good fishing, with buffalofish and catfish, sometimes weighing a hundred pounds, and trout being among the most popular kinds.

Wild fruits, nuts, and berries added variety to drab pioneer diets. In the hardwood sections of Kentucky, hickory nuts, black walnuts, chestnuts, and beechnuts were plentiful, and the wild cherry, plum, grape, and crab apple, as well as the papaw, persimmon, and black and red haw, grew extensively in much of the state. In some places wild strawberries, raspberries, blackberries, and mulberries abounded. Numerous roots, barks, and herbs were used either as food or as seasoning and flavoring. Sassafras tea, for example, not only provided a refreshingly pleasant drink in early spring, but was regarded as having the medicinal value of thinning the blood, which was thought to have thickened during the winter.

Native greens, sometimes referred to as sallet or pot herbs, enjoyed a special place among the pioneers. Part of their knowledge of which ones were edible had come down from colonial times. Plantain, for instance, had been so popular that settlers often planted its seeds in new clearings. The Indians also contributed to this aspect of plant lore. One settler in Kentucky stated that the women followed the cows and picked whatever they ate as a means of avoiding poisonous plants. Blue root was a favorite, but it required a bit of dock to give it balance. The women also gathered wild lettuce, which they used sparingly, and the tips of wild grape shoots. Tender poke leaves, fried in lard or boiled with bacon, and perhaps eaten with sugar, also had a wide appeal.

Always greeted with great joy was the discovery of a swarm of bees, and a bee tree was considered even more valuable than big game. The bee was not native but was the descendant of imports from England which had escaped from domestic hives and migrated westward to the frontiers, usually about a hundred miles in advance of settlement. A single bee tree might yield hundreds of pounds of honey and provide a family with sweetening for months. Pioneers often redomesticated the wild bees and established their own hives, usually called gums because the bees were housed in a hollow sour gum log.

The other major source of sweetening was maple sugar, which had been made by the Indians long before the arrival of the first Europeans. The pioneer notched the sugar trees after a thaw, usually in late January or early February, bored holes, inserted spouts into them, and constructed small wooden troughs to carry the sap to buckets. As the buckets filled, the sap was collected and taken to the boiling kettles. A good tree might yield from three to five gallons of sap a day. Thirty to forty gallons of sap normally produced one gallon of syrup after hours of boiling. When the syrup cooled, sugar crystals formed at the top of the residue, and "sugar molasses" were drained from the bottom.

Honey and maple sugar were desirable, but neither was as essential as salt, which was needed for seasoning and for preserving meats and butter. Kentucky, fortunately, had numerous salt springs and licks, which had been visited for untold ages by deer, buffalo, and other animals, as well as by the Indians. Among them were Drennon's Lick on the Kentucky River and Blue Licks on the Licking River. So vital was salt that during the Revolutionary War moves were made to construct a fort at Drennon's Lick to protect saltmakers there. When speculators who had staked out valuable salt properties failed to develop them, some Kentuckians even proposed that the state take the socialistic step of making them state property. Daniel Drake, in his classic *Life in Pioneer Kentucky*, recalled his anguish when, as a child, he was sent to borrow a small quantity of salt from a neighbor and then spilled most of it on his way home.

Extensive as they were, the pioneer could not, and did not, expect to live indefinitely by the bounties of Nature alone. He dreamed of a land under cultivation and of livestock grazing upon rich pasture-land. In his scheme of agriculture, corn immediately took precedence over all other crops because of the ease with which it could be cultivated, the variety of ways in which it could be served, and its suitability for a grain and livestock type of farming. The pioneer prepared for his first crop of corn by girdling the larger trees and clearing away the smaller growth on his land. He usually left the stumps standing until he had more time to grub them out, perhaps a year or two later. In cultivating the corn, he needed only a hoe, but he sometimes used a shovel plow. He could grind the corn into meal by means of a hominy block or by hand, but gradually horse mills and water-powered mills became the custom.

Conversion of the corn into food for the family rested primarily with the womenfolk. Any housewife who could not prepare a variety of tasty corn dishes could hardly qualify as a cook. Fresh from the field, the corn often appeared as roasting ears to be baked or boiled. Ground meal, with the addition of salt and water, formed the basis for the hoe cake, apparently named from the habit of Virginia slaves of baking the mixture on their hoes. The same ingredients were baked in hot ashes, to make ash cakes, or on a rock or board sloping toward a fire to produce the much beloved journey cake, or johnny cake, often carried by travelers because it kept well. For another popular form of corn bread, meal was leavened, mixed with eggs and buttermilk, and baked in a Dutch oven covered with coals. Corn breads were always better when eaten hot, and families ordinarily had hot bread with each meal.

Two other popular corn products were hominy and grits. Hominy was made by soaking whole grains of corn in lye water to remove the hulls, cooking them long enough to get rid of small flakes of hull but not long enough to destroy the hearts, and seasoning with lard or bear's oil. Grits, sometimes referred to as small hominy, had long been a common dish and were to the Southern frontier what groats were to the English people. Grits were prepared from coarse cornmeal, made by rubbing mature and hard kernels over the rough side of a piece of tin pierced with nail holes. Corn was also made into mush, dried and then parched, pickled for winter use, and served in almost any other way that the imagination of the frontier cook might suggest.

Corn had yet other uses related to the pioneer diet. One was as food for livestock, particularly cattle and hogs, which themselves contributed greatly to the variety of foods available. The other lay in the manufacture of corn whiskey. Since corn was too bulky to transport to distant markets and also spoiled easily, many farmers converted it into whiskey, which had a ready sale. They never failed, however, to keep a quantity for medicinal purposes and for use with meals, a prevalent practice in Kentucky and other frontier areas.

Wheat was probably no more plentiful in Kentucky than in other newly settled sections of the trans-Appalachian region. For one thing, it did not mature properly in new soil, and fields suitable for wheat must first be sown to other crops. Moreover, even after the erection of improved mills, flour continued to cost several times as much as cornmeal. Wheat growers, therefore, frequently limited their own consumption of flour to occasional biscuits, thickening for gravy, cakes, and pie crusts. The remainder they sold as a cash crop in local and distant markets.

As soon as possible the pioneer planted other vegetable crops, among which were beans, potatoes, pumpkins, cabbage, peas, turnips, lettuce, and cucumbers. Tomatoes were widely regarded as poisonous, and it was not until about 1830 or even later that a few daring individuals began to include them in their diets. Plantings also included sage, peppers, thyme, mint, mustard, horseradish, and tansy, used primarily for the preservation or seasoning of foods. This herb garden, considered the special preserve of the womenfolk, was usually planted close to the dwelling.

Aside from corn, few vegetables were more important than beans and potatoes. A favorite among the green beans was the cornfield or October variety. Late in the afternoon the housewife picked the beans to be used next day. In the evening she removed the strings and broke the beans into pieces. The next morning they were put on the stove, usually in an iron pot with plenty of bacon, and cooked until about noon, after which they simmered until supper, as the evening meal was universally called. Substituting for green beans in winter were "shucky" beans, which had earlier been strung on long cords and hung up to dry. More common in winter, however, were shelled dried beans, which were boiled with bacon or sometimes with ham hocks. The cook might prepare Irish potatoes by frying, boiling, or baking them, but she usually fried or roasted the sweet potatoes or mixed them with milk, eggs, and spices to make a pie filling.

Most pioneers who expected to make permanent settlements also planted fruit trees as soon as possible. The most common were apple, peach, pear, cherry, and plum. The peach was a special favorite because it matured rapidly. These trees provided fresh fruit in season and the base for jellies, jams, and preserves. The making of apple butter, preferably outdoors in a large copper kettle, was a special occasion. Apples and peaches were also dried for use in winter, when in many cases they were the only fruits available. Both were also converted into brandy, another important cash product of the pioneer farm, and apples provided the cider so beloved by many pioneers, as well as vinegar used both for pickling and for flavoring greens and other foods.

As the natural bounties were diminished, the pioneer became increasingly dependent upon his own resources. This was especially true in the case of meats, and domesticated stock, particularly hogs, cattle, and poultry, assumed ever greater importance. For many Kentuckians pork long remained the favorite meat. Many of the hogs of the mountainous regions could survive by feeding on mast in the woods and whatever else they could find, but more and more farmers fattened their animals on corn. Although they might kill a pig at any time during the year, they preferred the late fall and early winter, between Thanksgiving and Christmas, for slaughtering their hogs. In killing the animals, they usually shot them or stunned them with an ax and then cut their throats to bleed, but some preferred to stick them while they were yet alive in order that they might bleed better.

From the hog came an assortment of meats, including large hams, loin cuts, spareribs, sides of bacon, and other desirable parts. Most of the scraps were ground into sausage and seasoned with sage and red pepper. Many pioneers, however, preferred sausage made by a mixture of both lean and fat meats. Another type of sausage, known as headcheese or souse, included the head and feet of the hog. This sausage might be pickled and at the time of cooking rolled in cornmeal and fried. Hams were preserved by hickory smoking, a practice that had already made Virginia hams famous long before the first settlers arrived in Kentucky. In addition to the meats, the women rendered considerable quantities of lard at hog-killing time, for with the decrease of the bear population, hog lard became more and more a necessity.

Although pork was for many Kentuckians the most important of the domesticated meats, the English antecedents of a large part of the population meant that beef, too, would loom large in their diets. The first settlers paid little more attention to their cattle than to their hogs, with the result that most animals were coarse and rangy in appearance. In 1790, however, Matthew Patton, an emigrant from the South Branch of the Potomac River, introduced into the Bluegrass region the popular Patton cattle, a cross between native stock and blooded English cattle. The Patton cattle remained favorites with many stockmen long after the introduction of Shorthorn cattle into the Bluegrass in 1817. In the hill country, nevertheless, unimproved stock continued to predominate for many years to come.

The pioneer might have various forms of pork preserved for use throughout the year, but he apparently preferred to have his beef fresh. Cattle, therefore, were killed at almost any time during the year. Very often one family would share its beef with its neighbors, who would reciprocate when they did their own slaughtering. By thus scattering the beef killings, all had fresh meat several times during the year and saved the expense of salt necessary for preserving it. The cows added milk, buttermilk, and butter to the frontier diet. Butter was also a salable commodity, and by common custom in many areas the proceeds from it were considered to be the right of the housewife, who might use the income to purchase a few of the elegancies of life. Cheese-making was perhaps most common among settlers of German descent, who had a great fondness for smearcase, or German *schmier-kase,* today known as cottage cheese.

Chickens provided eggs for both eating and baking, but many found their way into a pot with thick dumplings for a special Sunday dinner. Fried chicken was also popular, particularly at social gatherings and picnics.

Beverages were at first severely limited. Coffee and tea, as well as chocolate, had to await the production of surpluses on pioneer farms or the accumulation of cash products from the forests, such as ginseng, which could be exchanged for articles not produced by the settlers. Beverages therefore consisted of teas brewed from native plants, such as the sassafras, and of products of the cider presses and stills, the latter including apple and peach brandy and corn whiskey.

Although the pioneer table might display both an ample amount and a considerable variety of food during the growing season, winter and early spring could bring lean months unless the family had taken adequate steps to prepare for them. Food preservation, therefore, formed a vitally important part of the work of the household. As has already been noted, the provident family cured, smoked, and preserved sufficient pork products during the slaughtering season to last much of the coming year. Occasional killings of beef and the hunting of wild game supplemented the supplies of pork.

Especially important among the vegetables preserved or stored for winter use were potatoes, corn, beans, pumpkins, cucumbers, and cabbage. Corn and beans, as has been noted, formed two of the great staples of the pioneer diet during the winter months. Pumpkins, one of the most useful of farm products, were easily stored under fodder shocks or other shelters. In winter they might be fried, put into corn bread batter, cooked with spices and sugar or honey to form a kind of butter, or made into filling for pies. Much cabbage was made into sauerkraut, particularly by those of German backgrounds.

The children of the family customarily gathered in large supplies of nuts for the long winter evenings, when they were cracked and eaten before blazing fires or used as ingredients in a variety of special foods. Many families also had small patches of popcorn, which never ceased to prove a delight to the young folk.

Despite the difficulties of the pioneering experience, relatively few families needed to suffer hunger or want except during unusual times of game shortages and crop failures. Careful planning and diligence carried their own rewards and enabled most pioneers to live with some degree of comfort. As a more sophisticated society developed, such as that which rapidly came to prevail in the Bluegrass region, eating habits underwent change. All the elegancies known to the sumptuous tables of the East and to the varied cuisines of Europe ere long found their way to the Goshen of the Western World. But many pioneer foods continued to held a special place in the tastes of Kentuckians and, in some cases with modifications, have endured to this day.

The Pioneer Kitchen

Marcia Cebulska

I know of no scene in civilized life more primitive than such a cabin hearth as that of my mother. In the morning, a buckeye backlog & hickory forestick resting on stone andirons, with a Jonny cake on a clean ash board, set before it to bake, a frying pan with its long handle resting on a split bottomed turner's chair, sending out its peculiar music, and the tea kettle swung from a wooden "lug pole" with myself setting the table, or turning the meat, or watching the Jonny cake, while she sat nursing the baby in the corner, and telling the little ones to "hold still" and let their sister Lizy dress them!

If the hearth of Daniel Drake's childhood was primitive, as he terms it, it was not, however, atypical of the kitchen facilities of the first homes of most Kentucky pioneer families. Although he does not mention it in the passage quoted above, the cooking was done in the same room as the spinning, the weaving, the eating, the sleeping; in short, all of the indoor living. On the other hand, the kitchen extended to the out-of-doors on occasions such as hog-butchering or maple-sugaring times. For these events, great kettles, weighing as much as 150 pounds, were set over outdoor fires and used to render the lard or boil down the sap.

Today we think of the kitchen as a room almost exclusively devoted to food preparation, storage, and sometimes consumption. For the great majority of settlers, the kitchen served the additional functions of sitting room, crafts room, dining room, and frequently bedroom. The hearth provided not only the heat for cooking but also the light by which to perform evening tasks and to commune, and the warmth around which to gather to keep out the winter cold. In summer, of course, the ever-present food odors and extra heat of the cooking fire were less welcome. The more affluent could build extra rooms and even buildings to house the many activities associated with transforming foodstuffs from their raw state to meals for the table. With prosperity appeared the summer kitchen, the dairy or springhouse, the icehouse, the smokehouse, and the bakehouse.

In the pioneer log cabin, cooking was done on the open hearth, that is, in a fireplace.[1] Just as the exterior of the house was built of materials native to the area of the homesite, so the fireplace was most often constructed of fieldstones found in the vicinity. In some areas, stone was quarried or bricks were made for this purpose, depending on the availability of raw materials. The usual exterior of the chimney was "cats & clay," that is, cattails or small poles arranged horizontally and bound with clay or mud. An improvement on this was the stone or brick chimney.

The opening or mouth of a fireplace used for cooking was generally larger than that of the atmospheric fireplace which graces the living room of today. The extra space was needed to house the kettles and pans that were in almost constant use. The hearth or floor of the fireplace also was larger, sometimes extending several feet into the room. Many cooking operations were performed on this extended part of the hearth rather than inside the fireplace. For example, coals could be raked out onto the outer portion of the hearth and a three-legged pan, or "spider," placed over the hot coals for frying. The "Jonny cake on a clean ash board" mentioned in Drake's letter

[1] The first iron cookstove made in this country was cast in 1765, but these were not in common use in middle-class homes until the mid-nineteenth century, well after the period of settlement of Kentucky.

is another example. Often smooth board or smooth stone was used to bake the unleavened varieties of corn bread, such as the johnny (journey) cake. The board or stone was propped up on the outer hearth, slanted toward the fire so that the top of the bread was baked by the heat emanating from within the fireplace. When one side was done, it was carefully turned to bake the other side. Many of Kentucky's early settlers came from families originally from Ireland and Scotland where this same process was performed with oat cake rather than corn cake.

A few items were cooked directly among the ashes and burning coals of the fire without the use of any utensil. Favorites for this type of preparation were Irish and sweet potatoes, squash, and ears of corn still in the shuck.

Porridge pots, tea kettles, and the like were hung over the fire at various heights depending on the degree of heat desired. What the kettle hung from depended on the availability of materials and the prosperity of the family. The crudest arrangement called for a piece of green wood to be suspended across the width of the fireplace as a sort of dowel. This was the "lug pole" mentioned by Drake. The pot or kettle was then hung either directly from the lug pole by means of an S-shaped "pot hook" or from a chain or wet rope, bringing it closer to the fire for higher heat. To keep the lug pole from burning, it had to be kept wet and occasionally replaced. The housewife was very cautious on this point; for a lug pole to break during meal preparation could mean the loss of a meal and danger to bystanders.

Safer and more permanent arrangements used metal, usually iron, equipment. One popular example was the crane with a swing arm. Operating somewhat like a large hinge, the swing arm allowed the cook to swing the kettle out of the fireplace for the purposes of adding more ingredients, tasting, serving, and so forth. Trammels and ratchets were more complicated pot hooks which incorporated a means of raising or lowering the pots hooked onto them.

The kettles and pots that hung from the crane or lug pole usually were made of iron, less commonly of copper, brass, or tin. They were for food preparation involving the use of liquid.

The stew or porridge pot usually was a large, footed iron kettle weighing as much as sixty pounds. This was a direct descendant of the medieval cauldron and the indoor cousin of the hog-processing and maple-sugaring kettles mentioned earlier. In such a pot were cooked soups, stews, bean dishes, and porridges. Examples of the types of dishes cooked in such a pot are our recipes for green beans and fricasseed rabbit. A stew made of game, in-season wild greens, and roots might cook all morning for dinner and later, possibly in the same pot, a porridge of Indian (corn) meal would be put on to cook over low heat all night for the next day's breakfast. With increased affluence, of course, a family could afford separate pots for separate purposes or even several pots of different sizes for the same purpose.

Smaller pots and pans resembled those of today in overall size and shape with two striking differences: legs on the bottom of the utensil and/or a long handle. The longer handle permitted the cook to stand a safe distance from the heat of the blazing fire, especially useful when she was cooking directly inside the fireplace. The legs enabled the bottom of the pot or pan to be above rather than directly on the coals, thus helping to prevent burning of the food. Trivets (three-legged stands of various heights) were used for utensils without attached legs, and sometimes a gridiron (a four-legged structure primarily used for broiling) doubled in this function, as well.

The long-handled frying pan and the spider were used for frying such foods as eggs, hominy, and meat (fried squirrel, for example), and for finishing up vegetables with bacon fat, as with poke sallet. A small pot might be used for heating up gravy, making a medicinal herb tea, or warming cocoa.

In the frontier home, most baking and roasting were done in what has come to be called in the United States a "Dutch oven." This utensil was a large, heavy pot or kettle with a tight-fitting lid either flush with or lower than the sides of the pot. Food was placed inside, then the oven was placed in the coals and hot coals placed on top of the lid to allow the heat to penetrate from all directions. In Great Britain and the original colonies this oven was used primarily for cooking breads, but in frontier Kentucky necessity (followed by taste) made its use more general. If the pioneer cook wanted to make a raised corn bread, she added a bit of lye to the batter and baked it in the Dutch oven. If it was a roast of meat for dinner, a pumpkin pie for supper, or a pot pie for company, the Dutch oven was the item most commonly used.

Some homes were provided with more than a Dutch oven for their baking needs. A bake oven might be built into the interior or exterior wall of the fireplace or housed outside of the home in a separate structure. It could bake more bread or pie at a time than the Dutch oven but also required considerably more effort, so it usually was used no more often than once a week.

First, a fire had to be built within. This fire would heat the bricks or stones that made up the oven walls, which would retain the heat for some time. After the fire died out, the ashes were swept out.

The oven was then tested for heat to ensure that it was not too hot and would not burn the goods. To test it, the baker might put a bit of flour or meal on the oven floor and count to see how long it took to turn brown. Another method was simply to put one's hand in and count how long one could stand the heat. If the oven temperature was right, the unbaked goods were put into the oven and the door shut. The oven door, made of wood or iron, might be sealed with clay to keep the heat from seeping out. The baker had to be a mistress of timing, for once the door was opened again, much heat would escape with no opportunity for reheating. Once the bread and pies were removed, the oven could then be used for items requiring a lower heat for baking, such as custards or puddings. Finally, in the remaining warmth of the oven, wood could be dried for future use.

The pioneer family brought with them in their wagon or on their flatboat the items which they considered necessary for cooking their food. These probably included a kettle or two, a long-handled frying pan, and a Dutch oven. Replacements or additions were not impossible to come by. Peddlers soon were making their way to even the most remote districts, selling or bartering cookware as well as other items. In a short time, also, each community had its store which sold or bartered cookware as well as dry goods, dyes, coffee, tea, and spices.

For those who could afford them, there were waffle irons, roasting spits, and reflector ovens. The waffle iron was not only a splurge in its purchase as a utensil, but also entailed a splurge in ingredients. Waffles called for white flour, sugar, eggs—items that were expensive and valuable to a pioneer. The waffle iron could be quite elaborate in design, producing waffles in the shape of hearts and imprinted with flower designs. It was equipped with a long handle for fireside use, and was occasionally footed.

Spits for roasting meats over the fire ranged from a simple iron rod turned by hand to elaborate mechanisms using complex systems of weights and pulleys. The simple iron rod often was the family's lug pole doing double duty. Using it meant spending a great deal of time tending the roast of meat or fowl, turning it often to ensure the meat getting done on all sides, and basting it from the pan placed beneath to catch the drippings. The complex systems of turning the spit were costly but labor-saving. Some were clock-driven, others used the hot-air drafts from the fire to power the rotation. One type even used the running motion of a small dog to turn the spit.

The reflector oven also was known as a "roasting kitchen," "tin kitchen," and "rabbit roaster." The reflector oven was placed with its one open side toward the fire. The shiny metal of which it was constructed reflected the heat onto the meat or poultry spitted in the center. Thus, the meat did not require turning to be roasted on all sides.

Cooking, baking, and roasting were but a few of the many food-processing tasks carried on in the pioneer kitchen. Many foods had to be preserved by drying, pickling or smoking, as described in the chapter on food preservation (pp. 286–301). There was also butter to be made, and in some families cheese.

The butter churn was standard equipment in almost every cabin. For the unfortunate family that did not possess one, butter could be made by the tiresome activity of shaking a large wooden bowl containing the cream or milk. The churn most often depicted in prints and most often found in museums is the plunge churn. It consisted of a barrel-like arrangement on the bottom, which contained the milk or cream to be churned, a dasher (a long shaft similar to a broomstick), a perforated disk attached to the lower end of the dasher, and a splasher top to keep the liquid from splashing out. After a long period of plunging with the dasher, butter was formed and its by-product, buttermilk. Except for the anticipation of the end, it was not an enjoyable chore. As Daniel Drake said of his boyhood churning days: "If I had as many dollars as times I have lifted the 'dasher' I might give up teaching, and devote the remainder of my days to writing nonsense for the amusement of my grandchildren. If I could have as many rational wishes gratified as I uttered wishes that the butter 'would come,' I should have nothing *more* to wish for in this life."

For cheese-making, the first necessity was milk, and the second, rennet. In the days before rennet was available for sale in stores, the cheese-maker had to make it herself. Rennet is an extract obtained from a calf's stomach by salting it, filling it with water (and spices if available), and letting it sit for two days. The resulting liquid was high in the rennet which, when mixed with milk and left to act, would turn the milk into curds and whey. The rennet not used immediately could be bottled or dried for future use. A cheese press, usually homemade, was used to squeeze out the whey from the curds. The cheese press basically was a large weight, flat on the bottom, usually lowered onto the curds and whey by means of a lever. A rock and a pole would do. After the curds were separated, the cheese was aged. Various ingredients could be added to the milk or rennet or curds to produce different kinds of cheese.

Many of the culinary activities of the pioneer woman were carried on not one at a time but simultaneously. The dinner kettle often was put on the fire before breakfast was eaten. After breakfast, while the beans and bacon cooked, butter could be churned and the pots and pans scrubbed with sand and put outside to be cleansed by the sun. All the while, there might be milk curdling in a bowl, slices of apple or pumpkin drying, and sausages or hams hung up to smoke. The end of it all, of course, was eating.

When the family gathered for a meal, it might be at an oak or maple table that had been crafted in the East and carefully transported to Kentucky in a covered wagon. Or the table might have been part of the old wagon itself, roughly refashioned by the man of the house. The home might boast family china and silver, but that would be rare. Most frontier folk ate from pewter or wooden trenchers, with utensils fashioned from pewter, wood, gourds, or shells. Some families, lacking even these humble artifacts, ate directly from the stewpot, using their hands.

Whether buckeye bowls or china were used, enjoying the meal was the culmination of many efforts. The meat had to be hunted or raised, the vegetables foraged for or cultivated. Then came the smoking, the drying, the churning, and the roasting. Finally, the table was set and the family joined together to enjoy the products of the frontier land and the arts of the pioneer kitchen.

WORK CITED

The quotations from Daniel Drake (1785–1852) are taken from his *Pioneer Life in Kentucky,* edited by Emmet Field Horine, M.D. (New York: Henry Schuman, 1948), a collection of letters written by Dr. Drake to his family, recounting daily life in the Kentucky of his youth.

The Inns and Spas of Early Kentucky

Mary McClinton Clay

During the last decade of the eighteenth century, Kentucky developed rapidly from a frontier wilderness into the cultural center of the country west of the Allegheny Mountains. Kentucky towns adopted a style of living nearly as fashionable as the urban areas of the East. Social and cultural exchange spurred this rapid advancement. The social life of a locality revolved around the tavern or inn, which was as important to its community as it was to travelers. Furthermore, the stagecoach line's success depended on the quality of the inns along its route.

In the backwoods, the homes of settlers along early roads offered lodging to travelers. F. A. Michaux and Thomas Ashe, who stayed in such lodgings in the first decade of the nineteenth century, described them as log huts where the traveler slept on the floor wrapped in his own blanket. Meals consisted of bread, Indian corn, dried ham, milk, and butter. Michaux observed that "Ninetenths of them . . . eat no other bread but that made from Indian corn; they make loaves of it from eight to ten pounds, which they bake in ovens, or small cakes baked on a board before the fire. This bread is generally eaten hot, and is not very palatable to those who are not used to it." Ashe complained that they "eat salt meat three times a day, seldom or never have any vegetables, and drink ardent spirits from morning till night."

Tavern and ordinary rates varied each year and in each county. In 1803, the Fayette County Board of Magistrates fixed the annual rates thus: "Breakfast, hot, one shilling, three pence; cold, one shilling; Dinner, hot, one shilling, six pence; Supper, hot, one shilling, three pence; Whiskey per half pint, four pence; Brandy per half pint, six pence; French Brandy per half pint, one shilling; Rum per half pint, one shilling; Madeira wine per bottle, nine pence; All other wines per bottle, six pence; Lodging per night, six pence; Oates per gallon, four pence; Corn per gallon, four pence; Hay and stableage, 24 hours, nine pence; Pasturage, 24 hours, nine pence; Cyder per quart, six pence, Strong beer per quart, six pence."

These rates were posted, along with rules of the house, in the public room of the tavern. Henry Fearon, staying at Lawes' Hotel in Middletown in 1819, recorded the following rules:

1st. All Gentlemaen to give their names to the bar-keeper.
2nd. No gentleman shall enter the Dining-room until the second bell rings.
3rd. No gambling allowed in the Bedrooms.
4th. The doors closed at ten o'clock, except on the night of public amusement.
5th. No *Gentleman* shall *take* the Saddle, Bridle, or Harness of another Gentleman without his consent.

Taverns not only provided lodging for travelers, but also diversion and a meeting place for townspeople. Michaux found the prevailing amusements in Lexington to be drinking, gambling, billiards, and cards. Taverns were especially crowded during the sittings of the courts of justice, when law suits comprised the usual topic of conversation. James Flint observed in 1822 that "among the succession of people at the tavern, many are polite and obliging in their behavior. Some are interesting in their conversation, and some talk of horses and horseracing. The latter kind of discourse is mixed with swearing." Taverns were also the scene of such public gatherings as political rallies, lectures, exhibitions, theatricals, musicals, balls, and sporting events. Love's Tavern in Frankfort once housed an animal show in the main dining room, although the elephant was obliged to stay outside. Duncan Tavern in Paris held theatricals as early as 1808.

The accommodations of taverns varied considerably, depending on location. In his *Letters from America,* James Flint gives an illuminating account of a typical Kentucky backwoods tavern in 1822.

> Like its owner, it commonly makes a conspicuous figure in its neighborhood. It is a log, a frame, or a brick house, frequently with a wooden piazza in front. From the top of a tall post, the sign-board is suspended. On it, a Washington, a Montgomery, a Wayne, a Pike, or a Jackson, is usually pourtrayed, in a style that might not easily be deciphered except for the name attached. On the top of the house is a small bell, which is twice rung before meals. Immediately after the second peal, travelers and boarders assemble round the table, where they commence eating *without preface.* In such promiscuous parties, the governor of a state, or a general of the militia, may be seen side by side with the wagoner. The larger towns having taverns of different rates of charges, a distinction of company is the natural consequence. We breakfast and sup on coffee or tea, accompanied with plenty of beef, bacon, chicken, and eggs. The hostess (or host if he is unmarried) takes her seat at the head of the table, and dispenses the tea. One or two *hired people* (or slaves, in slave-keeping parts of the country) wait at table. At dinner, wheaten and Indian corn breads, beef, pork, venison, wild turkey, geese, and poultry, are staple articles; with a profusion of vegetables, such as cucumbers, onions, cabbages, beans, and preserved fruits. Lodging in taverns has not generally all the convenience that could be wished for. It is common to see several beds in the same room, and these are simple bedsteads without hangings. There are no bells in the bedrooms, and other apartments; nor are menials accustomed to move at the signal of the stranger. Water is rarely to be met with in bedrooms; washing is, of course, performed under a shed behind the house, or at the pump. A full house is always the apology for causing two strangers to sleep in the same bed; the propriety of the custom will always be admitted by the person who arrives latest. It has been my lot to sleep with a diversity of personages; I do believe, from the driver of the stage coach, to men of considerable name. The noted cutaneous disease is certainly not prevalent; if it was, the beds of taverns which, like burying grounds, lay all on a level, would soon make the disease as prevalent in this country, as in some others in the old world.

In contrast, Samuel Brown in 1816 described Lexington taverns and boarding houses as "neat and well furnished. Wilson's Hotel [originally Postlethwait's and later the Phoenix Hotel] is excelled by none in America, for extensiveness, style and good living." The original building was a low log house fitted with fashionable, locally made furniture and illuminated by tallow candles. Rag rugs covered the floors.

Among other noted Kentucky taverns was Bell's Tavern near Mammoth Cave. Like most proprietors, the landlord, Billy Bell, was an educated and civically responsible man. His tables were known to have "groaned with the best food (venison, wild turkey, pheasant, fish from the river) the country can afford and the trimmings were suitable to the taste of the most fastidious epicurean. His favorite appetizer was 'peach and honey' [peach brandy mixed with honey] and he was lavish in its dispensation." Kentuckians also favored metheglin, as did other southerners. This drink was made from ground honey locust beans mixed with honey, herbs, water, and yeast, which was then allowed to ferment.

Sir Charles Lyell in 1846 found the Galt House in Louisville (built in 1832) "the best hotel we had been in since we left St. Louis." A Galt House menu for Christmas Day 1856 offered (for fifty cents a plate) "saddle of venison with current jelly; rib of bear with fancy sauce; wild turkey with cranberry sauce; stuffed red-head duck; woodduck with hunter's sauce; wild goose with poteine sauce; bridge of buffalo tongue a la Godar; arcade of pheasants with green peas; choice of four soups, two fish, fifteen vegetables, numerous cakes, puddings, nuts, apples, and Charlotte Russe with Punch au Rhein."

Surprisingly, a number of Kentucky's early inns still stand. Duncan Tavern in Paris, built in 1788, is now maintained as a museum by the Daughters of the American Revolution. The Old Stone Inn in Simpsonville (1791), Doe Run Inn, east of Brandenburg (1792), and Old Talbott Tavern, Bardstown (1779, pictured on p. 36), still serve excellent food. Stage Coach Inn in Guthrie (pictured on p. 9) is now a private residence. Others, such as Bright's Inn near Stanford, Elkhorn Tavern in Caldwell County, and Chiles Tavern in Harrodsburg, all dating from the early nineteenth century, although long gone, are still remembered in local legend, and some of their recipes are preserved by descendants of their proprietors. Other inns, restaurants, and hotels have taken their place, maintaining Kentucky's reputation for fine food and impeccable service.

The development of stagecoach travel through Kentucky during the first decade of the nineteenth century made much of the state easily accessible to travelers from other parts of America. As Kentucky's economic and social life evolved, the state's numerous salt licks and mineral springs were developed as fashionable "watering places" which became meccas for those seeking congenial associations during the summer months. The social season at Kentucky spas soon acquired as fashionable a reputation as that at Virginia's famous springs. The social season usually lasted from June to September. Northerners came to enjoy a warm June and Southern plantation owners came from the low country to escape the heat and malaria of the late summer. The spas also provided a haven for Central Kentuckians fleeing the infestuous cities during the cholera epidemics of 1833 and 1849.

The restorative benefits of the springs drew as large a clientele as did the social attractions. Among the various mineral waters boasted of were alum water, copperas, sulphur, and chalybeate salt. These proved beneficial for diseases of the liver, kidneys, and stomach, as well as asthma, gout, dyspepsia, rheumatism, bilious disorders, neuralgia, "autumnal fevers," and general debility. In addition to drinking the waters, a patient could be steamed in a shower or tub bath, and some spas offered pools for plunge bathing.

Despite the blanket claims of the spas' promoters, not all were convinced. Fortesque Cuming observed at Blue Lick in 1810 that the spas were "frequented . . . as both a cure and antidote for every disorder incident to the human frame. I believe them to be perfectly neutral; they are impregnated with sulphur, and smell and taste exactly like the bilge water in a ship's hold, of course, they are very nauseous. They act sometimes as a cathartick and sometimes as an emetick, but without causing either griping, or sickness of the stomach." At Olympian Springs, Cuming found the patrons more given to "cards, billiards, horse-jockying, &c, than to the use of the waters for medicinal purposes."

Most spa guests paid by the week or the month. In the 1820s and 1830s charges ranged from three to six dollars a week, depending on the accommodations. Children stayed for half price, and servants and horses cost their masters two dollars a week.

Many springs acquired the reputation of veritable pleasure grounds. N. Parker Willis described Harrodsburg Spring in 1853 as the "most unexpected mixture of paradise and public house. . . . You could be no-where more luxuriously comfortable . . . a good table, and a good society, are two luxuries which I believe you may always make sure of at Harrodsburg."

A typical day's routine at Harrodsburg Spring in the 1840s began with a walk before breakfast to see the sunrise. Breakfast was served at eight, followed by bowling, ten-pins, or billiards. Lunch was at one, after which everyone retired until the heat of the day was past. The arrival and departure of the stage occupied guests during the afternoon, and dinner began at seven, followed by dancing at eight.

Food served at the Mammoth Cave Hotel was typical of that served at other spas: "Venison steak, bass fried in corn meal, mast-fattened bacon, cured with hickory wood fire, snap beans cooked with green corn, pone bread from the skillet on the hearth, and cider and rum, French brandys and home made wines." The daughter of Judge John Rowan described the table at Harrodsburg Spring in 1829 as "the best that I had ever sat down at any place; *ice cream in profusion.*"

Kentucky's spas reached their height of popularity between about 1830 and 1860. The state boasted more than half a dozen watering places of national reputation and numerous others locally popular. One of the most noted was Olympian Springs in Montgomery County (earlier known as Mud Lick), which was developed early in the nineteenth century by Colonel Thomas Hart, father-in-law of Henry Clay. Greenville Springs near Harrodsburg opened during the first decade of the century, and in the 1820s its competitor, Harrodsburg Spring, began. Dr. Christopher Columbus Graham took over both institutions late in that decade and operated them until 1853 under the name of Graham Springs or Harrodsburg Spring, as the most fashionable resort in Kentucky. Crab Orchard Springs in Lincoln County rivaled Graham Springs as the Saratoga of the South. Paroquet Springs in Bullitt County (so named because of the large numbers of Carolina parakeets found in the area at that time), Cerulean Springs in Trigg County (originally a black sulphur spring which the great earthquake of 1811 changed to a light blue color), Drennon Springs in Henry County, Blue Licks in Nicholas County, Grayson Springs near Leitchfield, and Esculapia Springs in Lewis County were all prominent.

The Civil War forced many spas to close due to the lack of patronage and damages from fighting on their lands, and resort life went into a decline until the mid-1870s and early 1880s. Those that continued did so on a less grand scale than in antebellum days. With the Gay Nineties came a revival of some old spas and the opening of new ones. This was short lived, however, for the decade also brought circuses, county and state fairs, Chautauquas, railroad tours to other scenic parts of the country, and the development of patent medicines, which replaced the curative powers of the mineral waters. The final demise of watering places occurred between 1900 and 1915. With them went not only an era but a quality of life that was never to return.

SUGGESTED READING

Coleman, J. W., Jr. "Old Kentucky Watering Places." *Filson Club History Quarterly* 16, no. 1 (January 1942).
————. *Stage-Coach Days in the Bluegrass.* Louisville, Kentucky, 1936.
————. *The Springs of Kentucky.* Lexington, Kentucky, 1955.
Lathrop, Elise. *Early American Inns and Taverns.* New York, 1926.
Willis, N. Parker. *Health Trip to the Tropics.* New York, 1853.

Pleasant Hill's Shakers: A "Gathering" of Excellence

Elizabeth C. Kremer

The Shakers never had any intention of becoming known to the world for their cooking; nor did they intend to be ahead of their time in knowledge of nutrition. Their communities were designed as escapes from "the world"; and with their hearts tuned to Eternity, they renounced the things of their times. They established peaceful celibate communities where both sexes, freed from worldly cares, could obey Mother Ann Lee's injunction to "put their hands to work and their hearts to God." The result of seeking first such a kingdom of God, however, was the creation of earthly communities whose excellence astounded and intrigued "the world" they left behind.

Paradox runs through their history. They abhorred ornamentation, for instance, and thought of beauty as a devil's snare. Yet their insistence on simplicity and concern with functionalism produced striking loveliness in costume, furniture, and architecture. To such places as Pleasant Hill,[1] near Harrodsburg, visitors come from far

---

1 Pleasant Hill, which began in 1805, was formally disbanded in 1910, though Sister Mary Settles, the last of the Shakers, lived there until her death in 1923. Kentucky's other Shaker community, South Union, lasted from 1811 until 1922.

away to admire the restored community, to eat at the Trustees' House, and to acknowledge the ingenuity and integrity of the believers.

Shaker cookery is an example of such paradox. Shaker lemon pie, for instance, is a practical dessert; nothing is wasted. Mother Ann Lee, who founded the Shaker movement, took literally the injunction to "gather up the fragments so that nothing remains," and guests at Shaker villages were always asked to finish any helping they took. This pie features the whole lemon, sliced paper thin: an intriguing and nutritional dessert which is a culinary delight born of practicality and piety.

"The world" which the Shakers abandoned frequently came to them for food. Sometimes, it is true, the world's people came as "winter Shakers," seeking a way to get through the hard months before spring. But often those from the world were guests, curious investigators who came to scoff but went away, if not believers, at least admirers of their unique life and culinary brilliance. An 1837 visitor to one Shaker village commented on the delicious breads he was served for lunch, "some wheaten, some of Indian corn, and some made with molasses." His party, he reported, "could have gone on eating such bread and butter all day." *The Best of Shaker Cooking* (which records the visitor's praise) tells us that by the century's end Shaker cooking was known far and wide: "In the latter part of the nineteenth century the Shakers invited 'the people of the world' to their dinner tables, and fond recollections of these occasions have been passed along from one generation to another by word of mouth, by letter, and through accumulation of recipes from Shaker cooks."

John M. Cromwell recalled, in the *Cynthiana Democrat,* "a most bountiful meal taken with the Shakers" of Pleasant Hill on a bicycle tour in 1886: "After climbing the long hill we were in a receptive mood for a square meal, and the hour being high noon we decided to try our luck with the Shakers. Never shall I forget the meal we sat down to on that occasion. Like 'Oliver Twist' we 'asked for more,' but unlike him we were not denied."

The world also clamored for Shaker food products: crates of fruit were sent by railway as far as Texas; herbs were shipped to England. Indeed, herb lore was well known to the Shakers, some of it learned from the Indians. They cultivated acres of herbs—sage was a large crop—and gathered wild herbs from the woods (a task often assigned to the children at Pleasant Hill). The Shakers, we are told, "were among the first in this country to practice a systematic and more or less scientific gathering and classifying of herbs for medicinal uses"; they were also "the first people in this country to grow herbs on a large scale for the pharmaceutical market." They mastered large-scale processing of herbs, drying them or converting them into extracts or oils. They also used them liberally in foods with practical intentions: "Many Shaker recipes call for one or two herbs to flavor or to heal." The result was unparalleled excellence: "Many of the recipes are simple. However, because of the Shakers' extensive use of herbs and spices, their dishes were more exotic than other American cooking."

The Shakers' orchards were famous, and they originated several varieties of apples, including the quince apple, the Shaker pippin, the Shaker greening, and several drying apples. They learned to preserve their fruits, not only to maintain the community, but to market for profit. Such activities were especially important in Kentucky. Elder Henry C. Blinn, inspecting the Pleasant Hill community in 1873, described the trees he passed in riding to inspect livestock on a May morning: "On the way we pass through an orchard of some 1000 trees: half of which are apple & half peach. . . . We pass by acres of strawberries, gooseberries & other small fruits. The clover in the orchard was to the horse's knees." Shaker fruit trees were productive. Elder Blinn recorded that "one old cherry tree at this place afforded . . . 175 one quart bottles of preserves last year." Furthermore, not the least thing in these orchards was wasted. The clover through which Elder Blinn's horse waded had its use; in the village's storage cellar he viewed not only "jars of preserves & canned fruit . . . in abundance," he found also honey boxes "filled with honey of last year, and the bees are now making new. White clover is in bloom & some of the colonies have already swarmed three times."

Elder Blinn recorded the Shaker sisters' industry in marketing garden produce: "Our first walk this morning is to the Wash House to see sisters, who are engaged in preserving strawberries. This is sale work. They get 11½ dollars per doz—for quart bottles. They have the same price for cherries, Ice melon & other fruits. They use one pound of sugar to one pound of fruit." He also delighted in the richness of Pleasant Hill's May crops: apples, he noted, are "¾ inch in diameter. Peaches about the same. Cherries are ripe. Peas ready to pick. From our window we see the hills of sweet potatoes. A novel sight, indeed."

The Elder recorded, also, a sight seen in a walk "before breakfast" (he mentioned his meals frequently, and with favor): "Several beautiful flower beds," he noted, "attract our attention." He added the more practical observation that "the gardens are very extensive and everything is provided for the kitchen department with a liberal hand." Even the "beautiful flower beds" were part of the practical garden. The Shakers admired such things as roses for utility, as they valued violets for nutrition. They converted rose blooms to rose water or attar of roses, both offered for sale. One Shaker building in Ohio "was stacked in season with wagonloads of rose bloom"; lest there be a temptation to adornment, all flowers were plucked without stems.

From the beginning the practical Shaker gardens were places of beauty. As early as 1825 a visiting reporter for the *Richmond Inquirer* described the Pleasant Hill field as "a handsome garden tastily laid off." He also admired the believers as "a trafficking, humane, honest and thrifty people." "Everything about them," wrote this visitor from the world, "indicates uncommon neatness, ingenuity and industry."

The Richmond reporter admired the Shakers not only for their industry, but for their joy. The "countenances" of most men and women, he said, "when not at worship exhibit meek, contented, cheerful and happy minds." He was bothered by Shaker worship—where believers "shook out" the carnal life in turbulent dance, a vigorous and noisy ceremony he did not understand; but he did understand—and praise—the results of their life: industry, productivity, gentleness, and joy.

A Shaker community, set apart from the world and often misunderstood by it, took great care of its own, affirming a heavenly family in place of the earthly one abandoned. An example of this was the concern and respect the Shakers had for their older members. Both psychologically and nutritionally, they grasped much that the modern world is just beginning to appreciate. Shakers developed "especially nutritive diets for those over sixty." Yet, this group of senior citizens was not a dependent one, since Shakers "believed in every member— both old and young—working according to his strength and ability. They considerably lightened the load of their older members but never robbed them of their sense of usefulness."

Food prepared for the elderly included "soups, stews and broths, laden with vitamins, minerals and proteins, made of red beef, liver and kidneys." Greens and fruit were emphasized, as well as "great quantities of tomatoes, ample butter, milk, cheese and eggs." While recipes varied, they included such sickbed standards as calf's foot jelly and jellied veal as well as surprisingly hearty dishes such as kidney and steak pie and baked liver with onions. For variety there were curious items like tomato custard and for tempting the appetite such desserts as "Sister Abigail's Strawberry Flummery."

Although they exempted their elderly from it, the Shakers even experimented with vegetarianism. A ban on meat eating was attempted from 1837 to 1847. Eventually abandoned, the experiment had no lasting influence beyond the fortunate production of a number of excellent vegetarian recipes. One group who embraced "the bloodless diet," as it was called, claimed that "the whole family united and found as the years passed that the abundant diet of grains, vegetables, fruit, eggs, and milk products . . . answered every physiological need as well as satisfying the conscience of the consumer." Pleasant Hill's community made at least a partial step in the direction of this reform. Its journal for October 10, 1842, records that on Monday "we all unitedly quit the use of all strong drink, tea coffy and tobacco and also the use of swines flesh in part. We now make use of such drinks as we can raise on our own soil." But the change seems to have been temporary. Elder Blinn in his 1873 visit noted that the community "drink both tea & coffee," adding that "Elder Frederic's spirit of reform in dietetics has made but slight inroads into the customs of this society." He also recorded that "in the cellar we saw six barrels of lard, which came from their own beef."

This community had both a thriving livestock business and expertise in the dairy trade. One pasture the Elder inspected held "the cattle for beefe, one two & three years old." That the experiment in vegetarianism had passed is indicated by an anecdote he recorded on the same occasion: "Br. James thought they might sell some of them. 'Ah, nay,' said Elder Thomas, 'They will eat a mighty heap before spring & will want them right fat too." The cows, Blinn observed, were "excellent milkers. All full blood Durham." He described the Shakers' care of milk: "We pass their spring house, a small building in which they place their pans of milk. A stream of water runs through the building & spreads over the whole floor, making it one of the best places to keep milk cool."

These industrious and gentle Shakers of Pleasant Hill were troubled by "the world" during the Civil War: "The roar of artillery at intervals between Harrodsburg and Danville" records a journal on October 11, 1862, "announced that the work of death and destruction was going on within 8 or 10 miles of this sacred spot." They rose to this occasion—as to others—with service: "We have fed more than a thousand persons to-day. . . . They offer to purchase every thing they call for, but we have little for them except provisions, and we have uniformally declined any compensation for these, and they are lavish with their thanks for our hospitality." Both Union and Confederate soldiers experienced that hospitality. "A company of 100 United States cavalry" camped in the pasture "east of the East barn" to be fed breakfast and lunch. Troops under "Col. Gana of Gen.

Morgan's command" were fed "with the help of the brethren" and the sisters, who cooked and baked "with all the means at their command to keep a supply, till about 400 had eaten." With compassion and concern they cared for the intruders, mustering their industry and supplies to feed warring soldiers of the world they had renounced.

Shaker excellence in food stemmed entirely from theological convictions. Nutrition was valued because a strong body was essential in working for "the glory of God." Elder Blinn, whose journal describes so well the Pleasant Hill community, wrote that "if the food that we eat to sustain life has anything to do with the ruling of our mind or body . . . it becomes highly important, especially for those of the Christian faith, to examine the subject with great care." Craftsmanship—the job well done—was important because it was an offering. The Shakers admonished, "Do your work as though you had a thousand years to live, and as if you were to die tomorrow." Soup bubbling in heavy iron kettles in the kitchen and preserves sent to market in "the world" were work done before God.

Pleasant Hill's journals, recordings of daily activities written with careful hands, preserve memory of the industry involved in what the Shakers labeled "Business in general." There is concern with livestock, description of harvest from the garden, accounts of foraging in the country for annual wild plants. "Gathering" is a favorite word; "gleaning" after gathering is another. Sage, currants, elderberries, strawberries, cherries were regularly harvested for the community and its market, the world. These journals record various seasonal journeys: "Went to the cliffs after raspberries"; "Gathered blackberries at the cove spring." Catnip and strawberry leaves were used for tea, apples collected for drying or for processing as jelly or apple butter; pears and plums were preserved in season.

Sometimes the details of the Pleasant Hill schedule seem far in excess of simple industry. An 1855 entry states:

> July. Monday 2nd. we got up at the early hour of 2 O-clock and completed our washing against 10 O-clock. we all comenced gathering cherries, and by night fall we had put up 50 jars of boilt cherries for Ministry and sick people.
> Tuesday. 3rd. we got up at 3 O-clock and completed our ironing at an early hour and returned again to the cherry trees. gatherd and built 18 2 gal. jars for home use.

In other records only a simple entry sums up daily labor: "October 30. Tuesday. Ironed. killed a beef." The seasons went round, crops changed, but Shaker industry went on: "gathered apples after Ironing . . . made apple butter for our use . . . made apple butter for Sale also 3 barrels of vinegar."

Shakers were aware of the passage of time, and they accepted their responsibility: "You must not lose one moment of time, for you have none to spare" was one of their proverbs. Turning their attention to things eternal, they mastered much that is temporal. "The world" now beats paths to the doorsteps they have left—to view the remains of their excellence and to learn from them. "If you improve in one talent," says one of their proverbs, "God will give you more."

SOURCES

The Shaker Journals at Pleasant Hill record the daily labors of the community. Elder Henry C. Blinn's "A Journey to Kentucky in the Year 1873" is printed in *The Shaker Quarterly* 5, no. 4 (Winter 1965): 107-33. For detailed information about Shaker diet for the aging I am indebted to Caroline B. Piercy, *The Shaker Cook Book* (New York: Crown Publishers, 1953). My information about Shaker cooking and other Shaker communities was supplemented by Amy Bess Miller and Persis Fuller's *The Best of Shaker Cooking* (New York: Macmillan, 1970); *The Shaker Image,* compiled by Elmer R. Pearson, Julia Neal, and Walter Muir Whitehill (Boston: New York Graphic Society, 1974); and Marguerite Fellows Melcher's *The Shaker Adventure* (Princeton: Princeton University Press, 1941). The library at Pleasant Hill furnished the copy of the May 3, 1825, article in the *Richmond Inquirer.* The material from "Cromwell's Comments" in the *Cynthiana Democrat* was taken from my own collection of my father's writing.

Elegant Dining in Kentucky

Burton Milward

The Declaration of Independence was only two years old, the American Revolution was at its peak, and the sparse Kentucky population kept constant vigilance against the Indians who resented and resisted their intrusion. It was the winter of 1778. In the previous July, General George Rogers Clark and his small force of riflemen had defeated the Indians in the Illinois country and won comparative but temporary safety. The general felt it was feasible for the settlers at the Falls of the Ohio to build a fort on the shore and leave their island sanctuary in the river.

The fort was a simple structure, according to Reuben T. Durrett's account in J. Stoddard Johnston's *Memorial History of Louisville*—200 feet long and half as wide, with twenty-four double cabins and a two-story blockhouse at each corner, and as Christmas approached the settlers "determined to move into it and there celebrate their first Christmas in the wilderness.

"Hunters were sent into the woods to secure an ample supply of venison, and buffalo, and bear, and wild turkey, and opossum meats for a grand dinner, and the women lost no time in getting ready their dishes of hominy and cornbread and ash-cake, and pumpkin pie."

The northeast blockhouse was the banquet hall, and at noon, Colonel Durrett relates, the men, women, and children gathered around the long puncheon table, in the center of which was a whole baked possum. After dinner, the table was moved to the side, black Cato Watts and his old fiddle provided the music for the Virginia reel, and the sound of merriment broke the quiet of the wilderness.

Elegance in dining, as in other aspects of life, is a relative thing, depending upon the circumstances and the resources available, and that Christmas fete in the winter of 1778 was, indeed, an elegant affair.

By 1788 Colonel William Whitley had laid out a race course on his acres near the Crab Orchard, and by 1794 he had erected there the handsome brick residence that is now a state shrine. Even then, despite the increasing civilities of life, the Indian menace remained and Colonel Whitley led an expedition against the Chickamauga village of Nickajack in what is now Tennessee. Upon his return he honored his compatriots with a barbecue at Sportsman's Hill, where the table was set on the lawn and "well supplied with viands, vegetables & fruits" and a pair of shoats, roasted whole.

Whitley's race course, the first circular track in the West, attracted people from near and far, and he entertained them graciously. Thomas D. Clark, in his "Rivers of America" book, *The Kentucky*, relates that Whitley "pointed the way to high living" when he "gave a breakfast in 1813 for his friends who attended the morning races . . . which was all that a gourmet's heart could desire. There was chicken, soup with rice, baked Ohio River salmon, bacon, cabbage, beans, barbecued lamb, roast duck, applesauce, roast turkey, cranberry sauce, roast beef, broiled squirrel, leg of bear, baked opossum, sweet potatoes, roasting ears, hominy, boiled potatoes, baked sweet potatoes, stewed tomatoes, hot cakes, corn dodgers," and a large assortment of desserts and beverages, including, of course, old Kentucky bourbon.

While the hunter and the gardener provided the menu for the pioneer feasts, Kentucky was still in its frontier stage when families from Virginia and other eastern states were bringing in the furniture, china, and silver that would grace the handsome homes they were planning or already building. And the merchants of Lexington as early as 1787 were importing by flatboat and wagon such amenities as teapots, cups and saucers, linens, coffee, tea and chocolate, sugar, spices, and seasonings.

Nowhere was living more elegant and entertainment more gracious than at Colonel David Meade's "Chaumière des Prairies" in Jessamine County, for the old Virginia gentleman's whole way of life was epicurean. He and his family, with a retinue of servants and an abundance of possessions, came to the Bluegrass in the summer of 1796 and set about making their new estate a wonderland of landscaping. He was ever prepared for guests who came without notice and was, indeed, offended if any refused to remain for dinner.

On Christmas Day in 1818, it is said, there were a hundred guests at Colonel Meade's table, and on another occasion President Horace Holley and twenty of his faculty and students at Transylvania University were persuaded to remain for dinner. Virtually every notable visitor to Central Kentucky was welcomed at Chaumière, among them reportedly President James Monroe, Andrew Jackson, Zachary Taylor, and Aaron Burr. Colonel Meade's sense of hospitality caused him grief if anyone felt it necessary to send advance notice of his coming or awaited an invitation.

In all Kentucky's history, it is likely that no event occasioned more lavish entertainment than the triumphal tour of the Marquis de Lafayette, "the nation's guest," in the summer of 1825. In his journey from Louisville to Lexington to Cincinnati, nothing was left undone to prove that Kentucky hospitality was justly famed. At Frankfort, for instance, a banquet was served in the public square, where two huge circular tables, one within the other, provided places for 700 guests. Colonel Richard Taylor, proprietor of the Mansion House hotel, had charge of the dinner, and the cost was the then-extravagant sum of two thousand dollars.

In Lexington a ball and dinner were given at the Grand Masonic Hall which, although still unfinished, was lavishly decorated in patriotic motif. The pièce de résistance was a magnificent castellated cake, made by Mathurin Giron, the confectioner; a cake so magnificent, in fact, that none could bring himself to cut it and it was preserved for display at breakfast in the morning and then at the next meeting of the lodge. Lafayette, alas, feasted on it only with his eyes.

Monsieur Giron, accomplished as he was and still remembered for the delicacies he concocted and the parties given at his ballroom in Lexington, was, nevertheless, but one of numerous Frenchmen who fled the unrest of their own country and helped bring culture and culinary delight to Kentucky's towns. Many of them were men and women of education, intelligence, and charm who made their living in the West as teachers of music, dancing, and language, or engaged successfully in business and manufacturing.

The annual Independence Day celebrations throughout Kentucky, as well as in most cities in the country, were conducted with ceremonies and festivities rarely accorded them now. After all, the events of independence were fresh in the memory of many citizens, and veterans of the Revolution lived in many communities.

Samuel D. McCullough, in his reminiscences of early Lexington, describes how the Fourth of July was celebrated during the first decade of the nineteenth century, when he was but a boy. The day began with a parade led by drummers and fifers and the colorfully uniformed military companies; then came the citizens, men and women, boys and girls, in double file; members of the Masonic order; and finally the venerable veterans on foot and in carriages. From Main Street the procession moved out Limestone to the Maxwell Springs, on the present campus of the University of Kentucky, where the orators of the day spoke. Then "the drums beat the call to dinner."

"The fraternity of Free Masons were, as individuals, generally selected to wait on the tables, especially those of the Ladies," McCullough related, adding that "In my childish ignorance I wondered why those elegantly dressed gentlemen should act as servants along with their own servants. . . . After the festivities of the day were about to be concluded, and all, man and woman and child; the rich and the poor, the master and servants had eaten their fill; the 'fragments' that remained, far more than 'twelve baskets full' were carefully gathered up, consisting of bread, bacon, hams, lambs, beef, venison, all whole; besides an abundance of sweet-meats and comfits, and were religiously given to the poor."

Barbecue and burgoo are concoctions which date back to the pioneer days, for they could be made of whatever meats and vegetables might be available and were easily prepared. Over the years, however, they acquired a mystique that lingers yet, and each section of the state has had its noted burgoo makers and its favorite recipes, each better than any other. One of the assets of burgoo is that it is made best and most flavorfully in large quantity, and thousands have been fed on occasions ranging from the early patriotic and political celebrations to reunions of the Northern and Southern veterans of the Civil War, the annual Fancy Farm picnic in Graves County, and the Iroquois Hunt Club picnic at Grimes Mill.

The Fancy Farm festival dates back to about 1880, and in the early years the people came with their baskets of food which they spread together. As the gatherings grew larger, the women began to cook part of the food in the school kitchen and serve it family style in the dining room. Sheep were barbecued on open pits, vegetables came from the family gardens, and homemade pies, cakes, and ice cream were brought. Because the picnic was held each year a few days before the primary election, then in August instead of May, it became a "last-ditch stand" for many of the candidates, and people came by the thousands, and from many states, to enjoy the fun and food.

Today the meals are served in a modern cafeteria. Green beans, lima beans, corn, blackeyed peas, tomatoes, potato salad, slaw, homemade pickles, fried chicken, and barbecued pork and mutton are on the menu, with gallons of coffee and iced tea at hand. The meat is cooked on modern covered pits and approximately eighty sheep and a hundred and fifty hams and shoulders roast for twenty-four hours over the hot hickory coals. And at times the political oratory is as hot as the glowing embers.

Of all the men famed for skill in the art of burgoo making, the greatest, perhaps, was Gus Jaubert, who once, in 1895, provided thirty thousand gallons of the delection, plus thousands of pounds of barbecued meat, for more than two hundred thousand members of the Grand Army of the Republic at Louisville. Jaubert was known as "the Burgoo King," and when he died in 1920 his title and one of his huge iron kettles were inherited by J. T. Looney. It was for Mr. Looney that Colonel E. R. Bradley named the chestnut colt, Burgoo King, which won the 1932 Kentucky Derby.

Burgoo and barbecue, served out of doors around long pits of glowing oak and hickory and tremendous iron kettles, are honored in Kentucky history, as typical of Kentucky hospitality as the immaculate dining table of a handsome old residence, a table set with gleaming coin silver and graced with country ham at one end and roast turkey at the other.

It was in July of 1856 that Sarah Gibson Humphreys honored her husband, Joseph, with a stag dinner at their home, "Sumner's Forest," in Woodford County. The printed menu at each of the thirty places listed three kinds of soup; boiled meats—ham in champagne sauce, brisket in white sauce, leg of mutton, and pig's head with mint sauce; baked meats—beef, ham, duck, and calf's head; roast saddle of mutton and roast shoat; five entrees—chicken with mushrooms, croquettes, broiled kidney, oyster pies and sweetbreads; more than a dozen vegetables; four kinds of pastry, seven of dessert, and nuts and fruits. Digestion was aided by five vintage wines and coffee.

Five years later, at Ashland, Kentucky, Mrs. John Means entertained at tea for a newcomer to the community. Actually, she wrote, it was a supper for fifteen, and she "had oysters, tongue, chicken salad, Sally Lunn, hot biscuits, sponge cake, jelly cake, preserves and peaches and other good things in proportion."

In Mason County in 1887 Captain James M. Davis, "a plain farmer, not given to putting on style," made a handsome fortune dealing in tobacco. To celebrate his success he gave a dinner attended by fifty friends, and a newspaper of the time described it:

> The provision made for the entertainment was royal. The waters of the Chesapeake, the orange groves of Florida, the tropical fruits of the West Indies, the vineyards of sunny Italy and France, the plantations of Louisiana, the swamps of Michigan, the graperies of California, the fig groves of Smyrna, and the rich fields and pastures of Mason and Fleming were drawn upon to furnish a banquet good enough for Kings, Princes or Presidents. The guests were seated to tables groaning with oysters, quail, turkey, old Virginia ham, celery, fruits, cake and wine served by members of Captain Davis' family and in a style that would do credit to professional caterers. . . .
>
> It was remarked that none of the birds served at the feast had any shot marks upon them. This was explained by Captain Davis. He said that some time ago he informed some of his Maysville friends that the time would come when birds could be killed on his place with silver dollars and if silver dollars were not heavy enough, they could be brought down with twenty dollar gold pieces. . . .
>
> Haucke's string band from Maysville relieved the hours with excellent music during the evening, and contributed greatly to the enjoyment of the occasion [which lasted until the rising of the moon at 4 A. M.]

It was in the same decade that the ladies of Maysville's Methodist Episcopal Church, South, published *The New Kentucky Cook Book,* which conveniently gave in the back a menu for each day in the year. People obviously ate bountifully in those days, but the Thanksgiving Day suggestion was especially robust:

For breakfast: brains, steak, buckwheat cakes, roasted potatoes, light bread and coffee. For dinner: oyster soup, hot crackers, turkey stuffed with oysters, cranberries, pickles, celery, jelly, buttered light bread, sweet potatoes, macaroni, French pease on toast, and eggs, and for dessert, plum pudding with wine sauce, ice cream, almond custard cake, assorted cakes, coffee, fruits, nuts, and raisins. Small wonder the ladies listed "No supper" for that evening!

Just as early Lexington had its Monsieur Giron, so many Kentucky communities later had their noted confectioneries and restaurants. Of them all none was more highly regarded than Miss Jennie Benedict's in Louisville. Miss Jennie began her culinary career as a cateress but in 1900 took over a forty-year-old business on Fourth Street and opened her own dining room and soda fountain. In 1911 her business had grown to such an extent that she moved to larger quarters on the same street, where her meals were rivaled only by her "decorative candy" pieces and her cakes, which were shipped to all parts of the United States and many foreign countries. Discerning visitors thought their stay in Louisville incomplete without luncheon or dinner at Miss Jennie's, and many a housewife relied upon her *Blue Ribbon Cook Book,* first published in 1904 and reissued in revised editions.

Typical of the menus in the back of her book is this summer dinner: Fresh strawberries with caps, served on shaved ice, with powdered sugar; bouillon and croutons; soft-shelled crabs or lobster cutlets, cucumbers in cucumber cups, beaten biscuit, chicken livers en brochette with sauce, bread and butter sandwiches, hollandaise punch, broiled chicken, French pea croquettes, broiled tomatoes, hot rolls, water cress and orange salad, cheese sticks, individual ices, cakes and coffee.

"An Elegant Lunch" was the headline in the Frankfort *Capital* of February 27, 1890, over an article describing a party given by Captain and Mrs. L. D. Holloway in honor of several state officials, a party which, the paper stated, "has not been excelled by any thing of the kind seen in a private residence in Frankfort this season. The menu is shown at the top of page 57.

To the modern reader, Saratoga Chips may be a mysterious item. Virtually every hostess in the late 1800s and the early years of this century served Saratoga Chips or Saratoga Potatoes if her menu had any pretention to style. They were only potato chips, but back then they were considered a delicacy. These thin shavings of potato, dipped in ice water and then in boiling lard, were invented by a Negro chef at Saratoga, New York, about 1865, but were not commercially manufactured until about 1900. They frequently were served hot.

French cooking did not pass from the Kentucky scene with the death of Mathurin Giron and his compatriots. In Louisville, for instance, Le Cercle de l'Union Française gave annual banquets, and its Fête Nationale of 1906 was a pretentious affair, as seen from the gaily illustrated menu (p. 58).

Soup, Kentucky Burgoo.

———

Fish, Baked Red Snapper.

———

Roast Turkey, Cranberry Sauce.   Venison.
Roast Ham,   Quail on Toast.
Roast Loin of Beef.

———

Fried Oysters.   Raw Oysters.   Slaw.
Hard-boiled Eggs.   Broiled Middling.
Chicken Salad.

———

Celery.   Pickles.   Chow Chow.   Catsups.
Horse Radish.   Cheese.   Olives.
Crackers.

———

Saratoga Chips.   Lettuce.
New Tomatoes.   Radishes.   Cucumbers.
Young Onions.

———

Cakes.   Ice Cream.   Peaches.   Bananas.
Apples.   Lemonade.   Tea.
Strawberry Wine.   Corn Bread.
Coffee.   Buttermilk.

The next year Lexingtonians went all out to welcome "The Princess Alice," Mrs. Nicholas Longworth, daughter of President Theodore Roosevelt, and her husband, the distinguished congressman from Ohio. They, with a few companions, came from Cincinnati to Lexington, according to *The Lexington Leader* of May 5, "in Mr. Longworth's big three-seated touring car," to attend the final day's racing at the old Kentucky Association track. Though they arrived two hours late, in time only for the last race, the reception went according to schedule. They "were guests of the directors of the association at a buffet luncheon in the club house, to which possibly one hundred people had been informally invited. The spacious dining room . . . was tastefully decorated with potted plants, while pink and white carnations adorned the table. The menu, which was furnished by the Leland Hotel Company, was prepared under the supervision of Dollie Johnson Dandridge, former cook at the White House under President Harrison, consisted of country ham, barbecued Southdown mutton, beaten biscuit, Queen Elizabeth salad, chicken salad, cucumber, olive and lettuce sandwiches, salted almonds, coffee and cham-

MENU

Fete Nationale

XIVme Banquet Annuel

Donne par

Le Cercle de l'Union Française

le 16 Juillet, 1906.

a Louisville, Ky.

Hors d'Oeuvre Varie

Pot au feu

Boeuf bouilli garni

Preignac

Friture de Poissons Sauce. Tartare

Pommes Parisienne

Filet Mignon, Jardiniere

St. Emilion

Petits Pois

Poulet Roti

Coeurs de Laitue

Creme glacee Gateaux assortis, Fruits   Montebello

Roquefort

Demi Tasse   Cognac

Cigares

CHAMPAGNE MONTEBELLO

THIRD AVENUE GARDEN,
H. F. BRUENS. PROP.

paigne. Colored waiters, in immaculate linen, flitted here and there about the club house serving the guests."

Of all Kentucky's annual events, the Derby undoubtedly has provided the occasion and the inspiration for more lavish entertainment than any other. High officials from Washington, governors of many states and mayors of many cities, stars of the entertainment world, horsemen and horse lovers from throughout America and other lands, and titled men and women from abroad fill the guest lists of scores of parties during the first weekend in May. At the homes of wealthy sportsmen in Jefferson, Fayette and other counties the favored guests dine in splendor ranging from the bizarre to traditional and stately elegance. For some, Derby Day begins with the governor's breakfast, which for nearly half a century has been held, first at the Mansion at Frankfort and more recently at Spindletop Hall and on the Capitol grounds.

While the Derby itself is ample provocation for entertainment, extra incentive and public excitement occasionally are provided by the presence of such noble visitors as Lord Derby in 1930, the Duke and Duchess of Windsor in 1951, the Aly Kahn in 1958, Prince Rainier of Monaco in 1963, and the Princess Margaret and Lord Snowden in 1974.

Nothing remains today of the magnificent Green Hills mansion of James Ben Ali Haggin on Elmendorf Farm in Fayette County except the columned portico, but during the short life of the palatial residence it was the scene of some of the most elegant entertainment Kentucky has known. It was built by the elderly Mr. Haggin for his young second wife, Margaret Voorhies, and its completion was celebrated in 1902 by "one of the handsomest private functions ever given in the South. . . . The large rooms of the first floor were all thrown together, and the accommodations were made even more adequate by the erection of a large temporary pavilion with a hardwood floor in the rear of the dining room. This was used as the supper room, and later cleared for the dancing of the cotillion. . . .

"Guests entered from the porte-cochere, were taken in the elevator to the dressing rooms on the second floor . . . and entered the reception hall on the lower floor from the handsome staircase, where the receiving party stood."

The larger towns of the state have had no monopoly on tasteful and delightful entertainment. At Park City in Barren County, for instance, the wedding of Miss Margaret Ella Mentz and Paul J. Mahoney took place in 1891. The Mentz Hotel, of which the bride's father was proprietor, provided ample room for the festivities, with the dining room and parlors opened up for the marriage ceremony and for dancing, while in the upper hall, tables were set for 200 for a supper that was described by a contemporary newspaper reporter as "a dream of delight, prepared and served by Delmonico caterers of Louisville.

"Every substantial, every delicacy, every luxury was there in lavish profusion. The choicest viands tempted the appetite; the most superb dishes known to the culinary art were served in succession, while wines, delicate with the fragrance of masterful making and rich with the bouquet of years, speeded the passing hours all too happily."

So it was, too, at Kentucky's pioneer weddings, as Ben Casseday describes in his *History of Louisville*. The celebrating then may have been more exuberant and crude, the table and its setting primitive, but the feast that followed the ceremony was as elaborate as the circumstances would allow. There "was a substantial backwoods feast of beef, pork, fowls, and sometimes venison and bear meat, roasted and boiled, with plenty of potatoes, cabbage and other vegetables," accompanied by the ever-present product of home stills.

But when it came to weddings, few ever equalled those of the daughters of General and Mrs. William Preston of Lexington. The general had married the lovely Margaret Wickliffe, and after the Civil War they and their children lived at Glendower, the old Wickliffe place. The mansion was ideally suited for entertaining, and the Prestons, gracious and lavish hosts, made it the center of social life of Lexington.

The story is told, and not doubted, that the Preston dinners had so many courses, and the wine flowed so freely, that a guest might get drunk and sober up three times before the evening ended. It is remembered, too, that on one occasion a young lady who had the misfortune to spill soup on her gown during the first course quietly left the table, called her carriage, was driven home to change, and was back in time for dessert.

Of all the social events, though, the most memorable were the wedding receptions of the Preston daughters, and, of these, the betrothal of Susan Christie Preston to General William F. Draper of Massachusetts, in 1890, was typical. "The room in which the ceremony was performed was like a scene in fairy land," a local newspaper reported. "Elegant mirrors reached almost from floor to ceiling, rich lace curtains hung over the windows, old gold hues were the principal colors on wall and floor. . . . An exquisite bower of roses placed in the rear end of this apartment, between two windows, furnished a suitable setting for the bridal couple during the marriage ceremony."

After a half-hour of congratulations, the bridal party, the fifty guests and the "family connections" were

ushered into two large rooms and seated around several tables . . . laid with exquisite taste: Large cakes and bunches of flowers, elegant china, and the finest of cut glass, the glint of burnished silver and the soft lights. . . . About the festive board the congenial throng enjoyed the pleasures of the table for several hours. . . .

The supper . . . was served in courses as follows: Soft shell crabs. Spring chicken with trouffles. Snipe with champignons. Sweet breads in cases. Pattie des foi Gras. Roman punch. Creme de volail. Saddle of lamb. Lobster salad. Bone turkey. Baked ham. Nesselrode pudding. Bisque glace. Jelly and velvet cream. Fruits. Coffee. Appropriate wines were served . . . gohannisburg, sherry, claret and champaigne.

General Preston, it is likely, would not have considered such a repast overly sumptuous. It was he who is reported to have said that a turkey is an awkward bird—too big for one person but not quite enough for two.

SOURCES

Benedict, Jennie C. *The Road to Dream Acre.* Louisville, Kentucky, 1928.

Fryman, Mrs. Virgil T. "History of Lewisburg and Mill Creek, Mason County, Kentucky." Manuscript in Mason County Museum, Maysville.

Hardin, Bayless, ed. "Whitley Papers, Volume 9—Draper Manuscripts—Kentucky Papers." In *The Register of the Kentucky State Historical Society* 36, no. 116.

Hume, Edgar Erskine. *Lafayette in Kentucky.* Frankfort, Kentucky, 1937.

Jillson, Willard Rouse. *Some Kentucky Obliquities in Retrospect.* Frankfort, Kentucky, 1952.

McCullough, Samuel D. "My Early Reminiscences of Lexington, Kentucky." Manuscript, 1871, in Lexington Public Library.

Means Papers, M. I. King Library, University of Kentucky, Lexington.

Simpson, Elizabeth M. *Bluegrass Houses and Their Traditions.* Lexington, Kentucky, 1932.

Talbert, Charles G. *The William Whitley House.* Pamphlet reprint from *Filson Club History Quarterly* 25, nos. 2, 3, 4.

Kentucky newspapers consulted were *The Capital,* Frankfort; *The Lexington Herald, The Lexington Leader,* and *The Sunday Herald-Leader,* Lexington; and *The Maysville Bulletin.*

The writer wishes to express his appreciation to Dr. Jacqueline P. Bull and Mrs. Mildred Stanley, of the Special Collections Department, Margaret I. King Library, and to Mrs. C. C. Calvert, Jr., and the staff of the Mason County Museum, who located pertinent manuscript material and newspaper items.

Recipes

Entrées

In colonial America, meat was the symbol of the New World's bounty. Settlers wrote to their relatives across the Atlantic that they ate over a pound of meat daily—an astonishing figure to a virtually vegetarian Europe in which meat was a luxury item reserved for holidays and special occasions. Little has changed since then. Americans are still the envy of the world because we live in a land so prosperous that meat is an everyday food. To Americans, meat has always symbolized the good life.

Kentuckians have always been great meat eaters. From the days when George Rogers Clark provided a Christmas feast of baked possum, venison, buffalo, bear, and wild turkey, to today's barbecues of pork and mutton, there has been plenty of well cooked meat on Kentucky tables. Wild game, as Otis Rice points out, was the principal food of the explorers and the earliest settlers. The recipes here for bear's paws, pheasant, fricasseed rabbit, and fried squirrel are reminders of those early times.

For the Scottish and English settlers who followed, domesticated animals quickly replaced game as the staple. Pork, beef, mutton, and poultry were all plentiful, and this chapter gives ample evidence of the variety of traditional recipes that evolved and are still in use today. Chicken is a good example. There is Florence Peers's superb chicken dinner, complete with dressing, dumplings, and gravy. There are recipes for chicken fried, boiled, broiled, and baked; chicken pickled, creamed, croquetted, and stuffed; chicken garnished with almonds, delighted, casserolled, and even biscuited. In short, chicken any way you could possibly want it.

On the more serious side is ham. Kentucky country hams are recognized as one of the world's best preserved meats, on a par with the products of Smithfield, Virginia, the Ardennes, Parma, and Krakow, Poland. The basic curing process used in Kentucky originated in England, but in the course of two hundred years, hundreds of local variants have developed. Because Kentucky hams differ considerably from one region to another, recipes for cooking them also vary. Included in this chapter, therefore, are recipes for fried, boiled, baked, and kale-stuffed country ham, all traditional. But most unusual and actually Medieval in origin is the recipe for stuffed country ham, larded with kale and wild greens. The result is a dish that tastes and looks exceptional.

Barbecued pork does not have the lineage of stuffed ham, but it is traditionally more important. As Burton Milward notes, Kentucky barbecue, like burgoo, has "acquired a mystique that lingers yet." The popularity of these dishes is due in large measure to the fact that they are best cooked in quantity and therefore are the basis for feasts: political rallies, family reunions, community meals, and so on. They have become pleasurable secular rituals and thus endure along with politics, families, towns, and Kentucky.

Jay Anderson

GAME

BEAR'S PAWS

Bear's paws are by many considered to be a great delicacy, in fact the best part of the bear. Clean the forepaws very nicely, boil in salted water until tender, dip them in melted butter, egg, and then in bread crumbs, broil with frequent basting until lightly brown. Garnish with lemon slices and capers and send to the table any kind of a spice gravy. Sometimes the paws are pickled in vinegar and savory herbs for a day beforehand; then boil in bouillon and part of the marinade instead of water before broiling them.

From THE PRACTICAL COOKBOOK (1904)

PHEASANT

2 pheasants   2 cans cream of mushroom soup
1 small onion   2 tbsp. white wine
1 carrot

Cut pheasants into serving pieces. Roll in seasoned flour; brown in a small amount of oil. Add diced onion and carrot. Add soup, ½ can of water, and wine. Simmer for 1½ to 2 hours in a heavy covered pan on top of the stove, or bake at 325° in a buttered casserole covered with foil.

Mrs. James Adams, Prestonsburg Woman's Club

FRICASSEED RABBIT
An 1823 Recipe

The best way for cooking rabbit is to fricassee them. Take a couple of fine ones and disjoint them. Put them into a large stewpan, season them with cayenne pepper and salt, some chopped parsley and some powdered mace. Pour in a pint of warm water (or veal broth if you have it) and stew over a slow fire till the rabbits are quite tender, adding some bits of butter, rolled in flour, when the rabbit is about half done. Just before taking from the fire, enrich the gravy with a jill or more of thick cream with some nutmeg grated into it. Stir the gravy well, but take care not to let it boil after the cream is in, lest it curdle. Put the pieces of rabbit on a hot platter and pour the gravy over them.

Mrs. M. F. Osting, Woman's Club of Paducah

FRIED SQUIRREL

Clean the squirrel thoroughly, disjoint it, and cut the back into two pieces. Put in a large glass container with salt water and soak overnight in the refrigerator. Next morning, drain and dry the pieces and remove any loose membrane. Roll in seasoned flour. Heat oil or lard (not vegetable shortening) in a heavy skillet. Brown the pieces, turning once. Cover the skillet and cook about 30 minutes longer. Remove meat from skillet, pour off all but 3 tbsp. of fat, and add 2 tbsp. seasoned flour. When flour is brown stir in equal parts of milk and water and cook, stirring constantly, until thick.

Mrs. William Baldwin, Suburban Woman's Club, Lexington

MEATS

COLONEL WM. RHODES ESTILL'S RECIPE FOR CURING HAMS

Kill your hogs when the wind is from the northwest. The night before you salt the meat, take a string of red pepper and make a strong tea. (Let it remain on the stove overnight.) Put in the tea 2 heaping tablespoons of saltpetre to every two gallons. Take this strong tea and pour on the salt. Salt the meat lightly for the first time to run off the blood. Let the meat lie packed 3 days—longer, if the weather is very cold. Then overhaul the meat and put 1 teaspoon of pulverized saltpetre on the flesh side of each ham and rub in well. Then rub with molasses mixed with salt. Pack close for 10 days. After this overhaul again, rubbing each piece, and pack close again. Hang the meat in 3 weeks from the time the hogs were killed. Before hanging, wash each piece in warm water, and while wet roll in hickory ashes. Then smoke with green hickory wood, and tie up in cotton bags in February.

From THE BLUE GRASS COOK BOOK *(1875); contributed by Mrs. Alex Campbell, Jr., Lexington, great-granddaughter of Col. Estill*

OVEN FRIED COUNTRY HAM

Place sliced country ham in an iron skillet. Sprinkle a tiny bit of white sugar on the ham and ⅛ tsp. sugar in the skillet. Add 2 tbsp. water. Cook in a preheated 350° oven 20 minutes, turning once.

Marjorie McGee, Cave City Younger Woman's Club

CARE AND COOKING OF TRIGG COUNTY COUNTRY HAM

The uncooked cured country ham should be placed, stockinette or cloth bag intact, in a heavy grocery sack, tied very tightly at the top, and hung in a cool dry place. If it should develop mold, scrub it off when you are ready to use the ham.

FRIED COUNTRY HAM

Slice the ham into steaks 3/8 inch thick or less. Soak the steaks in milk or water at least 30 minutes, then trim the rind and any excess fat. Put the ham in a heavy frying pan and cover with water. Simmer slowly until the water is gone. Lightly brown the ham on both sides and remove from pan. To make red-eye gravy, add a little water to the pan drippings and simmer for 3 minutes, stirring constantly. Spoon the gravy over the ham, or on hot biscuits or grits.

BOILED COUNTRY HAM

Soak the ham overnight in cold water. Next morning, wash the ham and scrub off any mold with a stiff brush. Trim off any hard edges. Cut off the hock and save it for seasoning or soup. Fill a large roaster half full of fresh water and add 1 tbsp. brown sugar per pound of ham. Bring the water to a boil, put the ham in, skin side down. Cover and simmer 20 to 25 minutes per pound. Remove the roaster from heat, leave it covered, and allow the ham to cool in the water overnight. This is part of the cooking process. Remove the skin and trim the fat, leaving a layer about 1/2 inch thick. Glaze as desired. Brown the glaze in a 400° oven.

BAKED COUNTRY HAM

Wash, scrub, and soak the ham overnight as in the boiling method, above. Place the ham, skin side up, in an open roasting pan with some water in the bottom of the pan. Place a piece of foil over the top and attach it loosely to the pan. Place in a preheated 325° oven and bake until a meat thermometer registers an internal temperature of 160°. Be certain that the thermometer is stuck into the thickest part of the ham without touching any bone. When fully cooked, remove the skin, glaze the ham, and brown it as with boiled ham.

Mrs. Smith Broadbent III, Cadiz Woman's Club

BAKED COUNTRY HAM

15-lb. aged country ham,	2 tbsp. dry mustard
3 to 5 years old	1 tsp. black pepper
Dough blanket:	½ cup bourbon
4 cups flour	apple cider
1 cup brown sugar	*Glaze:*
2 tbsp. ground cloves	1 cup honey
2 tbsp. ground cinnamon	grated peel of ½ orange

Soak the ham in a lard can for 2 days, changing the water daily. Wash the ham in warm water and remove any mold with a wire brush. Cut the rind from the ham. Make the dough blanket by combining the dry ingredients with the bourbon. Add enough cider to make an easily handled dough. With rolled dough, cover the fat side of the ham. Place in a roasting pan and put in a cold oven. Bake at 325° for 20 to 25 minutes per pound. Baste the ham every 30 minutes. When done, remove and discard dough blanket. Spread ham with glaze and return to the oven for 45 minutes.

Mrs. Charles Campbell, Greenville Woman's Club

COUNTRY HAM

Soak the ham in cold water overnight. Next morning scrub it and place in a roaster with 5 cups cold water. Cover roaster and put in a cold oven. Bring the oven temperature to 500° and bake 10 minutes; turn off the oven but do not open the door. After 3 hours, bring oven temperature again to 500° and bake for 10 minutes. Turn the oven off and leave the ham inside overnight without opening the door. Next morning take the ham from the roaster, remove skin, and glaze as desired. Brown.

Mrs. G. F. Ernst, Lexington Woman's Club

BARBECUED HAM

5-lb. ham, sliced	4 tsp. ground cloves
½ cup melted butter	¼ cup prepared mustard
1 bottle cooking sherry	4 tsp. paprika
½ cup brown sugar	8 cloves garlic, minced

Combine all ingredients and pour over ham. Marinate several hours or overnight. Bake at 325° until the sauce is thick, about 2 to 3 hours.

Mrs. Lyle Harlow, Stamping Ground Woman's Club

STUFFED HAM

18-lb. hickory smoked ham   8 small green onions
2 lbs. kale or wild greens

Bake ham until well done. Cook cleaned greens for 15 minutes, drain, and chop fine. Add the finely chopped onions and tops to the hot greens. With a long wide knife make deep slits in the warm ham and fill with the stuffing. Let stand overnight. When sliced you have ham and greens together.

Miss Mary Martina Scott, Beechmont Woman's Club, Louisville

Miss Scott noted that ham prepared in this manner has been a part of the traditional Easter Sunday dinner in her family as long as she can remember. It is served with mashed potato salad, baked apples, corn muffins, yellow or white cake, and a mug of float.

PEPPERS STUFFED WITH DEVILED HAM

6 green peppers
3 cans deviled ham
1 16-oz. can tomatoes,
    partially drained, or
    4 medium tomatoes,
    peeled and chopped

1 10-oz. package sharp cheddar
    cheese
12 soda crackers, crumbled
dash of pepper
1 heaping tbsp. cornstarch
butter

Wash peppers, cut in half lengthwise, and remove seeds and membranes. Parboil until slightly tender and drain well. In a saucepan combine deviled ham and tomatoes. Reserving enough cheese for topping, dice the remainder and add it to the mixture. Add crackers and season with pepper. Bring to a boil, stir in cornstarch dissolved in a little water, and cook until thick. Place peppers in a shallow buttered baking dish and fill with the mixture. Place a slice of cheese and a little butter on top of each half. Bake at 350° until cheese is melted and the top is slightly brown. Serves 6.

Alberta Early Klopp, Erlanger Woman's Club

ROAST SUCKLING PIG

Most people associate roast suckling pig with the Hawaiian luau, but our forefathers in Eastern Kentucky, like their forefathers in England, were roasting suckling pigs long ago. Today it is difficult to obtain a suckling pig but 50 years ago almost every family raised their own pigs. Often a sow had a larger litter than was needed or more than it was feasible to feed to maturity. The extra pigs were sold or traded, and occasionally one was roasted for a family treat.

15- to 18-lb. suckling pig
softened butter
salt and pepper
1 cup flour
Sausage stuffing:
1 lb. bulk sausage
4 cups cooked rice or
    dry bread crumbs

2 tbsp. chopped celery leaves
2 tbsp. sausage drippings
1 tbsp. chopped parsley
1 tbsp. poultry seasoning
1 tsp. salt
1 tsp. pepper
water

First prepare the sausage stuffing: Cook the sausage and drain off the fat, reserving 2 tablespoonfuls. Add remaining ingredients, using only enough water to moisten. Mix thoroughly and set aside.

The butcher will prepare the suckling pig by scraping and cleaning it. Force the mouth open and insert a piece of wood to keep it open while roasting. Wash the pig in cold water and dry thoroughly. Stuff with sausage dressing and sew up the opening. Place on a rack in an open roasting pan, with forefeet extended. Fold the hind legs under and tie or skewer them in place. Rub the pig with butter, sprinkle with salt and pepper, and dust with flour. Roast at 325° for 3 to 3½ hours, basting every 15 minutes with hot water and drippings. Protect the ears and tail with foil until the last 30 minutes of baking time, or they will crack. Put an apple in the mouth before serving.

Mrs. William Richards, Harlan Woman's Club

KENTUCKY PORK SAUSAGE

4 lbs. lean pork
2 lbs. pork fat (backbone
    fat preferred)
6 tsp. salt
6 tsp. pulverized sage leaves

3 tsp. black pepper
¾ tsp. red pepper
2 tsp. thyme
1 tsp. nutmeg

Grind lean meat and fat together; add other ingredients, kneading them in with your hands. Cook and taste a small test cake. Add more seasoning if desired. Shape into loaves. Wrap in waxed paper and refrigerate. When ready to use cut into ½-inch slices or shape into patties. Cook in a hot skillet, browning on both sides. Be certain the meat is thoroughly cooked before serving. Most delicious with fried apples and corn cakes or waffles with maple syrup.

Mrs. Elizabeth Tipton, Erlanger Woman's Club

FRIED SALT PORK

Select "fat back" or "side meat" with a streak of lean. Slice thickly and cover with boiling water; return water to a boil, then remove and drain the meat. Dip meat in cornmeal seasoned with black pepper and paprika. Fry in hot shortening until golden brown. Drain on a paper towel. Allow 3 slices per serving. A must accompaniment to poke sallet (page 158).

Harlan Woman's Club

CHATEAUBRIAND

6- to 7-lb. tenderloin of beef   1 clove garlic
bits of salt pork   salt and freshly ground pepper

Trim the tenderloin, removing all fat and tendons. Be particularly careful to cut off the silver membrane. Cut off about 6 inches at the butt end and about 5 inches at the pointed end; the piece of tenderloin left should weigh about 5 pounds. Lard the beef with bits of salt pork and tiny slivers of garlic. Rub it with salt and freshly ground black pepper. Broil 8 minutes on each side, turning frequently in order not to char it. This is best served rare but may be broiled to the desired doneness. Serve on a large silver platter surrounded by mounds of sautéed mushroom caps, deviled carrots, minted large green peas, and tiny potato balls fried in deep fat. Carve the beef at the table. Serves 8 to 10.

Mrs. Walter M. Kimbell, Woman's Club of Frankfort

EMPEROR'S BEEF ROLL

1 round steak	¼ tsp. each marjoram leaves and ground thyme
Marinade:	3 cups toasted bread cubes
½ cup soy sauce	2 tbsp. chopped fresh parsley
1 cup water	⅔ cup chicken broth (or 1 bouillon cube dissolved in water)
1 tbsp. brown sugar	
2 tbsp. lemon juice	*Sauce:*
2 tbsp. salad oil	1 tbsp. cornstarch
¼ tsp. Tabasco sauce	1 small can chopped mushrooms
¼ tsp. black pepper	
1 clove garlic, chopped fine	⅔ cup chopped water chestnuts (optional)
Stuffing:	
¼ cup chopped onion	⅔ cup chopped bamboo shoots (optional)
½ cup thinly sliced celery	
⅓ cup butter	
1 scant tsp. salt	
¼ tsp. black pepper	
½ tsp. sage	1½ cups cooked rice

Trim meat and cut around the edges through membrane. Cover meat with plastic wrap and place it on a breadboard or counter top; flatten it to about ¼ inch thickness with a meat pounder or rolling pin; pound both sides. Peel off plastic and put meat in a shallow baking dish or pan. Combine all ingredients for marinade and pour over meat. Marinate, covered, for at least 2 hours, basting occasionally or turning. Remove meat from marinade and place on a wire rack to drain. Reserve the marinade.

While meat is marinating, prepare the stuffing. Cook onion and celery in ½ cup water for 3 minutes. Add butter and stir until melted. Mix with remaining stuffing ingredients, moistening with chicken broth as needed. Spoon stuffing onto meat to within ½ inch of edges. Roll up lengthwise and secure firmly with skewers or toothpicks. Return to baking dish with reserved marinade. Cover and bake at 350° about 1½ hours or until tender, basting occasionally. Place on a platter, remove skewers, and slice. Thicken marinade with cornstarch blended in a small amount of water; add mushrooms, and water chestnuts and bamboo shoots if desired. Serve the sauce over the cooked rice and meat.

Mrs. Sherry Lynch, Danville Woman's Club

VIENNESE POT ROAST (Sauerbraten)

This recipe is a modernized representation of the sauerbraten so typical of the cooking of the German people who came into northern Kentucky in the late nineteenth century. A particularly large group settled in Covington, where the Ohio River reminded them of the Rhine River in their homeland.

5- to 6-lb. beef roast	1 large onion, quartered
1 large marrowbone	1 shallot, diced
½ cup white vinegar	1 tbsp. shortening
2 cups red wine	3 or 4 tbsp. flour
1 cup apple juice or cider	salt and pepper
2 tbsp. brown sugar	2 hard-boiled eggs
2 tbsp. pickling spices	½ lb. fresh mushrooms
2 bay leaves	1 tbsp. margarine

The beef, which may be a rolled roast, must be marinated for 3 days and may be cooked the day before serving. In a large crock or earthenware bowl combine vinegar, wine, apple juice or cider, sugar, pickling spices, bay leaves, onion, and shallot. Add beef and marrowbone. Refrigerate 3 days, turning meat each day so that all sides are well marinated. Lift beef from marinade and brown thoroughly on all sides in shortening in a large kettle or Dutch oven. Add marinade, cover, and simmer for 3 hours. Sprinkle flour on a pie tin and brown it in the oven until almost burned. Watch it carefully and stir often to brown it evenly. Remove meat from marinade. Stir a little marinade into the flour and then stir the mixture into the liquid in the kettle and add salt and pepper to taste. When the meat is cool, slice and arrange it in a large casserole. Pour the sauce over it. Top with whole mushrooms, sautéed in margarine, and hard-boiled egg slices. Refrigerate. When ready to serve, reheat in a 350° oven about ½ hour, or until heated through. Serves 8 to 10.

Mrs. Donald Flottman, Covington Art Club

SOUR MEAT

3- to 4-lb. English cut or   ¾ cup vinegar
    shoulder roast of beef   ½ cup sugar
shortening   flour (optional)
salt to taste

Brown meat on both sides in shortening, sprinkle with salt, cut into serving pieces, and return to pan over heat. Combine vinegar and sugar and add this mixture to the meat in about three steps, stirring and watching carefully that it does not burn. After all the liquid has been added, put the meat in a 300° oven for 2½ to 3 hours or until fork tender. A little flour-and-water thickening may be added to make gravy. Serve with homemade noodles (page 106). Serves 5 to 7.

Mrs. John H. Krusenklaus, Highland Woman's Club, Louisville

STEAK AND ZUCCHINI SUPPER

1 lb. round steak, cut into   ½ cup water
   thin strips   ½ envelope (about 2 tbsp.)
1 tbsp. cooking oil   spaghetti sauce mix
1 10½-oz. can mushroom   3 to 4 medium zucchini
   gravy

In a skillet quickly brown steak strips in hot oil. Add gravy, water, and spaghetti sauce mix; stir until well mixed. Cover and cook over low heat 20 minutes, stirring occasionally. Add sliced zucchini. Cover and continue cooking 10 to 12 minutes, or until zucchini is tender but still crisp. Serve over noodles or rice. Serves 4.

Mrs. Thomas Collins, Lexington Woman's Club

POOR MAN'S BEEF STROGANOFF

2 to 3 lb. round steak, cubed   1 pkg. dry onion soup mix
2 cans cream of mushroom   ¾ cup sherry
   soup

Combine all ingredients, mixing well, and place in a large casserole. Cover and bake at 325° for 2 to 3 hours. Serve with rice.

Karen McCane, Heritage Heights Woman's Club, Augusta

STUFFED GREEN PEPPERS

6 green peppers
1½ cups coarse bread crumbs
milk
1 lb. ground meat
2 ribs celery, chopped
1 tbsp. chopped onion
3 eggs, beaten
1 tsp. salt
¼ tsp. pepper

Sauce:
1 quart tomatoes, peeled
 and chopped
4 ribs celery, chopped
1 medium-sized onion,
 chopped
1 tbsp. chopped green pepper
3 tbsp. vinegar
1 cup brown sugar, packed
 solid
salt to taste

Wash peppers. Cut a slice from stem end. Remove seeds and heavy membrane. Place peppers close together in a saucepan and add about 1½ inches of water. Cover and parboil until tender. Soak bread crumbs in a little milk; squeeze dry. Add meat, celery, and onion. Stir in eggs, salt, and pepper. Stuff peppers with the mixture and place them in a casserole with ¼ cup water. Bake 45 minutes in a 350° oven.

Make a sauce by combining tomatoes, celery, onion, and chopped green pepper. Cook in a skillet over medium heat until thick. Add vinegar and brown sugar. Adjust seasonings. The sauce should be both sour and sweet. Continue cooking 5 to 10 minutes or until sauce is the consistency of unbeaten egg white. Pour over the stuffed peppers and serve. This sauce is also good over plain meat loaf. Serves 6.

Mrs. Paul R. Wickliffe, K.F.W.C. President, 1935–1938

MEAT LOAF

2 lb. ground beef
1 lb. pork sausage
2 large cooked potatoes,
 chopped

2 small onions, chopped
2 eggs, beaten
1 cup cracker crumbs
salt and pepper to taste

Combine all ingredients and place in a 9- by 5-inch loaf pan. Bake in a 325° oven 1 hour or until done. Cut into 12 slices.

Mrs. Dean Duvall Orr, Clinton County Woman's Club

BEEF 'N CHEESE BISCUIT RING

2 lb. ground beef
1/3 cup chopped onion
1 can condensed cream of
   celery soup
1/2 cup tomato juice

3/4 cup beef bouillon
1/4 cup catsup
1 tsp. chili powder
cheese biscuits (page 117)
1/4 cup sliced olives

Brown the ground beef and onion in a large skillet; pour off excess fat. Add remaining ingredients except biscuits and olives. Let simmer while making biscuits. Spoon meat into the center of a platter and surround with hot cheese biscuits. Garnish with stuffed olives. Serves 6.

Mrs. Charles W. Jackson, Woman's Club of Elizabethtown

HAMBURGER QUICHE

1/2 lb. ground beef
1/2 cup mayonnaise
1/2 cup milk
2 eggs
1 tbsp. cornstarch

1 1/2 cups chopped cheddar or
   Swiss cheese
1/3 cup sliced green onion
dash of pepper
1 unbaked 9-inch pastry shell

Brown meat in a skillet over medium heat. Drain and set aside. In a bowl blend mayonnaise, milk, eggs, and cornstarch until smooth. Stir in meat, cheese, onion, and pepper. Pour into pastry shell. Bake in a 350° oven 35 to 40 minutes, or until golden brown on top and a knife inserted in the center comes out clean. Serves 6 to 8.

Charlene Appleman, Heritage Heights Woman's Club, Augusta

BEST EVER CHILI

2 lb. ground beef
1 cup chopped onion
1 cup chopped green pepper
1 cup sliced celery
2 15-oz. cans (about 4 cups)
   kidney beans

2 16-oz. cans (4 cups) tomatoes,
   cut up
1 6-oz. can tomato paste
2 cloves garlic, minced
1 to 1 1/2 tbsp. chili powder
2 tsp. salt

In a Dutch oven cook beef, onion, green pepper, and celery until meat is brown and vegetables are tender. Drain kidney beans, reserving liquid. Add beans and remaining ingredients to meat and vegetables. Cover; simmer 1 to 1 1/2 hours. If mixture becomes too thick, stir in some of the reserved bean liquid. Serves 8.

Mrs. Justin Alexander, Cumberland County Woman's Club

ITALIAN SPAGHETTI

1 onion, chopped	1 pt. homemade chili sauce
bacon fat	salt and pepper
1 lb. ground beef	1 8-oz. pkg. thin spaghetti
1 pkg. French's Italian	cheddar cheese
Spaghetti Sauce mix	

Brown onion in bacon fat, add ground beef, and stir, breaking it into small chunks, until meat is browned. Add salt and pepper, spaghetti sauce mix, and chili sauce. Cook very slowly for about 1 hour. Cook spaghetti in boiling salted water to which 1 tbsp. butter has been added. Drain spaghetti and place on plates; top with sauce and grated cheese. Serve with rye bread. Serves 4.

Mrs. R. L. Mullins, Williamstown Woman's Club

HUNGARIAN GOULASCH

Slice a peeled onion and cook it until brown in three tablespoonfuls of fat fried out of salt pork; take out the onion and turn in a pound and a half of lean, uncooked veal cut in inch cubes; stir and cook the meat until slightly browned, then rejecting the fat, if there be any in the pan, dispose the meat in a casserole; add about a pint of broth, or boiling water, and a teaspoonful of paprika, cover the dish and set to cook in the oven. In the meantime add more fat to the frying pan, and when hot, brown in it about a dozen balls cut from pared potatoes, and a dozen small onions; when the onions are well browned, add them to the casserole, and after the meat has been cooking an hour, add a teaspoonful of salt and the potatoes, and, if desired, two tablespoonfuls of flour mixed to a thin paste with cold water. Let cook in all about two hours. Serve from the casserole.

From NATIONAL COURSE IN HOME ECONOMICS (1917);
contributed by Miss Margaret Carl, Erlanger Woman's Club

PAPRIKA VEAL WITH NOODLES

1	large onion, sliced	2	tbsp. flour
2	tbsp. shortening	1	cup milk
1½	lb. veal flank steak	1	cup water
1	heaping tbsp. paprika	1	pkg. noodles, cooked and
1	cup boiling water		drained

Brown onion in shortening; add veal and brown well on both sides. Add paprika and boiling water. Cover and let simmer 1 hour. Remove meat and slice it. To the pan drippings add flour, brown it, and add milk and water. Stir until smooth. Add ½ cup gravy to the drained noodles, and stir well. Place on a large platter and lay sliced veal around the edge. Spoon a little gravy over all and serve. Serves 6.

Mrs. Carl E. Bee, Woman's Club of Elizabethtown

LIVER MUSH

1 tsp. beef bouillon powder	10 oz. liver
2 tsp. salt	1 cup cornmeal
3 cups water	bacon slices
5 oz. boneless stewing beef	

In a 2-quart saucepan, dissolve beef bouillon powder and salt in 2 cups of the water. Add beef, cover, and simmer until tender, about 2 hours. In a small covered skillet, cook liver in the remaining cup of water until very tender, about an hour over medium heat. Discard any liquid left from liver. Reserve liquid from beef; add enough water to make 2 cups. Allow meats to cool, then put through a food chopper, using the fine blade. Return reserved liquid to saucepan; add chopped meat and bring to a boil. Slowly add cornmeal, stirring rapidly. When thickened (about 3 minutes) remove from heat and pour into 1½-quart loaf pan. Refrigerate from 4 to 48 hours as desired.

To serve, fry as many slices of bacon as you will use of the mush. Remove bacon to paper towel and keep warm. Fry slices of mush (about ⅝ inch thick) in bacon fat, turning once. When mush is nicely browned, place it on a warm serving plate and top each slice with a piece of bacon. This is good served for either breakfast or lunch. Serves 14.

Miss Esther A. Compton, Williamsburg Woman's Club

BAKED LIVER WITH ONIONS

2 tbsp. shortening
salt
1 lb. sliced beef liver
flour

1 tbsp. leaf sage
2 tbsp. chopped onion, or 1
small onion, sliced

Melt shortening in an 8- by 4-inch loaf pan. Hack the liver (cut it and remove the membrane) and salt it to taste. Dip each piece in flour and arrange in a pan. Sprinkle with sage, pulverized in the hand, and onion. Barely cover with hot water and bake at 300° until liver is tender. This takes at least an hour. Slices should be turned once or twice while baking. Serves 4.

Miss Virginia Belcher, Greenville Woman's Club

POULTRY

FRIED CHICKEN

2½-lb. fryer
1 tbsp. salt
½ cup buttermilk
½ tsp. soda
1½ cups flour
½ tsp. freshly ground pepper
1½ tsp. salt

3 cups Crisco oil
Gravy:
2 tbsp. flour
2½ cups milk
½ tsp. black pepper
1 tsp. salt
½ tsp. nutmeg

Select a chicken weighing not more than 2½ lb. and with very little fat. Cut into desired pieces and cover with cold water to which 1 tbsp. salt has been added. Let soak at least 30 minutes. Drain and wash in cold water, then dry. Combine buttermilk and soda; pour over the chicken, turning pieces to coat well. Put flour, salt, and pepper in a bag; drop chicken pieces into the bag and shake well. Fry in oil that has been heated to 400° in an electric frying pan. When all pieces are in the pan, reduce heat to 375°. Cook for 15 minutes or until brown on the under side; turn and continue cooking for 20 minutes. Drain on paper towels. To make cream gravy, pour off oil, leaving about 2 tbsp. oil and brown crumbs. Add 2 tbsp. flour; brown well. Let flour mixture cool slightly, then slowly add milk, black pepper, salt, and nutmeg. Cook and stir until gravy thickens.

Mrs. Leslie Blakey, Lexington Woman's Club

FRIED CHICKEN

bacon grease
2- to 3-lb. fryer

salt and pepper
flour

Melt about ½ inch of bacon grease in an iron skillet. Wash chicken pieces, season with salt and pepper, and roll in flour. Brown chicken in hot fat, turning once. Place a lid on the skillet and continue to cook slowly for about 1 hour. Drain chicken on brown paper. Pour off grease and use pan drippings to make gravy.

Mrs. Malcolm McGregor, Suburban Woman's Club, Lexington

BROILED CHICKEN

This recipe, brought to Kentucky from Alabama, was a specialty at Richardson House in Williamsburg for 20 years.

1 fryer, quartered
½ tsp. salt
¼ tsp. pepper
Basting sauce:
1 cup sherry

½ tsp. lemon juice
¼ tsp. nutmeg
¼ tsp. curry powder
1 cup butter

Two hours before time to cook the chicken, combine ingredients for the basting sauce and heat until butter is melted. Set aside.

Rub the chicken with salt and pepper; place in a broiler pan, skin side down. Cook at 350° for 25 minutes, basting with sauce every 5 to 10 minutes. Turn the chicken; cook and baste for 20 minutes. If the skin is not brown after 20 minutes, set broiler on low and broil for 5 minutes, basting often. When the chicken is tender and golden brown, place it on a platter and dust with paprika. Pour remaining sauce over the chicken and serve immediately. Serves 4. Fluffy white rice is a perfect side dish.

Mrs. A. A. Richardson, Williamsburg Woman's Club

BAKED PECAN CHICKEN

2½- to 3-lb. frying chicken,
    cut into serving pieces
1 cup biscuit mix
½ cup chopped pecans
1 tsp. paprika

1 tsp. salt
1 tsp. poultry seasoning
1 cup sour cream or ½ cup
    evaporated milk
½ cup margarine, melted

Wash and pat dry the chicken pieces. In a flat dish combine biscuit mix, pecans, paprika, salt, and poultry seasoning. With a rubber spatula or broad knife, spread sour cream over chicken pieces or coat them with evaporated milk. Then roll them in the dry mixture and place them skin side up, not touching, in a greased shallow baking pan. Sprinkle with any remaining mix and drizzle with margarine. Bake 40 minutes or until tender in a preheated 400° oven. Do not turn. Serves 4.

Mrs. Harley C. Davis, Richmond Younger Woman's Club

CHICKEN CROQUETTES

1 small onion	butter the size of a goose egg
chicken broth	(about 4 tbsp.), melted
scant 2 cups bread crumbs	2 cups ground baked chicken
3 eggs, separated	1 beaten egg
salt and pepper	cracker meal

Scald broth with the onion in it; discard the onion. Place bread crumbs in a bowl and pour enough broth over them to moisten well. Beat eggs, whites and yolks separately, until light; add to soaked crumbs. Add salt and pepper to taste and butter. Put the mixture in a pan and cook over low heat, stirring constantly, until eggs are set. Remove from heat and let cool. Add chicken. If mixture is too stiff, add more broth or some cream. Chill well. Shape into croquettes, roll in egg, then in cracker meal. Chill again. Bake at 375° or fry in deep fat at 375°. Drain on brown paper.

Note: Prepared stuffing mix can be used instead of bread crumbs.

Mrs. Ben E. Clement, Marion Woman's Club

This recipe was used by Mrs. Clement's grandmother, who at the insistence of her daughters in the 1870s taught a cooking class for them and a few friends. One of the students was Jennie Benedict, who became one of Louisville's outstanding caterers. She often baked fruit cakes for friends so it was natural for her to think of cooking as a way to add to the family income when they needed help in 1893. With a loan of $381 she outfitted a kitchen in a backyard cottage. She catered school lunches and many private parties, not only in Louisville but in many states. Before opening the tearoom with soda fountain which was her last business, she studied at the Boston School of Cooking, was employed as a home economist by the gas company, wrote a newspaper column for a short time, and published two cookbooks. After retirement Miss Benedict wrote an autobiography.

FLORENCE PEERS'S CHICKEN DINNER

For years the name Peers and poultry were synonymous in Louisville. Located across from Churchill Downs at the corner of Fourth and Central, the Peers Poultry House was owned and operated by Mr. Charlie Peers and his six sons. To maintain their reputation for the best fresh poultry and the freshest eggs in town, Mr. Peers and his sons made weekly trips to the rural area of Jefferson and surrounding counties to purchase springers, ducks, geese, turkeys, and eggs, and on occasion country hams.

If you wanted to choose your bird personally you could go to their warehouse, make your selection, and wait about 10 minutes for it to be killed, scalded, and cleaned. On a cold day you could keep warm by standing near the pot-bellied stove in the center of the building.

Peers's poultry was delivered anywhere in the city by the boys, who were also responsible for feeding, watering, and dressing the birds. During Derby week and at the Thanksgiving or Christmas holidays, the poultry house was one of the busiest places in Louisville. Often on Christmas Eve the boys were out making deliveries long after midnight.

The old poultry building has been replaced by a parking lot. The hustle and bustle of trucks unloading hundreds of chickens and turkeys, and the feathers floating through the air are gone, never to return in our automated world. But Florence Peers's traditional chicken dinner lives on.

1 large fat hen and giblets and, if possible, the egg bag with any eggs left in the hen	salt and pepper to taste 1 small onion 3 ribs celery 1 pinch thyme

Carefully wash the hen, giblets, and egg bag. Place in a large kettle, cover with water, add salt, pepper, onion, celery, and thyme. Simmer until tender. Remove hen from broth and place in a baking pan. Save and measure the broth for dressing, dumplings, and gravy, one-third for each.

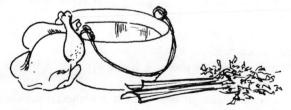

DRESSING

2 loaves bread, toasted and
   crumbled
2 eggs, beaten
1 large onion, chopped
2 tbsp. rubbed sage

2 ribs celery, chopped, and
   remains of cooked celery
   from broth
1/3 of the chicken broth (above)

Mix all ingredients except broth. To broth add an equal amount of water; pour into crumb mixture and mix well. Place by spoonfuls in the hen and around it in the pan. Place hen in a 350° oven and bake approximately 45 minutes. While hen is baking make the dumplings.

DUMPLINGS

1/3 of the chicken broth (above)
3 cups flour

2 tsp. salt

Put broth in a large kettle with an equal amount of water; bring to a boil. Combine flour and salt in a large mixing bowl; add cold tap water a little at a time to make a thick, heavy dough. Work dough with floured hands until it is not sticky. On a floured surface roll to about 1/8 inch thickness. Cut in strips 1 inch wide and 3 inches long. Drop dumplings, one at a time, into the boiling liquid. Stir occasionally. When all dumplings are in, reduce heat and simmer for 20 minutes.

GIBLET GRAVY

1/3 of the chicken broth (above)
giblets
4 tbsp. flour
1 cup cold water

3 hard-boiled eggs (and any
   eggs and egg bag from the
   hen)

Chop giblets and add to the broth. Bring to a boil. Mix flour and water; when broth is boiling hard, add thickening until desired consistency is reached. Let cook about 3 minutes longer. Remove from heat; add hard-boiled eggs, sliced or quartered.

By the time the gravy is ready the dressing and dumplings should be done. This chicken was always served with mashed potatoes, slaw, green beans, fresh tomatoes, and other vegetables in season. Dessert was usually cake and ice cream, or strawberry shortcake.

Mrs. Charles W. Peers, Jr., Fern Creek Woman's Club

CHICKEN BREASTS WITH HAM STUFFING

3   chicken breasts, halved,
    skinned, and boned
½   cup corn bread crumbs
½   cup light bread crumbs
½   cup ground cooked ham
    (country ham if possible)
    or ham hocks
2   tbsp. chopped parsley
1   tsp. dried onion flakes

¼   tsp. salt
⅛   tsp. pepper
¼   cup melted margarine
½   cup chicken bouillon
1   can cream of mushroom soup
½   cup dry vermouth
½   tsp. paprika
2   tsp. cornstarch
¼   cup water

With a rolling pin, lightly roll chicken breasts between two sheets of waxed paper until as thin as possible. Mix bread crumbs, ham, parsley, onion flakes, salt, and pepper. Toss lightly with the melted margarine and bouillon until moistened. Put approximately 1/6 of the stuffing into the middle of each piece of chicken. Fold chicken around stuffing as neatly as possible, using toothpicks if necessary. Place pieces, fold side down, in a greased 12- by 7- by 2-inch baking dish. Mix soup and vermouth, and pour over chicken. Sprinkle with paprika. Bake in a 350° oven 1 hour, or until tender and browned. Place chicken on a heated platter. Mix cornstarch and water, and stir into sauce. Cook, stirring until thick. Serve sauce separately. Good with brown or wild rice. Serves 6.

Mrs. Frank Gunn, Horse Cave Woman's Club

PICKLED CHICKEN

4   chickens, 3½ to 4 pounds
    each
1½ qts. cider vinegar

4   tsp. pickling spices
    (optional)

Simmer chickens in water until tender enough for meat to fall from bones. Chill broth and remove fat. Put meat in a stone jar and pour over it cold vinegar and 3 cups of the broth; add spices if desired. Refrigerate or keep in a cool place. The chicken will be ready for use in two days. This is a popular luncheon or Sunday evening dish. Chicken prepared this way also makes a delicious salad with the addition of chopped egg, chopped celery, chopped pickles (either sweet or dill), and mayonnaise.

Mrs. John W. Stevens, Metropolitan Woman's Club of Lexington

CHICKEN LEILANI

4 or 6 chicken breasts, boned
   and pounded
salt and pepper
4 or 6 slices cooked ham
1 12-oz. jar apricot preserves

2 tbsp. cornstarch
1 no. 2 can pineapple tidbits
1 no. 2 can peaches
¼ cup 90-proof brandy

Season chicken with salt and pepper. Lay a piece of ham on each breast. Roll up and fasten with a toothpick. Brown in butter for a few minutes. Blend cornstarch, apricot preserves, and juice from pineapple and peaches. Place chicken in this liquid. Cover and simmer about 1 hour or until tender, stirring frequently. Add peaches and pineapple tidbits during the last 20 minutes of cooking. Place chicken rolls on a serving dish, pour hot brandy over them, and ignite the brandy. Serves 4 to 6.

Mae Burnett, Woman's Club of Elizabethtown

CREME DE VOLAILLE

When Dr. and Mrs. H. L. Donovan moved to Maxwell Place, the president's home on the University of Kentucky campus, she brought with her the recipe for "Creme Divoli." She often served it to her luncheon guests and it soon became "the dish" at luncheons and bridge clubs.

3 cups ground cooked chicken
1 small onion, ground
3 cups chicken stock
1 cup cracker crumbs
3 eggs

3 or 4 sprigs of parsley
salt and pepper
dash of cayenne pepper
1 cup medium white sauce
1 hard-boiled egg, riced

Mix the chicken, onion, stock, crumbs, eggs, parsley, and seasonings; beat well. Pack firmly into a buttered melon mold. Seal tightly and steam in a pan of water for 1½ hours. Serve piping hot with a covering of white sauce sprinkled with the egg. Surround with peas and carrot balls. Serves 10.

Mrs. Albert A. Pogue, Woman's Club of Frankfort

Mrs. Donovan's recipe substituted 1 cup white sauce for the chicken stock. She added peas and mushrooms to the additional sauce used for covering.

CREME DE VOLAILLE

1 chicken	parsley
2 eggs	1 cup thin white sauce
2 tbsp. cream	1 tbsp. gelatin
salt and pepper	1/4 cup sliced mushrooms
onion	

Stew the chicken, remove skin and bones, and grind the meat. To the ground meat add eggs, cream, seasonings and white sauce to which the softened gelatin and mushrooms have been added. Put into a well-buttered mold and steam 1¼ hours. Serve with additional white sauce to which peas, mushrooms, and pimientos have been added. Serves 8.

Mrs. B. L. Adkins, Chautauqua Circle, Somerset

Mrs. Meredith Cox, Woman's Club of Richmond, doubles the amount of chicken and eggs, seasons to taste, and steams it for 3 hours. She does not put white sauce in the chicken mixture, but does use it as a covering, as above. Serves 8.

ROAST GOOSE AND STUFFING

12-lb. goose	½ tsp. pepper
lemon juice	½ tsp. ground mace
salt	½ tsp. freshly grated nutmeg
1 cup chopped onion	2 tbsp. poultry seasoning
goose liver, finely chopped	¼ cup chopped parsley
½ cup butter	1 cup dry white wine
4 cups bread crumbs	juice of 1 lemon
4 cups peeled, chopped	1 tbsp. rosemary
apples	1 tbsp. salt
1 cup raisins	beifuss leaves (see below)
1½ tsp. salt	

Rub the goose inside and out with lemon juice and salt. Remove any loose heavy fat. Sauté onions and liver in butter for several minutes; add bread crumbs and cook until brown. Stir in apples, raisins, seasonings, and parsley. Toss all together lightly. Stuff the goose and sew up cavity or secure with skewers. Prick skin all over with a fork to let fat out during cooking. Place the goose on a rack in a roasting pan. Prepare a basting liquid of white wine, lemon juice, rosemary, and salt. Pour some of this over the goose and cover it with leaves of beifuss, also called mugwort *(Artemisia vulgaris)* if you have it. (This is an old German custom; beifuss leaves and buds were also added to the stuffing.) Otherwise cover lightly with foil.

Roast in a preheated 325° oven, basting frequently, for about 4 hours. Drain fat from pan at least twice. About 1½ hours before the goose is completely roasted, remove foil to allow the skin to brown. The goose is done when the legs pull easily from the body and juices run pale yellow when the fleshiest part of the drumstick is pricked.

If you are preparing this feast for your return from midnight service, put the stuffed goose in a 325° oven about nine o'clock and baste frequently until you leave for church. Let the roasting continue, and on your return, by one or one-thirty, the goose will be ready. It can wait 30 or 40 minutes in the hot oven with heat off if the door is left ajar. Serves 8.

Mrs. H. C. Bohon, Harrodsburg Woman's Club

MARTHA RAMSEY'S ROAST TURKEY

Select a good, firm, clear, creamy looking turkey. Clean it and place it in a roasting pan; rub it thoroughly with melted shortening. Set oven at 500° and roast the turkey 20 minutes. Reset oven at 250° and bake until tender, 45 minutes per pound. Cook in a double (self-basting) roaster; or, if a single roaster is used, baste every 15 minutes. Add hot water and 1 teaspoon butter as often as necessary to keep enough liquid in the pan for basting.

Mrs. Steely Terrell, Ossoli Woman's Club, Corbin

SARAH'S TURKEY LOAF

2 eggs	2 tbsp. chopped green pepper
1 cup milk or broth	2 tbsp. chopped pimientos
2 cups cooked, finely diced turkey	2 tbsp. chopped celery
	½ tsp. salt
1 cup bread crumbs	¼ tsp. paprika

Beat eggs and add milk. Lightly stir in remaining ingredients. Pour into a buttered loaf pan. Let stand until bread crumbs are completely soaked. Bake in a 300° oven 30 minutes or until brown. Unmold, slice, and serve. Serves 8.

Mrs. W. H. Nance, Woman's Club of Elizabethtown

SEAFOODS

FRIED CATFISH

catfish
salt and pepper
egg or milk

cornmeal
fat for frying

Fry small fish whole. Large fish should be filleted before frying. Wash and drain the fish; sprinkle with salt and pepper. Dip in beaten egg to which 1 tbsp. water has been added, or in milk. Then coat with cornmeal. Fry in ¼ inch hot fat until brown on one side, then turn and brown on other side, 3 to 5 minutes more.

Mrs. Leslie Blakey, Lexington Woman's Club

BAKED WHITEFISH

3 to 4 lb. whitefish
1 can tomato soup

2 ribs celery
½ green pepper

Clean fish and wipe dry. Rub inside with salt, place in a buttered baking dish, and cover with a sauce made by cooking soup and finely chopped vegetables together until they are tender. Bake at 350° for 1 hour. Serves 4 to 6.

Mrs. Howard F. Bary, K.F.W.C. President, 1950–1952

CURRIED FISH

2 lb. fresh cod, halibut, or
    other large fish
4 tbsp. butter or other fat
1 tbsp. chopped green pepper
1 small onion, chopped
¼ cup chopped celery

3 tbsp. flour
½ to 1 tsp. curry powder
3 drops Tabasco sauce
salt to taste
2 tbsp. chopped parsley

Simmer fish about 10 minutes in a small quantity of water in a shallow pan; drain, reserving liquid. Meanwhile, melt butter and sauté green pepper, onion, and celery a few minutes; blend in flour and add cooled fish liquor with enough water to make 2 cups. Add curry powder, Tabasco, and salt, and cook 3 minutes, stirring constantly. Remove skin and bones from cooked fish and arrange it on a hot platter with a border of fluffy rice. Pour sauce over fish and sprinkle with parsley. Serves 4.

Mrs. J. Matt Sparkman, Murray Woman's Club

FISH GOURMET

1 pkg. frozen fillet of sole, thawed	1 can frozen shrimp soup, thawed
pepper	Parmesan cheese
butter	paprika

Place fish on a buttered pie plate; sprinkle with pepper, dot with butter. Spread soup over fish; sprinkle with cheese and paprika. Bake at 400° for 25 minutes.

Mrs. Blair Scott, Metropolitan Woman's Club of Lexington

PAN FRIED OYSTERS

1 pint select oysters	⅛ tsp. pepper
2 eggs	½ cup bread crumbs
2 tbsp. milk	½ cup cracker crumbs
1 tsp. salt	

Drain oysters. Beat together eggs and milk. Add seasonings to crumbs. Dip oysters one at a time first in egg mixture, then in crumbs. Fry in hot deep fat (375°) until golden brown. Serves 3 to 4.

Mrs. Monroe Riehlman, Fern Creek Woman's Club

SCALLOPED OYSTERS

¼ cup melted butter	2 tbsp. sherry
2 cups coarse cracker crumbs	1 tsp. Worcestershire sauce
2 dozen oysters with liquor	¼ tsp. coarse black pepper
⅓ cup cream	

Combine butter and cracker crumbs. Drain oysters, reserving liquor. Mix liquor, cream, sherry, Worcestershire sauce, and pepper. Place one-third of the crumbs in a buttered shallow baking dish; top with a layer of oysters. Pour half the cream and liquor mixture over the oysters. Repeat layers. Top with remaining crumbs. Bake at 425° for 10 to 15 minutes or until crumbs are lightly browned.

Mrs. S. G. Hembree, Ossoli Woman's Club, Corbin

A similar recipe was contributed by Mrs. Monroe Riehlman, Fern Creek Woman's Club.

SHRIMP CREOLE

1½ lbs. fresh or frozen shrimp
¼ cup finely chopped onion
¼ cup finely chopped green
  pepper
1 clove garlic, finely chopped
¼ cup butter

3 tbsp. flour
1 tbsp. chili powder
1 tsp. salt
dash of pepper
2 cups cooked tomatoes
¼ cup red cooking wine

Peel shrimp, devein, and wash. Large shrimp may be cut in half. Sauté onion, green pepper, and garlic in butter until tender. Blend in seasonings and flour, add tomatoes, and cook until thick, stirring constantly. Add shrimp and simmer uncovered for 15 minutes. Add wine and simmer 5 minutes longer. Serve with green salad and French bread. Serves 4 to 6.

Mrs. Betty M. Durrett, Woman's Club of Elizabethtown

IMPERIAL CRAB

½ cup butter, melted
2 lb. crabmeat, lump or
  regular
1 cup mayonnaise

1 small can pimientos,
  chopped
2 tbsp. prepared mustard
salt and pepper to taste

Combine all ingredients and mix well. Put the mixture into crab or baking shells or a baking dish. Rub the top with additional mayonnaise and bake at 350° until brown. Serves 8.

Joseph C. Covington, Bowling Green

This recipe came from the gourmet file of Mr. Covington's mother, Mrs. Dora Thomas Covington.

MEAT CASSEROLES

SIRLOIN CASSEROLE

2 lb. beef sirloin cut in bite-
  size pieces
2 tbsp. cornstarch stirred into
  ¼ cup cold water
1 can cream of mushroom
  soup

1 can cream of chicken soup
1 can cream of celery soup
1 large can mushrooms
½ package dry onion soup mix
1 tbsp. prepared mustard
¼ cup sherry

Place raw meat in a 9- by 13-inch baking dish. Mix cornstarch and water with remaining ingredients and pour over meat. Bake 2½ hours at 350°. Cover casserole during the first 2 hours; remove cover last half hour. Stir occasionally, adding water if necessary. Serves 8.

Mrs. Veryl F. Frye, Jr., Somerset Junior Woman's Club

GROUND BEEF BARBECUE

2 lb. ground beef, crumbled	1 tsp. lemon juice
½ medium onion, diced	1 can tomato soup
1 rib celery, diced	½ cup catsup
1 tsp. salt	1½ tbsp. brown sugar
¼ tsp. pepper	1 small green pepper, diced
1 tbsp. Worcestershire sauce	

Brown the beef, onion, and celery, and add salt and pepper. Simmer ½ hour. Place ground beef mixture in a greased oblong baking dish. In a large bowl mix remaining ingredients. Pour this over ground beef and mix well in the baking dish. Bake 1 hour in a preheated 350° oven.

Florence Colvin, Heritage Heights Woman's Club, Augusta

CRUSTY CORN CASSEROLE

1 lb. ground beef	*Cornbread topping:*
1 tbsp. fat	½ cup flour
½ cup chopped onion	1½ tsp. baking powder
2 cups fresh or canned corn	1½ tsp. sugar
1 cup tomato soup	½ tsp. salt
½ cup sliced olives	½ cup cornmeal
½ cup chopped green pepper	1 egg
salt and pepper	½ cup milk
	2 tbsp. oil

Brown the meat in fat. Add onion and cook until tender. Add remaining ingredients except topping. Pour into a greased 1½-quart casserole. Make topping: Sift together flour, baking powder, sugar, and salt. Stir in cornmeal. Beat egg with milk and oil; add to dry ingredients. Mix until just moistened. Spread over meat. Bake in a 350° oven 35 to 40 minutes. Serves 4 to 6.

Mrs. T. R. Haag, Sr., Buechel Woman's Club

WESTERN HOSPITALITY

3 to 4 lb. round steak, in cubes
flour
salt and pepper
½ cup oil
garlic to taste
1   6-oz. can tomato paste
1¼ cups dry red wine

3   cups water
½ tsp. thyme
1   bay leaf
1   can mushroom pieces
1   pkg. noodles, cooked and
      drained
grated cheddar cheese

Dredge meat in seasoned flour and brown in hot oil. Stir in garlic, tomato paste, wine, water, thyme, and bay leaf. Cook until tender, about 3 hours, over low heat. Add mushrooms and noodles. Place in buttered baking dish. Freeze overnight or longer. Bake at 350° for 1½ hours. Sprinkle cheddar cheese on top for last few minutes of baking.

Mrs. Evon Legg, Columbia Woman's Club

WIGGLE

1 lb. bacon
2 lb. ground beef
1 tbsp. chili powder
salt to taste
2 onions, coarsely chopped
1 bunch celery, coarsely
   chopped
2 green peppers, chopped
1 can peas

1 can tomatoes
1 ten-cent package [8 oz.]
   wide noodles, cooked
1 large can mushrooms
flour
1 ten-cent can [4 oz.] grated
   cheese
buttered bread crumbs

Dice and fry bacon until brown; remove from skillet and set aside. Brown the ground beef with chili powder and salt in 4 tbsp. bacon fat. Add onions, celery, green pepper, and bacon. In a large casserole, layer the meat mixture, peas, tomatoes, noodles, and mushrooms, sprinkling each layer lightly with flour. Cover with grated cheese and top with buttered crumbs. Bake at 350° for 1½ hours. Serves 15.

Mrs. George Hart, Eddyville Woman's Club

This recipe is from the 1930s. At that time the total cost was less than ten cents per serving.

BROCCOLI-SPINACH-SAUSAGE CASSEROLE

¾ lb. bulk sausage
1 pkg. frozen chopped
   broccoli
1 pkg. frozen chopped spinach
½ cup mayonnaise
½ can cream of mushroom
   soup, undiluted

1 can water chestnuts, drained
   and sliced
1 tbsp. lemon juice
½ tsp. dill
tomatoes, peeled and sliced
½ cup grated sharp cheese
1 can fried onion rings

Sauté the sausage, breaking it up with a fork, until barely done. Drain well. In a separate pan cook broccoli and spinach 3 to 4 minutes and drain. Mix mayonnaise with soup, and combine with sausage, vegetables, water chestnuts, lemon juice, and dill. Put the mixture into a casserole. At this point the dish may be frozen for future use. When ready for baking, cover top with tomatoes, sprinkle with cheese, and bake 30 minutes at 350°. Remove from oven and cover with onion rings. Bake 5 minutes longer. Serves 6.

Mrs. Talmage G. Rogers, Greenville Woman's Club

WILD RICE CASSEROLE

1 lb. bulk sausage
1 lb. mushrooms, sliced
1 cup chopped onion
2 cups long grain and wild
   rice
¼ cup flour
½ cup heavy cream

2½ cups condensed chicken
   broth
oregano, thyme, marjoram,
   salt, and pepper to taste
½ cup slivered blanched
   almonds, toasted

Brown sausage in a skillet; remove and drain on paper. Pour off fat, reserving 3 tbsp. Sauté mushrooms and onions in reserved fat. Return crumbled sausage to the skillet. Meanwhile, cook rice according to directions on the box, but for only 15 minutes. Drain. In a separate pan, mix flour and cream until smooth, add chicken broth, and cook until thick. Combine sauce, rice, sausage, and vegetables; mix well. Add seasonings to taste. Pour into a large buttered casserole. Bake at 350° for 25 to 30 minutes or until bubbly. Sprinkle almonds around the edge of the casserole and serve. This casserole may be made ahead of time. If it becomes dry while standing or baking, add more chicken broth. Serves 8.

Mrs. James Farris, Bullitt County Woman's Club

SAUSAGE AND CORN BREAD PIE

1   lb. bulk sausage
3   tbsp. flour
½   tsp. salt
2½   cups tomato juice
½   cup cooked corn
1   cup cooked green peas

Corn muffins:
1   cup sifted flour
½   cup cornmeal
2   tsp. baking powder
1   tsp. salt
1   egg
¾   cup milk
¼   cup shortening

Brown the sausage in a heavy skillet. Drain off fat. Remove from heat and stir in flour and salt, blending well. Gradually add tomato juice and stir until thickened. Add corn and peas. Mix well. Combine dry ingredients for corn muffins. Cut in shortening, mixing thoroughly, and add egg and milk to make a batter. Bring meat mixture to a boil and drop spoonfuls of batter around the edge of the skillet. Reduce heat and simmer 20 minutes or bake at 425° for 20 minutes. Serves 8.

Mrs. David Prow, Junior Woman's Club of Campbellsville

RICE CASSEROLE

1   lb. bulk sausage
1   envelope chicken noodle
    soup mix
½   cup uncooked rice
4½   cups boiling water

1   onion, chopped
1   green pepper, chopped
pinch of dried parsley
dash of paprika
¼   cup almonds

Cook and drain sausage; add soup mix, rice, and water. Cook 7 minutes. Add vegetables, seasonings, and almonds. Pour into a buttered casserole. Bake at 350° for 1 hour. Serves 10.

Mrs. Sam Neace, Sr., Erlanger Woman's Club

HAM SQUARES

1   lb. ground cooked ham
½   lb. ground beef
1   cup soft bread crumbs
¾   cup milk
1   egg
2   tbsp. chopped onion

2   tsp. parsley
1   tsp. dry mustard
salt and pepper
2   cups creamed peas
¼   tsp. curry powder

Combine all ingredients except creamed peas and curry powder, and mix thoroughly. Lightly pack into a buttered 10- by 6-inch baking dish. Bake uncovered at 325° for 1 hour. Spoon off drippings. Allow to stand 5 minutes before cutting into squares. Sprinkle with curry powder and pour creamed peas over the squares. Serves 6.

Mrs. Jimmie Blumenstein, Erlanger Woman's Club

BROCCOLI AND HAM SOUFFLÉ

12 slices bread	6 eggs, slightly beaten
12 slices American cheese	3½ cups milk
2 pkgs. frozen chopped	2 tbsp. minced onion
broccoli	4 tsp. prepared mustard
2 cups chopped ham	½ tsp. salt

Cut bread with a doughnut cutter and reserve the rings. Place the scraps of bread on the bottom of a greased 9- by 13-inch pan. Place cheese over the bread scraps. Cook broccoli and drain. Place broccoli over cheese and sprinkle with chopped ham. Space bread rings on top. Mix eggs, milk, onion, mustard, and salt, and pour over the top. Allow to stand in refrigerator 6 hours, or make one day ahead. Bake in a 325° oven 55 minutes. *Important:* Let stand 10 minutes before cutting into squares to serve. Serves 12.

Mrs. George P. Schiffer, Covington Art Club

REUBEN CASSEROLE

6 cups crushed potato chips	1 16-oz. can sauerkraut,
⅔ cup hot water	drained
2 eggs, beaten	2 cups chopped corned beef
2 tbsp. Russian dressing	8 oz. Swiss cheese, sliced
½ tsp. caraway seeds	¼ cup chopped olives

Combine potato chips, water, eggs, dressing, and caraway seeds. Spread ⅓ of mixture on the bottom of a greased 12- by 8-inch baking dish. Top with half each of the sauerkraut, corned beef, and cheese; repeat the four layers. Top with remaining mixture. Bake uncovered at 350° for 25 to 30 minutes, or until heated through and top is crisp and golden. Garnish with olives. Serves 6 to 8.

Mrs. Paul Lindsay, Lexington Woman's Club

LEVAS' EGGPLANT MOUSSAKA

Levas' Restaurant, Lexington, was established in 1920 by Mike Levas. His sons Evangelos and John carry on the family tradition of fine Greek food. Moussaka is a Levas' specialty.

1 large eggplant (about 2 lb.)	1 tsp. dried sweet basil
flour	½ tsp. cinnamon
1 cup vegetable oil	1 tbsp. brown sugar
1 large onion, minced	salt
1 clove garlic, minced	2 eggs
1 lb. ground lean lamb	2 cups milk
1 6-oz. can tomato paste	½ cup grated Romano cheese
diluted with 1 can water	

Wash eggplant; do not peel. Cut in half lengthwise, then cut into ¼-inch crosswise slices. Dust with flour. Brown in heated oil, turning once. Place on brown paper to drain and sprinkle lightly with salt. Sauté onion and garlic in the same oil until soft but not brown. Add meat and stir, breaking it into small chunks. Simmer 10 minutes. Add tomato paste and water, sweet basil, cinnamon, sugar, and salt; simmer 10 minutes longer. In a greased casserole alternate layers of eggplant and meat sauce. Beat eggs and milk until blended. Pour over eggplant and meat. Top with grated cheese. Bake uncovered at 350° for 30 minutes. Allow to stand for 15 minutes. Cut into squares. Serves 6.

CHICKEN DELIGHT

1 cup chopped celery	½ cup slivered almonds
1 fryer, stewed and boned	salt and pepper
1 cup cooked rice	herb seasoning
1 can cream of chicken soup	MSG
2 tbsp. chopped onion	parsley flakes
¾ cup mayonnaise	2 tbsp. butter
1 can water chestnuts,	1 cup bread crumbs
drained and sliced	

Cook celery in water 1 minute; drain. Mix all ingredients except butter and bread crumbs, using seasonings to taste. Pour into a buttered casserole. Dot with butter and sprinkle bread crumbs on top. Bake at 350° for 45 minutes.

Carolyn Lakes, Jackson County Woman's Club

CHICKEN CASSEROLE SUPREME

1 4-oz. pkg. dried beef (salty)
3 chicken breasts, boned and
    halved
6 slices bacon

1 small can button mushrooms,
    drained
1 can cream of mushroom soup
1 cup dairy sour cream

Shred the dried beef into the bottom of a buttered shallow baking dish. Wrap a slice of bacon around each piece of chicken breast and place on top of beef. Sprinkle with black pepper. (The dried beef provides enough salt.) Combine drained mushrooms, mushroom soup, and sour cream; pour over chicken. Cover with a lid or heavy foil pressed down over the baking dish. Bake at about 350° for 2 to 3 hours, or until meat is fork tender. Serves 6.

Mrs. J. R. English, Woman's Club of Elizabethtown

CHICKEN 'N BISCUITS

4 chicken breasts, boned,
    skinned, and halved
¼ cup self-rising flour
⅛ tsp. pepper
1 tsp. paprika
1 can onions, drained
1 can cream of mushroom
    soup
1 cup sour cream
½ cup sliced stuffed olives

Biscuits:
1 cup self-rising flour
1 tbsp. sugar
¼ cup shortening
⅓ cup milk
Crumb mixture:
¼ cup butter
½ cup bread crumbs
1 tsp. poppy seeds
¼ tsp. poultry seasoning
2 tbsp. sliced stuffed olives

Place chicken breasts in a casserole; sprinkle with flour, pepper, and paprika. Add onions, pour soup over all, and bake covered for 1 hour at 350°. While chicken is baking, make biscuits: Mix flour and sugar. Cut in shortening. Stir in milk. Turn onto a floured board and roll into a rectangle. Prepare crumb mixture: Melt butter in a saucepan; add remaining ingredients. Mix well. Spread over biscuit dough and roll as for jelly roll. Cut in 1-inch slices. Refrigerate until ready to use.

When chicken has baked 1 hour, remove from oven and cover with sour cream and olives. Place biscuits on top. Bake at 400° for 20 to 25 minutes, or until biscuits are browned.

Mrs. Marvin Doyle, Park City Woman's Club

CHICKEN CORNELIA

1 frying chicken, cut in serving
   pieces, or 4 breasts, if
   preferred
salt and pepper
paprika

1 can cream of mushroom soup
1 cup cream
½ cup white wine
2 tbsp. chopped parsley

Season the chicken with salt, pepper, and paprika; place in a buttered casserole. In a bowl mix soup, cream, and wine until well blended. Spoon over chicken and sprinkle with parsley. Bake at 350° for 1½ hours.

Mrs. Richard Cooper, Somerset

HOT CHICKEN SALAD

2 cups diced cooked chicken
½ tsp. salt
¼ cup minced green pepper
2 tsp. lemon juice
1 tsp. Worcestershire sauce
¾ cup grated sharp cheese
1 cup finely chopped celery

2 tbsp. chopped pimiento
½ cup mayonnaise
½ can cream of chicken soup,
   undiluted
½ cup slivered almonds
crushed potato chips

Mix all ingredients except potato chips and place in a well-greased 2-quart baking dish. Top with potato chips. Bake at 350° for 30 to 40 minutes. Serves 6.

Mrs. Elmer DeMott, Woman's Club of Elizabethtown

CHICKEN CASSEROLE

2 cups diced cooked chicken
1 cup mayonnaise
2 cups diced celery
1 cup cracker crumbs

2 cans cream of chicken soup
6 tbsp. chopped onion
1 cup slivered almonds

Combine all ingredients, reserving ½ cup almonds. Place mixture in a shallow buttered baking dish. Sprinkle with reserved almonds. Bake at 300° for 1½ hours. Serves 8.

Mrs. Hubert Fulks, Woman's Club of Elizabethtown

TURKEY-RICE CASSEROLE

2 medium onions, chopped

¾ cup margarine

2 cans cream of chicken soup

2 soup cans water

1 can mushrooms, sliced

2 cups uncooked quick rice

3 to 4 cups chopped cooked turkey

salt to taste

Sauté chopped onion in margarine. Add all other ingredients and mix well. Turn into a buttered casserole. Bake covered at 350° about 50 minutes. Uncover for the last 5 minutes of baking time. Serves 12.

Durie B. Chaney, Woman's Club of Elizabethtown

HOT BROWN

This popular dish originated at the Brown Hotel, Louisville, in the late 1920s. The original Hot Brown was quite different from today's version. Although technically a sandwich, it is actually a hearty entrée.

Sauce:

2 tbsp. butter

¼ cup flour

2 cups milk

¼ tsp. salt

½ tsp. Worcestershire sauce

¼ cup sharp cheddar cheese, grated

¼ cup grated Parmesan cheese

1 lb. turkey, thinly sliced

8 slices trimmed toast

4 slices tomato

8 strips bacon, partially cooked

4 oz. grated Parmesan cheese

Melt butter in a saucepan; add flour and stir well. Add milk, cheeses, and seasonings, and cook, stirring constantly, until thick.

Cut toast into triangles and place on a baking sheet or individual baking dishes. Arrange turkey slices on the toast and cover with hot cheese sauce. Top with tomato slices and bacon strips. Sprinkle with Parmesan cheese. Bake at 425° until bubbly. Serves 4.

To freeze: Omit tomato slices; wrap in foil. When ready to use, remove foil and bake at 375° for 45 minutes.

Ham may be substituted for the turkey or used in addition to it.

Mrs. Robert J. Cope, Lexington Woman's Club

SHRIMP MY WAY

2 cans shrimp, drained
⅓ cup minced onion, heated in butter until yellow
1 or 2 cloves of garlic, minced
1 cup uncooked rice
1 can whole tomatoes (3½ cups)
2 cans consommé

1 small bay leaf
3 tbsp. parsley
½ tsp. ground cloves
½ tsp. marjoram
½ tsp. pepper
1 tsp. salt
1 tsp. chili powder

Mix all ingredients and place in a buttered 1-quart casserole. It is important to use all spices. Cover and bake 1 hour in a preheated 350° oven. If dish becomes too dry or guests are late, add more consommé. Serves 4.

Mrs. James D. Philbrick, Lexington Woman's Club

QUICK TUNA CASSEROLE

1 7-oz. can solid pack tuna
1 can cream of chicken soup
1 can chicken rice soup
¾ cup cream or half-and-half
1 small can chopped pimientos

1 small can chopped mushrooms, undrained
1 can chow mein noodles
salt and pepper to taste
potato chips

Drain and flake the tuna. Combine all ingredients except potato chips. Mix well and pour into a 1½-quart buttered casserole. Top with crushed potato chips. Bake at 325° for 1 hour. Serves 8.

Mrs. H. S. Anderson, Stanford Woman's Club

CHEESE & EGG DISHES

CHEESE SOUFFLÉ

3 tbsp. butter
2 tbsp. flour
1 cup milk

½ tsp. salt
3 eggs, separated
1 cup grated cheese

Melt butter, blend in flour, gradually add milk, and stir over medium heat until thick. Remove from heat. Add salt, beaten egg yolks, and cheese, and stir until cheese is melted. Fold in stiffly beaten egg whites; pour into a well-greased casserole. Set casserole in a pan of hot water and bake at 300° for 45 to 50 minutes. Serves 4.

Mrs. O. B. Hundley, Erlanger Woman's Club

CHEESE PUDDING

In the 1920s the Lynn Hotel in Hodgenville, owned and operated by the Wimsetts, was a family-style hotel which drew Sunday dinner crowds from a wide area of Kentucky. In addition to Kentucky country ham with red-eye gravy, fried chicken, fresh vegetables, and homemade ice cream, there was always the traditional Hodgenville casserole known as cheese pudding. In recent years the Hodgenville Woman's Club has served it on many occasions and always at the annual Lincoln Day celebration, which draws many famous people to the town. When it was served to the late Vice-President Alben Barkley, he asked for a second helping. A few years later when President Eisenhower was served cheese pudding, he requested not only a second helping but the recipe as well. The recipe has been published in several periodicals and in the *Senate Cookbook*.

1 cup soda cracker crumbs	1 7-oz. can pimientos, grated
2 cups medium white sauce	½ lb. American cheese, grated
4 eggs, hard cooked, grated	buttered crumbs

Mix cracker crumbs with white sauce; stir well to be sure all are moist. In a buttered casserole place a layer of crumbs, a layer of eggs, a layer of pimientos, and a layer of cheese. Repeat layers. (If cracker crumbs are not well moistened add a little milk.) Top with buttered crumbs. Bake at 350° for 30 minutes.

Martha L. Hamilton, Hodgenville Woman's Club
Mrs. Stuart Huffman, Campbellsville Junior Woman's Club
Mrs. W. Ed. Hamilton, K.F.W.C. President, 1964–1966

CHEESE PUDDING

½ cup margarine	1 lb. grated sharp cheese
10 slices bread, trimmed and cubed	1 tsp. dry mustard
	½ tsp. salt
3 eggs, separated	½ tsp. red pepper
2 cups milk	

Melt margarine. Add bread cubes, beaten egg yolks, milk, and cheese. Add seasonings. Beat egg whites until stiff and fold into egg and cheese mixture. Pour into a buttered baking dish. Let set 12 hours in refrigerator, or freeze if desired. Bake at 350° to 375° for 45 minutes or until set. Serves 8 to 10.

Mrs. Cloys A. Hobbs, Mayfield Woman's Club
Mrs. Luther Ambrose, Berea Woman's Club

CREOLE EGG CASSEROLE

1 medium onion	dash each of salt, Tabasco
1 small green bell pepper	sauce, Worcestershire
5 ribs celery	sauce, chili powder
½ cup butter	8 eggs, hard boiled, cold
1 can tomato soup	cracker crumbs
1 can cream of mushroom soup	grated sharp cheese
1 4-oz. can sliced mushrooms	

Chop the onion, pepper, and celery and sauté in butter. Add undiluted tomato soup and simmer for 20 minutes. Add undiluted mushroom soup, drained mushrooms, and seasonings; simmer 5 minutes. Rice the cold eggs and place in a casserole; cover with sauce. Sprinkle cracker crumbs and a small amount of grated cheese on top. Bake at 450° for 15 minutes.

This can be made a day ahead and heated when ready to serve. It may also be frozen before baking.

Mrs. Thomas Magraw and Mrs. John L. Street, Cadiz Woman's Club

This dish was a specialty at the old Cadiz Hotel when it was operated by Mrs. Magraw's mother.

A similar recipe was contributed by Mrs. Smith Broadbent III, Cadiz Woman's Club, who substitutes a 28-oz. can of tomatoes and 1 tbsp. sugar for the tomato soup in the creole sauce, and uses 1 cup medium white sauce instead of mushroom soup and mushrooms. She also layers the sliced eggs and sauces.

BAKED EGGS

bread crumbs	butter
6 eggs	cream or rich milk
salt and pepper	

Butter a baking dish and sprinkle sides and bottom with fine bread crumbs. Break in eggs, one at a time, and season to taste with salt and pepper. Dot with butter. Cover with cream or rich milk. Bake 20 minutes at 275° to 300°. Serve at once. Serves 6.

Mrs. Walter Quinn, Woman's Club of Henderson

STUFFINGS, MEAT ACCOMPANIMENTS & SAUCES

CORN BREAD OYSTER DRESSING

turkey neck and giblets
1 rib celery
¾ cup butter
2 cups chopped celery
1 large onion, chopped
½ cup parsley, chopped
1 pan corn bread
½ loaf stale bread

1 small can oysters, drained,
   or 1 cup fresh oysters,
   drained
2 eggs, beaten
1 cup chopped nuts, floured
1½ tsp. dried sage
salt and pepper to taste

Make a stock by simmering turkey parts in water seasoned with 1 rib celery. Sauté chopped celery, onion, and parsley in butter until tender. Crumble corn bread and stale bread in a large bowl. Add sautéed vegetables and remaining ingredients except stock. Toss with a fork until thoroughly mixed. Add ½ to 1 cup stock, according to moistness desired. This will stuff a 15-pound turkey.

Mrs. Francis H. Vittetow, Heritage Woman's Club, Frankfort

BREAD CRUSTS FOR BALLS OR DRESSING

If you have scraps and broken crusts which cannot be toasted, do not throw them away, but soak them until soft, with warm water. Add pepper, salt, and butter, according to taste. Make into balls like an egg and lay them in a pan with a roast of beef; turn them when brown and serve with a rich gravy, and you will think it a rich, nutritious dish. . . . [And] it will be such, in fact.

From DR. CHASE'S RECEIPT BOOK AND HOUSEHOLD PHYSICIAN,
OR PRACTICAL KNOWLEDGE FOR THE PEOPLE (1883);
contributed by Mrs. John T. Tully, Radcliff Woman's Club

FRIED CHICKEN BISCUITS

None of our contributors mentioned fried chicken biscuits. To make these delicacies, use the dumpling recipe on page 106 or page 85 and roll the dough ½ inch thick. Fry, in the same fat used to fry the chicken, until brown on both sides. Split and serve covered with cream gravy.

NOODLES

3 egg yolks	1 tsp. salt
1 egg	2 cups flour
3 tbsp. cold water	

Beat egg yolks and whole egg until very light. Beat in water and salt. Stir in flour. Divide into 3 portions. On a lightly floured board or pastry cloth roll each piece as thin as possible (paper thin). Place between 2 towels or chamois skins until partially dry. Roll dough as for jelly roll and with a thin sharp knife cut into strips of desired width. Shake out the strips and allow to dry completely before using or storing in an airtight container. Makes 6 cups or 10 oz.

Mrs. Patrick DeLuca, Lexington Woman's Club

DUMPLINGS

2 cups flour	3 eggs
2 tbsp. butter or margarine	1 tsp. salt
½ cup boiling water	2 tsp. baking powder

Put 1 cup flour in a mixing bowl; make a hole in the center; place butter in the hole and pour in the boiling water. Stir until smooth. Add beaten eggs and remaining flour to which salt and baking powder have been added. Blend well; add more flour if needed to make the dough stiff enough to roll. Turn onto a floured board. Roll as thin as possible, cut into small squares, and drop one at a time into boiling broth. Simmer 15 to 20 minutes.

Mrs. Arville Castle, Paintsville Woman's Club

FRIED APPLES

5 or 6 apples	⅓ cup sugar
4 tbsp. bacon drippings	

Partially or fully peel the apples. Remove cores and slice about ⅛ inch thick. Heat bacon drippings to medium hot; add apple slices and fry until golden brown. If apples are a very firm, early season variety, add 2 tbsp. water to steam them as they fry. When almost done, add sugar and continue cooking until apples are soft and semitransparent. Delicious served with sausage, eggs, and hot biscuits at breakfast. Serves 6.

Mrs. Arville Castle, Paintsville Woman's Club

CINNAMON APPLES

4 medium Winesap apples	½ cup cinnamon drops
1 cup sugar	1 tsp. lemon juice
½ cup water	

Pare the apples and place in salted water to prevent discoloration. In a saucepan combine sugar, water, and cinnamon drops. Heat slowly to the boiling point, stirring until sugar is dissolved. Add drained apples and cook slowly until tender, 10 to 12 minutes. Carefully lift apples from syrup and place on a platter to cool. Add lemon juice to syrup and boil rapidly until thickened; spoon this glaze over the apples. If you prefer clear rather than rosy apples, substitute 3 sticks of cinnamon for the candy and use Grimes Golden apples. Serves 8.

Mrs. Thomas McCardwell, Falmouth Woman's Club
Mrs. Steely Terrell, Ossoli Woman's Club, Corbin

CRANBERRY MOLD

1 lb. cranberries	2 cups sugar
1 cup water	¼ tsp. salt

Simmer cranberries and water until berries pop. Put through a sieve. Add sugar and salt; mix gently and pour into a mold. Let set until cool and firm. Refrigerate until ready to serve. This can be made several days before using.

Mrs. R. A. Guerdon, Metropolitan Woman's Club of Lexington

MUSTARD SAUCE

½ cup sugar	½ tsp. salt
2 eggs, beaten	1 tbsp. butter
4 tbsp. dry mustard	½ cup cider vinegar
½ cup cream	

Stir sugar into beaten eggs. Add mustard, cream, salt, and butter. Over moderate heat gradually add vinegar, stirring constantly. Cook until thickened. Serve over meat. Reduce amount of mustard if sauce is to be used as a salad dressing.

Mrs. Willis P. Coleman III, Florence Woman's Club

MEAT LOAF TOPPING

3 tbsp. brown sugar   1 tsp. dry mustard
¼ cup catsup   ¼ tsp. nutmeg

Combine ingredients and heat to the boiling point. One-half hour
before meat loaf is done, baste with topping.

Mrs. C. W. Gleaves, Lexington Woman's Club

SORGHUM BARBECUE SAUCE

¼ cup sorghum   1 8-oz. can tomato sauce
1 tbsp. prepared mustard   ¼ cup chopped onion
1 tbsp. vinegar   ¼ tsp. Tabasco sauce

Combine all ingredients in a saucepan. Bring to a boil and boil 1
minute. Makes ⅔ cup sauce.

Barbara Perry, Morgan County Woman's Club

AUTHENTIC BARBECUE DIP

From early times in Western Kentucky, pit barbecue has been a
staple item for picnics, camp meetings, family reunions, and political
rallies. Pork, mutton, and beef cooked slowly over hickory coals are
frequently basted with this dip or sop. Western Kentucky was dotted
with little barbecue stands like that of Mr. Robinson in old Eddyville,
where the tourists and local people could purchase real pit barbecue
for eating in or taking home.

1   quart cider vinegar   ½ lb. butter
1¼-oz. box red pepper   ¼ lb. lard
1¼-oz. box black pepper   1 tbsp. brown sugar
1¼-oz. box paprika   salt to taste
Combine ingredients and heat to a slow boil. Use for basting.

Winifred M. Tanner, Eddyville

An old fashioned barbecue at the Smith Broadbents' in Trigg County, always planned for a night with a full moon, is truly an experience to remember. The guests gather in a creek bottom along a swiftly flowing stream on the farm. Generators hidden deep in the woods provide power for the Japanese lanterns that surround the picnic area, and numerous chimney-covered candles line the path to the tables of food. The meal is often preceded by a hayride.

Traditional Kentucky barbecued pork and mutton, burgoo, slaw, baked beans, potato salad, homemade bread, and trays of sliced tomatoes fresh from the garden line the wide tables. When you are sure your plate can hold no more, you are greeted with "fried on the spot" cornmeal cakes, huge pots of boiling corn on the cob, and vats of frying fish. Of course there is dessert, a choice of watermelon which has been thoroughly chilled in the creek or hot fried fruit pies. After the meal the evening is completed with games, stunts, and skits created by Mr. Broadbent for the participation of all guests.

Breads

Good bread has been an inalienable right for Kentuckians for two hundred years. When Daniel Boone and Felix Walker made their historic trip in 1775, Americans were used to an allotment of one pound of flour per person daily—and that will make a lot of bread! In New England and the Middle Colonies, yeast breads made with rye and wheat flour predominated. In the South, cornmeal breads were more common. Corn lacks gluten, so Southern cooks used soured buttermilk and small quantities of lye water (the colonial counterpart of our modern baking sodas and powders) to raise their corn bread. Kentucky's population was made up of settlers from all sections of the country, so its bread traditions represent a good cross-section of early American foodways.

The Northern contribution is exemplified in the recipes for brown bread, pumpkin bread, yeast batter bread, the two versions of Grandmother's White Bread, and whole wheat bread. All of these are classics, brought into the Commonwealth by the English settlers who established themselves so firmly on the broad plains of the Bluegrass region and the Pennyroyal. The English were great bakers and their tastes and techniques became an essential part of Kentucky's gastronomic heritage. Some of this skill can be seen in the recipes for yeast made from hops (the English were also great beer drinkers) and the "Eight Points in Bread Making."

The Southern impact on Kentucky's bread traditions is extremely well illustrated here. Based primarily on cornmeal, a legacy of the Indians who evolved maize, they indicate the ingeniousness with which the potential inherent in corn was realized. There are hoe cakes, cornmeal batter cakes, cracklin' corn bread, and hushpuppies, all of which date from the pioneer period. Bake ovens were few and far between then, so these breads were cooked in skillets. And there are breads originally designed to be baked in heavy casseroles and Dutch ovens directly over the coals of a hearth fire: Southern spoon bread, Shaker corn sticks, and corn light bread. Finally, there are some superb old recipes for oven-baked breads, using soft wheat flour: biscuits of all sorts (including that elegant Southern specialty, beaten biscuits), rolls and muffins. Some of these, such as Lucille Eversole Hall's recipe for hot dinner rolls, from which she has made 5,000 rolls in the last decade, have truly stood the test of time. Others show the effects of the changes in food technology that have come about in this century: icebox rolls and refrigerator rolls.

This chapter concludes with a section of sweet breads ranging from apricot bread and banana bread to loaves made with oranges, nuts, and even prunes. There is a world of difference between these modern luxury recipes and the humble hoe cake. But both are representative of Kentucky foodways today.

Jay Anderson

QUICK BREADS

BAKING POWDER
An 1886 Recipe

4 oz. bicarbonate of soda   2 oz. cornstarch
9 oz. cream of tartar

(All measurements are by weight.) Mix well and sift 17 times. This is absolutely pure and a 50 percent saving.

Mrs. Wayland Rhoads, Greenville Woman's Club

BRIGHT'S INN HOE CAKES

Bright's Inn was built in 1815 by Captain John Bright. Located about a mile and a half from Stanford, in Lincoln County on the Wilderness Road, it was a stagecoach stop where weary travelers could find rest and excellent food. A meal was 25 cents, with whiskey free. Isaac Shelby, George Rogers Clark, and Henry Clay were among the many frequent guests of the inn.

Each year Captain Bright would take slaves and a six-horse team and wagon and go to the mountains, where he and George Rogers Clark owned 5,000 acres of land, to make salt. While the slaves were making salt, Bright would hunt deer and bear. Bright's Inn became famous for its bearmeat roasts and corn pone cooked in a Dutch oven. Annually the captain took the salt from his mines and a quantity of whiskey made on the farm to New Orleans by flatboat. There he traded them for sugar, coffee, tea, and other things that were not available in Kentucky. One time he brought back a stove, which was considered such a wonder that women came from miles around to see it.

Hoe cakes, cooked over hot coals in the fireplace, were one of the specialties of Bright's Inn. They are still served at Christmas and other holidays by Marjorie Bright Walker of Stanford, a great-great-granddaughter of Captain John Bright. They are excellent with roast beef or turkey and gravy.

2 cups coarse-ground (grist)   ¾ cup cold water
    cornmeal   milk

Mix meal and water and let stand until water is absorbed. Thin with enough milk for easy handling. Form into 2-inch balls in hand, flatten with fingers to a thickness of about ¼ inch, and bake in a little grease (bacon grease is good) on a hot iron griddle until brown on both sides. Serve with butter or gravy.

Mrs. W. M. Bright, Stanford Woman's Club

CORN-MEAL BATTER CAKES

One pint corn-meal, three quarters of a pint of sour milk, one small tea-spoonful of soda in the milk, stirred till it foams, one egg or two would be better; salt to taste. Have the griddle hot and well greased. About one tea-spoonful of flour added to the meal is an improvement.

Miss Kate Spears, HOUSEKEEPING IN THE BLUE GRASS (1874);
contributed by Mrs. Henry C. Bohon, Harrodsburg Woman's Club

CRACKLIN' BREAD

2	cups cornmeal	3	eggs, well beaten
6	tbsp. flour	1	tbsp. butter
2	tsp. sugar	1	cup milk
1	tbsp. baking powder	½	cup cracklin's (or crumbled
2	tsp. salt		crisp bacon)

Mix all ingredients well and pour into a hot, well-greased iron skillet. Bake in hot oven (425°) about 30 minutes.

Mrs. Lucille S. Brown, Owner of Doe Run Inn

The cracklin's used by Mrs. Brown's grandmother were made at hog killing time, always a special event. A great amount of extra work for the adults but a good time for the children because there were friends and neighbors to help. After the meat was trimmed and the lean scraps made into sausage, the fat was cut in small pieces about an inch square and cooked in an iron pot until the cubes were golden brown. The rendered fat became lard and the golden brown pieces were put into a lard press and came out in a large round cake. Cracklin's were used to make corn bread or soap, or were fed to the chickens.

DOE RUN INN

Doe Run Inn, east of Brandenburg, built in 1792, was the first corn grinding mill in the county. Tom Lincoln, father of Abraham Lincoln, is said to have worked on the mill, either as a carpenter or as a stonemason, when it was enlarged in 1821. In 1892 it was converted into a summer vacation residence for Owensboro and Louisville families. After being used for grain storage early in this century, it was reopened and enlarged in the 1920s as an inn. The location of the inn with its thick limestone walls, large fireplaces, and a swiftly running stream nearby, give the feeling of yesteryear.

Mrs. Louis Waller, Brandenburg Woman's Civic Club

SHAKER CORN STICKS

Corn sticks were a specialty at Pleasant Hill, the Shaker settlement near Harrodsburg.

½ tsp. salt	1 cup plus 2 tbsp. cornmeal
½ tsp. soda	1 egg, well beaten
3 tsp. sugar	½ cup buttermilk
½ tsp. baking powder	

Sift together dry ingredients; add egg and buttermilk. Mix well. Bake in greased and heated iron corn stick pans at 450° until brown. Makes 22 small corn sticks.

Miss Julia Neal, Bowling Green

HUSHPUPPIES

2 cups cornmeal	1½ cups sweet milk
2 tsp. baking powder	½ cup water
1 tsp. salt	1 large onion, chopped fine

Sift the dry ingredients; add milk and water. Stir in chopped onion. Add more meal or milk as necessary to form a soft but workable dough. With hands, mold tablespoonfuls of dough into cakes and fry in about 1 inch of fat until well browned, 1½ minutes on each side. Drain on paper and serve very hot.

Mrs. George Ridings, Jr., Richmond Younger Woman's Club

SPOON BREAD

1 cup cornmeal	2 eggs
1 heaping tsp. salt	2 tbsp. baking powder
1 cup boiling water	1 tbsp. butter
1 cup cooked grits	1 cup milk

Sift meal with salt and pour boiling water over it. Let cool. Stir in grits. Add well-beaten eggs, baking powder, butter, and milk. Pour into a greased casserole and bake at 375° for 45 minutes. Serve hot.

Mrs. Mattie Young, Beaver Dam Woman's Club

A footnote on Mrs. Young's recipe admonishes the user to pass the bread several times during the meal.

SOUTHERN SPOON BREAD

3 cups milk	1 tsp. salt
1¼ cups cornmeal	1¾ tsp. baking powder
3 eggs, well beaten	2 tbsp. butter

Stir cornmeal into rapidly boiling milk. Cook until very thick, stirring constantly to prevent scorching. Remove from heat and allow to cool. When mixture is cold and very stiff, add well beaten eggs, salt, baking powder, and melted butter. Beat with electric beater for 15 minutes. Pour into well-greased casserole. Bake 30 minutes at 375°. Serve hot from the casserole with plenty of butter.

Mrs. W. L. Greenup, Florence Woman's Club

Mrs. Robert Haggerty, Maysville Woman's Club, uses only 1 cup cornmeal and 1 tsp. baking powder. She beats the eggs separately and folds the whites in just before baking at 325° for 1 hour. Mrs. Margaret M. Hobson, Bowling Green, substitutes 2 cups boiling water for part of the milk. She pours it over 1 cup cornmeal and the salt, adds other ingredients, blends well, and bakes it in a heated iron skillet at 350° for 25 minutes.

CORN LIGHT BREAD

Corn light bread is an old favorite in Western Kentucky, especially when served with baked or fried ham. It is always served at Thanksgiving and Christmas and often at other times of the year.

2 cups cornmeal	1 tsp. soda
1 cup flour	2 cups buttermilk
½ cup sugar	3 tbsp. melted bacon fat
1 tsp. salt	

Mix dry ingredients; add buttermilk and melted fat. Pour into a greased 5- by 9-inch loaf pan and bake at 300° for 1 hour and 15 minutes. Let cool in pan. Turn out and slice about ¼ inch thick. This is especially good with pork barbecue or chicken. It can be frozen.

Mrs. Don Bishop, Junior Woman's Club of Campbellsville

A similar recipe with 1 well beaten egg added was sent by Mrs. J. Matt Sparkman, Murray Woman's Club.

BISCUITS

2 cups flour	½ tbsp. white vinegar plus
3 tsp. baking powder	milk to equal ⅔ cup
1 tsp. salt	⅓ cup cooking oil

Combine dry ingredients in a medium size bowl. Combine vinegar, milk, and oil; pour into dry ingredients all at once. Stir until dough clings together. Knead on floured surface 10 times. Roll to ¼ inch thickness. Cut and place on a greased baking pan. Bake in preheated 375° oven until brown. Serve hot.

Florence Colvin, Heritage Heights Woman's Club, Augusta

SODA BISCUITS

2 cups all-purpose flour	½ tsp. salt
½ tsp. soda	4 tbsp. shortening
¾ cup buttermilk	

Sift flour and measure it; sift again with soda and salt. Rub shortening into dry ingredients until it is as fine as coarse cornmeal. Add enough buttermilk to make a soft dough. Turn onto a floured board. Knead slightly. Roll ½ inch thick with a rolling pin and cut with a floured biscuit cutter. Prick with a fork. Place biscuits on an ungreased baking sheet and bake at 475° for 12 to 15 minutes. Makes 12 2-inch biscuits.

Mrs. Joe Shields, Woman's Club of Frankfort

FOOLPROOF BISCUITS

2 cups flour	1 tsp. salt
2 tsp. baking powder	½ cup shortening
½ tsp. soda	1 cup buttermilk

Sift dry ingredients; cut in shortening. Add buttermilk and enough additional flour to make a workable dough. Roll and cut. Bake at 450° until light brown. Makes 2 dozen.

Mrs. Garnett Gilbert, Bowling Green Woman's Club

BEATEN BISCUITS

6 cups sifted flour (soft wheat   2 tbsp. sugar
    flour is best)   1 cup lard
1 tsp. salt   1 cup cold milk
1 tsp. baking powder

Sift dry ingredients together. Blend in lard; add milk. Work on beaten biscuit roller about 20 minutes or until dough is smooth and satiny and the blisters will pop. Roll to desired thickness; cut with a 1½-inch biscuit cutter. Place on baking sheet. With a fork prick each biscuit three times, making sure the fork goes all the way through the biscuit to the pan. Bake at 350° for 30 to 40 minutes. Makes 6 dozen small biscuits.

Mrs. C. M. Wade, Woman's Club of Elizabethtown
A similar recipe was contributed by Mrs. Owens Gulley, Sharpsburg

CHEESE BISCUITS

¼ cup shortening   2   cups biscuit mix
⅓ cup shredded cheddar cheese   ⅔ cup milk

Cut shortening and cheese into biscuit mix. Add milk and stir with a fork to make a soft dough; beat 15 strokes. Drop by table-spoonfuls onto a greased baking sheet. Bake at 425° for 12 to 15 minutes. Makes 12 large biscuits.

Mrs. Charles W. Jackson, Woman's Club of Elizabethtown

HERB BREAD

1 loaf unsliced sandwich bread   dash red pepper
1 cup butter   ¼ tsp. paprika
½ tsp. celery salt   ¼ tsp. salt
½ tsp. thyme   1 tbsp. summer savory

Preheat oven to 350°. Mix butter and herbs. Cut off crusts on sides and top of bread. Slice loaf in half lengthwise; then slice cross-wise in 1-inch slices, cutting only three-fourths of the way through. Spread herb-butter mixture on all sliced edges. Wrap in aluminum foil. Bake 25 minutes. For crisper bread, open foil the last 5 minutes.

Mrs. Charles Ashby, Woman's Club of Madisonville

YEAST BREADS

EIGHT POINTS IN BREAD MAKING

1. Good wheat flour. Some varieties of wheat, such as are deficient in gluten, will not make good flour.
2. A good miller to grind the wheat. The breadmaker should be sure to find a good miller.
3. The wheat should not be ground when very dry. Choose a "wet-spell" for the grinding.
4. The flour should be seived before using, to separate the particles.
5. Good yeast. This made from new hops. Stale hops will not, with certainty, make lovely yeast.
6. Thorough kneading. After it has had enough, knead it a little longer.
7. Do not let dough rise too much. Nine out of ten breadmakers in this country let their bread "rise" until its sweetness has been destroyed.
8. The oven can be too hot as well as too cool. The "happy medium" must be determined and selected.

There are three kinds of bread, viz.: sweet bread, bread, and sour bread. Some housewives make sour bread. A great many make bread. But few make sweet bread. Sweetness in bread is a positive quality, that not many breadmakers have yet discovered.

From THE AMERICAN FAMILY COOKBOOK (ca. 1870); *contributed by
Mrs. George Bradley, Woman's Club of Elizabethtown*

YEAST

1 ounce hops*	8 ounces flour
4 ounces white sugar	1 quart Irish potatoes, mashed
3 ounces salt	3 quarts cold water

Simmer the hops and water together until the water is reduced to 2 quarts and 1 pint; strain and divide the liquor, placing one half in a vessel with the flour, sugar, and salt, and half in another vessel containing the mashed potatoes. Heat each portion twenty minutes, then stir all together, and put away in a jug to ferment. Shake it

* Hops are grown on a vine on the garden fence. If you do not have a vine they can be bought at an herb store.

frequently. It will be ready for use in twenty-four hours. Two tablespoons or half a gill will be sufficient for a quart of flour.

From THE LITTLE GEM COOK BOOK (1882); *contributed by Mrs. George Bradley, Woman's Club of Elizabethtown*

More about Yeast

When you wish to use it for baking send a small vessel to the cellar for the desired quantity and re-cork at once. One-half hour in a hot kitchen may spoil it. It will keep for a month in a cool cellar. (A refrigerator doubles its life-span.) During the summer months dry yeast should be used.

From COMMON SENSE IN THE HOUSEHOLD (1873)

Dry Yeast

After yeast has worked for two days, add good white cornmeal until thick enough to make into cakes about one-half inch thickness. Place to dry in shade, where air will pass freely, so as to dry them as soon as possible, as fermentation goes on as long as there is any moisture; turn cakes frequently, when thoroughly dried put in a paper sack and keep in a dry place. It requires about 1½ cakes (biscuit cutter size) to make four medium sized loaves of bread.

From PRACTICAL HOUSEKEEPING (1890)

Compressed yeast was marketed before 1880, but unsold yeast often spoiled in the grocery store or the homemaker's refrigerator. The same problem was faced by the military services during World War II, so a packaged product was developed that could be kept on any cool, dry shelf. The first dry yeast needed the addition of sugar to start the action of the yeast as well as warm water to dissolve it. Today's active dry yeast needs only the warm water, and since it is much finer grained you can eliminate the dissolving entirely.

DERBY BREAKFAST YEAST BISCUITS

1 cup warm buttermilk	2 tbsp. sugar
1 cake or package yeast	2½ cups flour
½ tsp. soda	½ cup shortening (lard is best)
1 tsp. salt	

Dissolve yeast in warm buttermilk; set aside. Sift soda, salt, sugar, and flour into a bowl; cut in shortening. Add yeast mixture; stir until blended. Knead and roll ½ inch thick. Cut; dip in melted butter and place in a greased pan. Let rise 1 hour. Bake at 400° for 12 minutes.

Mrs. Linville Field, Robertson County Woman's Club

Angel Biscuits: Mrs. Joseph Dew, Vine Grove Woman's Club, doubles all ingredients except yeast, which is increased to 1¼ cakes and is dissolved in 2 tbsp. warm water. She adds 2 tsp. baking powder to the dry ingredients.

Rise Biscuits: Martha Kelsch, Heritage Heights Woman's Club, Augusta, rolls the dough ¼ inch thick and spreads it with softened butter, cuts, then stacks 2 rounds buttered sides together.

Buttery Biscuits: Mrs. Charles Hembree, Lexington Woman's Club, dissolves 1 pkg. dry yeast in 1⅓ cups warm water and adds 5 cups biscuit mix. After kneading, she follows Mrs. Kelsch's method. If biscuits are made for future use, bake only 6 minutes and brown when reheating.

SHAKER SALLY LUNN

This recipe comes from the Shaker settlement at South Union.

1 cup milk	1½ cakes yeast
3 tbsp. sugar	3 eggs, beaten
2 tsp. salt	6 cups flour
1 cup butter	4 tbsp. butter, for brushing

Scald milk. Add sugar, salt, and butter; stir until butter melts. Cool to lukewarm and crumble yeast into milk mixture. Stir in well-beaten eggs. Add flour gradually and beat well. Let rise in a buttered bowl until double in bulk. Knead lightly and place in a Sally Lunn pan (tube cake pan). Brush well with soft butter and bake at 350° for 1 hour. Makes one large loaf. Serves 12.

Miss Julia Neal, Bowling Green

YEAST BATTER BREAD

½ cup rolled wheat or whole   1   cup boiling water
   wheat flour   1   pkg. dry yeast
2   tsp. salt   ¼ cup warm water
¼ cup butter   2¾ cups flour
¼ cup molasses

In a large bowl, mix rolled wheat, salt, butter, and molasses. Pour boiling water over mixture and let cool until lukewarm. Dissolve yeast in warm water and stir into the wheat mixture. Add 1 cup flour; beat with electric mixer at medium speed for 2 minutes. Stir in second cup of flour; beat about fifty strokes. Stir in remaining flour. Batter will be sticky. Spread batter in a buttered 9- by 5-inch pan. Brush with melted butter. Cover with a damp cloth. Let rise in a warm place until double in bulk, about 1 hour. Bake at 375° about 50 to 55 minutes.

Eva Duncan, Woman's Club of Elizabethtown

EVERSOLE HOT DINNER ROLLS

This recipe has been handed down through the Eversole family of Owsley County and is becoming a tradition at the Covington Art Club meetings. In the past ten years Lucille Eversole Hall has made over 5,000 rolls for club luncheons and dinners.

1 pkg. dry yeast or 1 cake yeast   1 tsp. salt
2 cups warm water   2 eggs, slightly beaten
6 cups flour   5 tbsp. butter, melted
6 tbsp. sugar

Dissolve yeast in warm water. Mix flour, sugar, and salt by sifting twice. Mix in dissolved yeast, slightly beaten eggs, and butter. Mix well for 2 minutes. Cover with buttered wax paper. Let stand in warm place until double in size, about 2½ hours. Punch down and knead on lightly floured board for 2 minutes. Roll out and cut with a small biscuit cutter; turn in melted butter. (This is additional butter.) Stretch each piece and fold in half. Place on lightly buttered pan, 2 inches apart. Let rise until double in size. Bake in a preheated 450° oven until lightly browned.

Mrs. Wesley Hall, Covington Art Club

SPOON ROLLS

1 pkg. dry yeast
2 cups lukewarm water
¼ cup sugar
¾ cup melted shortening

1 egg
4 cups self-rising flour
¼ cup self-rising cornmeal

Dissolve yeast in water; add remaining ingredients. Mix well and refrigerate until ready to bake. Spoon into well-greased muffin tins. Bake at 425° for 20 minutes.

Mrs. Virgil D. Grayson, Somerset Literary Club

MAYBELLE'S ICEBOX ROLLS

1 cup hot mashed potatoes
⅔ cup shortening
1 cup potato water
2 eggs
1 tbsp. salt

1 scant cup sugar
1 pkg. dry yeast
¼ cup water
6 cups flour

Mix mashed potatoes and shortening with 1 cup boiling water in which potatoes were cooked. Let cool. Beat eggs, add salt, sugar, 1 cup flour, and potato and shortening mixture. Dissolve yeast in warm water and add to mixture. Let rise. Add 4 or 5 cups flour and let rise again. Shape into rolls or refrigerate until needed. (Work down each day if refrigerated. Dough will keep about four days before getting "yeasty.") Let rolls rise and bake in 425° oven 10 to 15 minutes.

Recipe of the late Mrs. Lawson Faxon; contributed by
Winifred M. Tanner, Eddyville Woman's Club

ICEBOX ROLLS

1 cake yeast
⅓ cup lukewarm water
¼ to ½ cup sugar
½ cup lard or other shortening
½ cup boiling water

½ cup cold water
1 egg, beaten
3 cups flour, unsifted
½ tsp. salt

Dissolve yeast in lukewarm water with 1 tsp. sugar. Cream remaining sugar and shortening; pour boiling water over the mixture. Add cold water, beaten egg, and dissolved yeast. Sift in flour and salt, and mix well. Refrigerate overnight. Place the portion of dough to be used on a floured board and shape as desired or roll and cut. Dip rolls in melted butter and place in pans. Let rise at room temperature until double in bulk. Bake at 400° to 425° for 12 minutes. The dough will keep in the refrigerator for several days.

Mrs. John Vertrees, Woman's Club of Elizabethtown
Mrs. Malcolm McGregor, Suburban Woman's Club of Lexington

Mrs. Ben Ashmore, Madisonville Woman's Club, doubles the recipe but uses only ½ cup sugar. A similar recipe was contributed by Mrs. M. J. Cundiff, Bullitt County Woman's Club.

MAW MAW'S HOT ROLLS

1 cup milk	1 cake compressed yeast
4 tbsp. sugar	1 egg, beaten
4 tbsp. shortening	3 cups flour
1 tsp. salt	

Scald milk. Add sugar, shortening, and salt; stir to blend. Cool until lukewarm. Break yeast into a teacup. When milk is cool, mix a few spoonfuls with yeast to dissolve it, then add yeast and beaten egg to milk. Add 2 cups flour gradually, stirring until smooth; add remaining cup of flour or enough to make a soft dough. Place in a greased bowl, cover with a damp towel, and let rise until double in bulk, about 1 hour. Punch down and let rise again. Punch down again, turn onto a floured board, and roll to about ¼ inch thickness. Shape as desired. Dip in melted butter and place in muffin cups for clover leaf rolls; or cut biscuit size, fold, and pinch edges together to make Parker House rolls. Cover and let rise until double in bulk. Bake at 425° for 15 to 18 minutes.

Mary Staggs, Morehead Woman's Club

Cornmeal Refrigerator Rolls: Mrs. John McCubbin, Campbellsville Woman's Club, doubles the milk, sugar, shortening, egg, and flour. She dissolves the yeast in ¼ cup warm water and substitutes ½ cup cornmeal for ½ cup flour.

SALT RISING BREAD

Starter:

2 medium potatoes
3 tbsp. white cornmeal
1 tbsp. salt
1 tbsp. baking powder
1½ tsp. soda
1 cup milk, scalded

Dough:

2 cups warm water
2 tbsp. sugar
1 tbsp. salt
3 tbsp. melted fat
1½ tsp. baking powder
¾ tsp. soda
8 to 10 cups flour

Peel and slice potatoes into a quart jar. Add cornmeal, salt, baking powder, and soda. Pour a small amount of warm water over this, stir, and add scalded milk. Stir again, put a lid on the jar, and keep in a warm oven or warm water for about 8 hours, or until foamy on top. Do not fasten the lid, as it might explode. The starter should be made the night before the bread baking.

Put starter in your mixing container and add dough ingredients and enough flour to make a fairly stiff dough. Beat thoroughly and keep in a warm place until the sponge doubles in bulk. To it, add more flour to make a stiff dough. Knead well and make into two loaves. Place in greased pans and allow to rise until even with the top of the pans. Preheat oven to 385° and bake 10 minutes; lower oven temperature to 350° and bake 25 minutes longer. Turn out on a cloth and allow to cool.

This bread freezes well when wrapped in foil or placed in air-tight bags.

Mrs. Albert Covington, Mr. Joseph Covington, Bowling Green

Kate Covington presided over Covington Hall, which was situated on a thousand-acre farm three miles from Bowling Green. She had a work schedule for Rosa and old Aunt Jenny for each day of the week: Monday, washing was done. Tuesday, they ironed. Wednesday, sewing and mending. Thursday was baking day. Friday was cleaning day. Saturday, Mrs. Covington went to town while the servants polished silver and put the finishing touches on the Sunday dinner. And Sunday was, of course, church day. Thursday was the best day of all, because the house was filled with the marvelous aromas of baking. Mrs. Covington took complete charge of making the salt rising bread by the recipe given. It is good hot from the oven, wonderful cold, and the best you ever tasted spread with country butter. (Mrs. Dudley, our other contributor of salt rising bread, recommends fresh country buttermilk to wash it down.) Mrs. Covington often made as many as 10 to 12 loaves at a time by multiplying the ingredients that are added to the starter by 2, 3, 4, or 5.

SALT RISING BREAD

Yeast:

½ cup milk

2 tbsp. cornmeal

Bread:

1½ cups milk

1 tbsp. sugar

4 .to 5 cups flour

1 tsp. salt

3 tbsp. lard

Heat ½ cup milk until a skim forms. Add cornmeal; mix thoroughly. Cover well and let set in a warm place overnight. The next morning it should be bubbly and fluffy. Proceed with your bread making.

Scald 1½ cups milk; cool to lukewarm. Add sugar and enough flour to make a thin cakelike batter. Add yeast. Mix well and cover with a cloth; set in a warm place to rise. When risen, add salt, lard, and enough flour to make a stiff biscuit dough. Let rise again for about an hour or until light. Knead well, shape into a loaf, roll in melted lard, and place in a well-greased 4- by 8-inch pan. Set the pan in a deeper pan containing warm water. Cover and let rise again until double in bulk. Bake at 375° for 10 to 15 minutes, until light brown; lower the temperature to 250° and continue baking 1 hour.

Mrs. E. S. Dudley, Covington Art Club

GRANDMOTHER'S BREAD

1 pkg. dry yeast

1⅓ cups warm water

⅔ cup milk

2 tbsp. lard

2 tbsp. salt

2 tbsp. sugar

5 cups sifted flour

oil

Dissolve yeast in water. Heat milk to scalding and add lard, salt, and sugar. Stir. Cool until tepid. Add milk mixture to yeast alternately with flour; mix well after each addition. Grease the top of dough with oil. Grease sides and bottom of a bowl and place dough in it. Cover with a towel and put in a warm place; let rise until double in bulk, about 1½ hours. Place in a well-greased bread pan and let rise once more, about ½ hour. Bake at 375° for 1 hour. Remove from oven, butter top of bread, and turn pan on side to cool.

Mrs. Eddith Wicker, Eddyville Woman's Club

GRANDMA'S OLD FASHIONED WHITE BREAD

2½ cups milk	1 cup warm water
1 potato, cooked and mashed	3 pkg. yeast
2½ cups brown sugar	3 eggs
1 tbsp. salt	1 cup wheat shorts or wheat
½ cup shortening	germ
½ cup honey	10 to 14 cups flour

Scald milk; stir in sugar, potato, salt, shortening, and honey. Cool to lukewarm. Sprinkle yeast on warm water and stir to dissolve. Add yeast, eggs, and wheat shorts to milk mixture. Add about 3 cups flour and beat until smooth. Add remaining flour; turn in hand mixer until a ball forms, 3 minutes or longer. Grease dough on all sides, cover, and let rise until double in bulk. Turn onto a lightly floured board; knead until dough is smooth and elastic, 8 to 10 minutes. Divide into 5 equal parts, shape into loaves, and place each in a 9- by 5-inch loaf pan. Cover; let rise in a warm place until double in bulk, about 1 hour. Bake at 425° for 45 minutes.

Ethel Fetterly, Magoffin County Woman's Club

WHOLE WHEAT BREAD

2 pkg. dry yeast	2 tsp. salt
½ cup lukewarm water	1 tsp. baking powder
2 cups buttermilk	1 tsp. soda
¾ cup sugar	¼ cup wheat germ
¾ cup oil	2 cups whole wheat flour
1 egg, well beaten	8 to 10 cups white flour

Dissolve yeast in water. Combine buttermilk, sugar, oil, egg, salt, baking powder, and soda in a large mixing bowl. Stir in yeast. Add wheat germ, whole wheat flour, and enough white flour to make a stiff dough. Knead well until bubbles form, adding flour as needed. Divide in two parts and put each into a greased bowl. Turn dough over in the bowl, cover, and let rise until double in bulk. Shape into loaves. Place in four 9½- by 5½-inch loaf pans; cover and let rise again until double. Bake at 350° for 30 minutes. Cool on a rack.

Mrs. R. B. Hudspeth, Greenville Woman's Club

DILLY BREAD

1 pkg. dry yeast	2 tsp. chopped dill weed
¼ cup warm water	1 tsp. salt
1 cup creamed cottage cheese	¼ tsp. soda
2 tbsp. sugar	1 unbeaten egg
1 tbsp. instant minced onion	2 to 2¼ cups flour
1 tbsp. butter	

Soften yeast in warm water. Heat cottage cheese to lukewarm and combine with sugar, onion, butter, dill, salt, soda, egg, and yeast. Add flour to form a stiff dough. Cover; let rise in warm place until light, 50 to 60 minutes. Stir down dough. Put in a greased casserole and let rise again, 30 to 40 minutes. Bake at 350° for 40 to 45 minutes.

Mrs. Thomas B. Bond, Ghent Woman's Club

ENGLISH MUFFINS

¾ cup milk	1 egg, beaten
½ cup water	4 cups flour
1 cake yeast or 1 pkg. dry yeast	⅓ cup dry skim milk solids
¼ cup warm water	1 tsp. salt
3 tbsp. shortening, melted	½ cup cornmeal (about)
1 tbsp. honey	

Scald milk with ½ cup water; remove from heat and cool to lukewarm. Soften yeast in ¼ cup warm water. When milk is lukewarm add yeast, shortening, honey, and beaten egg. Sift flour with milk solids and salt; add to liquid ingredients, mixing to a soft dough. Turn onto a floured board and knead 5 minutes, adding more flour if necessary for easy handling. Dough should remain soft. Put dough in a greased bowl and brush the top with shortening. Cover with a clean cloth and let stand until double in bulk, about 1 hour. Roll on floured board to about ½ inch thickness and let rest 3 minutes. Cut with a floured cutter; place muffins on a cookie sheet that has been sprinkled with cornmeal. Sprinkle more cornmeal on top of muffins. Let rise 30 minutes. Heat skillet on low burner, or 300° in electric skillet. Carefully move muffins to skillet, allowing room for them to "grow." Cook 5 to 7 minutes on each side. Split and toast; serve with butter and jam.

Mrs. Willis P. Coleman III, Florence Woman's Club

YEAST PANCAKES

2 cups sifted flour	1 pkg. dry yeast
¾ tsp. soda	¼ cup warm water
1 tsp. baking powder	3 eggs, well beaten
3 tbsp. sugar	¼ cup vegetable oil
1 tsp. salt	1½ cups buttermilk

Sift flour, soda, baking powder, sugar, and salt into a large bowl. Soften yeast in warm water. Add eggs, oil, and buttermilk to yeast. Add to flour mixture all at once and stir just until blended. Batter will be thick. Bake at a temperature slightly lower than for regular pancakes. Pour a scant ¼ cup batter onto the hot griddle and spread into a 5-inch pancake. Let the center bubbles break before turning with a broad spatula. When underside is lightly browned, remove to a heated plate. Makes 16 5-inch pancakes.

Note: Batter may be made the night before. Cover tightly and store in the refrigerator. Batter will keep for five days.

Maude Hancock, Horse Cave Woman's Club

SWEET BREADS

PUMPKIN BREAD

2 cups sugar	½ tsp. baking powder
1 cup oil	1 tsp. soda
3 eggs	1 tsp. cloves
2 cups mashed pumpkin	1 tsp. cinnamon
3 cups flour	1 tsp. nutmeg
½ tsp. salt	

Beat sugar and oil; add eggs, one at a time. Beat in pumpkin; add sifted dry ingredients. Pour into three well-greased loaf pans and bake at 325° for 50 minutes.

Mrs. William Major, Woman's Club of Madisonville

PRUNE BREAD

1¾ cups flour	1 egg
¾ cup sugar	2 tbsp. melted bacon grease,
½ tsp. salt	shortening, or oil
1 tsp. soda	chopped pecans or English
8 to 10 cooked prunes, chopped	walnuts (optional)
⅔ cup water	

Sift dry ingredients. Add prunes, water, egg, and shortening. Stir well. Stir in nuts, if desired. Pour into a greased loaf pan, 8½ by 4½ inches. Bake at 325° for 1 hour, or until golden brown and toothpick inserted in center comes out clean. Cool. Wrap well in plastic wrap or aluminum foil. Slice thinly and serve with butter or cream cheese, or plain. Makes a good party bread.

Mrs. Patch Woolfolk, Lexington Woman's Club

ORANGE DATE NUT BREAD

1 orange	1 tsp. soda
2 tbsp. melted shortening	1 tsp. baking powder
2 eggs, beaten	1 cup pitted dates, chopped
1 cup sugar	¾ cup broken nut meats
2 cups flour	1 tsp. vanilla
½ tsp. salt	

Squeeze orange and add enough water to orange juice to make 1 cup. Add shortening to orange juice. Stir in beaten eggs. Measure and sift together dry ingredients; add to orange mixture. Grind orange rind and add it with dates and nuts. Stir in vanilla. Mix well. Pour into two 7½- by 3½-inch greased loaf pans. Bake at 350° for 1 hour.

Mrs. A. W. Fullerton, Jr., Florence Woman's Club

APRICOT BREAD

1 cup dried apricots, chopped	¼ tsp. soda
1 cup sugar	1 tsp. salt
2 tbsp. shortening	½ cup orange juice
1 egg	¼ cup water
2 cups flour	¼ cup nuts, broken
2 tsp. baking powder	

Place chopped apricots in a cup and fill the cup with water; soak at least 30 minutes. Cream the sugar, shortening, and egg. Sift together dry ingredients and add to creamed mixture alternately with orange juice and water. Stir in apricots and any water that has not been absorbed. Add nuts. Pour into a greased and floured 9½- by 5½-inch loaf pan and let rest for 15 to 20 minutes. Bake at 350° for 50 minutes.

Mrs. M. H. Dunn, Stanford Woman's Club

BROWN BREAD

2 tsp. soda
3 tbsp. sorghum molasses
1 cup white flour
2 cups graham flour

1 cup brown sugar
1 tsp. salt
2 cups buttermilk
nuts and raisins (optional)

Dissolve soda in molasses, then mix in remaining ingredients. Steam in 4 well-greased number 2 cans for 3 hours.

Mrs. Earl F. Metcalfe, Covington Art Club

[To steam breads and puddings:] The cans should not be filled more than two-thirds full. The covering should be tied with a string; otherwise the bread in rising might force off the cover. For steaming, place the cans on a trivet in a kettle containing boiling water, allowing the water to come half-way up around them, cover closely, and steam, adding, as needed, more boiling water.

Boston School of Cooking (1923)

Note: Steaming can also be done in a pressure cooker, following the manufacturer's instructions.

BANANA BREAD

4 tbsp. butter
1 cup sugar
2 eggs
2 cups flour

1 tsp. soda
¼ tsp. salt
2 to 3 ripe bananas, mashed
¾ cup chopped nuts

Cream the butter and sugar. Add eggs; beat well. Add sifted dry ingredients and fold in bananas and nuts. Bake in a 5- by 9-inch loaf pan at 350° for 30 minutes.

Mrs. T. R. Haag, Sr., Buechel Woman's Club

Mrs. Rufus Brandenburg, Woman's Club of Elizabethtown, uses a similar recipe with double quantities.

WHIPPED CREAM WAFFLES

1½ cups sifted flour
¼ tsp. salt
¼ cup sugar
1½ tbsp. baking powder

1 egg
1 pint sterilized whipping
    cream
2 tbsp. oil

Chill a large mixing bowl and beaters of electric mixer before starting. In another bowl sift together dry ingredients. Beat egg in chilled bowl, then add cream and whip until peaks form, 10 to 15 minutes. Fold dry ingredients into whipped cream; fold in oil. Cook on hot, lightly oiled waffle iron. Makes 4 large waffles.

Mrs. Ted Greene, Lexington Woman's Club

COFFEE CAKE

2 cups sifted flour	1 egg
3 tsp. baking powder	*Topping:*
1 tsp. salt	½ cup brown sugar
¼ cup sugar	2 tbsp. flour
½ cup lard	¾ cup chopped nuts
1 cup milk	

Preheat oven to 400°. Sift together flour, baking powder, salt, and sugar. Cut in lard until mixture has the texture of coarse meal. Add milk and egg; stir until flour is well dampened. Spread in a well-greased 9-inch square pan. Mix topping ingredients and sprinkle over the batter. Bake 25 minutes.

Mrs. Lester W. White, Fountain Run Woman's Club

Cinnamon Coffee Cake: Mrs. Charles Hagan, Lexington Woman's Club, makes the basic coffee cake recipe, using half of all ingredients except 3 tsp. baking powder. She adds ½ tsp. cinnamon to the batter and sprinkles cinnamon-and-sugar over it before baking in a 9-inch round pan at 350°.

STREUSEL TOPPING FOR COFFEE CAKE

3 tbsp. butter	¼ cup dry milk
½ cup brown sugar, packed	1½ tsp. cinnamon
¼ cup white sugar	⅓ cup chopped pecans
¼ cup flour	

Cut butter into sugars; add remaining ingredients. Sprinkle over your favorite coffee cake batter before baking.

Mrs. James N. Farris, Bullitt County Woman's Club

Beverages

"THIS HOSESOME BEVERAGE"

Marie Campbell

The most favored and famous beverage made in Kentucky from Kentucky products, and one of the state's chief money crops, is corn whiskey. As is usual with the story of beginnings entrusted to memory of the folk rather than set down in writing at or near the time of occurrences, there are variants of the story as to just where, when, and by whom whiskey was first made in Kentucky. Was it somebody at Fort Harrod in 1774? Was it Elijah Pepper in what is now Woodford County in 1776? Elijah Pepper was the grandfather of James E. Pepper, a great name in the annals of whiskey distilling in Kentucky, and the Pepper distilleries used "Old 1776" as a trademark. Some disputed the Pepper claim and said it was not until years later than 1776 that Elijah made his first run of singlings. Others insist that the first whiskey distiller in Kentucky was John Ritchie, who set up his still at Linn's Fort east of Bardstown in 1777 and took a flatboat load of whiskey down to New Orleans in 1780.

No matter who made the first Kentucky whiskey and at whatever time and place, the reasons for making whiskey in Kentucky are

This essay is excerpted from a portion of a forthcoming book on Kentucky folklore by Dr. Campbell, to be published by the University Press of Kentucky.

clear: There was a crop surplus (in this case of grain) beyond family needs. Markets for such surplus were totally lacking or so distant that transportation costs consumed any hope of profit from grain marketed as such. Many Kentucky settlers brought a family tradition of whiskey-making. Especially was this true of the Scotch and Irish, who brought their distilling methods from their old homes in Britain when their families settled in America and now brought these same methods with them to Kentucky. Settlers also brought a taste for whiskey, and Monongahela whiskey from western Pennsylvania or whiskeys from other sections of the East were hard to get in ample supply. Then, too, in Kentucky's rivers and never-failing springs there was an abundant supply of water peculiarly suited to producing superior whiskey. The importance of the quality of water in whiskey-making was an Old World tradition with Scotch and Irish distillers— one apparently still practiced in Scotland. This tradition helps to explain the location of many of the large distilleries along the lower Kentucky River, which flows through the limestone soil of the Bluegrass.

Much of the distilling of whiskey in frontier Kentucky was a home industry. Many frontier families owned and operated a still and thought no more of it than "cooking up a meal's victuals," grinding a turn of corn, or boiling sorghum syrup to make molasses. A craftsman of the Bluegrass writing his memoirs says, "Nine tenths of the farmers had a small Still house on Each Farm, and did not make more than two Barrels of Whiskey per week." His percentage may be too high, but it is certain that on many Kentucky farmsteads a still house was one among the little village of outbuildings.

These small home distilleries not only supplied whiskey for use "amongst the family" but also provided a way of converting the corn crop into a marketable and profitable product. During the years when the Ohio River and the Wilderness Road were the only routes into and out of the Kentucky country, ginseng and whiskey were the only commodities that would pay overland transportation costs across the mountains, to say nothing of leaving a margin of profit. And, when the lower Mississippi, controlled by the Spanish, was closed to American shipping, whiskey could be slipped past the blockade when no other commodity could be.

Within the frontier region, whiskey was an important medium of exchange for barter and cash sale. Early issues of the *Kentucky Gazette* list whiskey among commodities for sale in Lexington and many advertisers through the years mentioned whiskey among goods that would be accepted in exchange for services or other commodities.

One notable example of whiskey's being "as good as money" is the fact that Thomas Lincoln, when he sold his Kentucky farm in 1817 to move to Indiana, received as the greater part of the sales price four hundred gallons (ten barrels) of whiskey.

In the early days, making or selling whiskey was not considered reprehensible, even when done by government officials or by preachers. In fact, a Baptist preacher is the person most often credited with having discovered by accident in 1789 the process of making bourbon whiskey. This preacher was the Reverend Elijah Craig, one of the two Craig brothers who led their "Travelling Church," singing hymns and preaching along the way, over the mountains and through the wilderness to settle in Kentucky. Elijah Craig, with James and Alexander Parker as partners, ran a grist- and fulling mill near Georgetown, and a distillery as well. At the Craig-Parker distillery, according to one legend, Craig happened to store whiskey made from sour mash in charred oak kegs which, it was discovered, mellowed the sharp taste, changed the color to amber, and removed foreign particles. Another story says that Daniel Stewart, who lived near Lexington, was perhaps earlier than Craig with this discovery.

At any rate, Kentucky bourbon whiskey became internationally famous and was the source of many distillers' fortunes. In New Orleans, Kentucky bourbon was offered at a premium. In 1819 that port received over 200,000 gallons of whiskey per month from Kentucky. Apparently the whiskey was named for Bourbon County, where at present whiskey can be sold legally only in the town of Paris.

In Kentucky, whiskey was at first made from rye as in the eastern settlements, and there are various accounts of the shift to using corn. One legend has it that the rye crop in Kentucky was a failure one year and local distillers had to use corn for their mash.

In Kentucky—on the whole frontier for that matter—whiskey has played many roles. One of these has been its use for medicinal purposes. The belief in the medicinal properties of whiskey—preventive, curative, or as a general aid toward having more "get-up"—has been widespread and enduring, so much so that every restrictive legislative act relating to whiskey has had some medical loophole. And much of the lore of folk medicine involves the use of whiskey. As a preventive, whiskey has been used to ward off all sorts of ailments, ranging from the common cold to Asiatic cholera, as in the terrible cholera epidemic of 1833. Among folk prescriptions for the cure of specific ailments are a multitude of remedies, including a great variety of homemade liniments and tonics, the content of which is largely alcohol—a principle widely exploited by the patent medicine business.

There are many apocryphal stories about how many gallons of whiskey it took to raise a family without a cow. To illustrate the point that whiskey was considered a necessary household commodity, there are numerous variants of the tale about a Kentuckian who, seeing another on his way to the gristmill with a sack of corn, commented, "Look at that feller going yonder to grind a turn a corn. Bet right now he ain't got a pint of liquor in his house."

Folk songs also reflect the notion of the daily dram of whiskey for one's health, somewhat in the light of a food supplement to tone up the system and promote good appetite and good spirits. Whiskey was doled out to children and to slaves as a preventive health measure. For river men and other workmen, whiskey was considered a part of the ration to be provided, though in the days of the steam packet many captains doled out whiskey rations very sparingly to the roustabouts till the end of the trip. Then it was served freely in buckets with tin dippers. A South Union Shaker journal makes a notation, dated July 1828, that "this was the first hay harvest ever taken in this country without the help of whiskey."

Among the most vivid glimpses of the part whiskey played in Kentucky life are those found in the memoirs of Ebenezer Hiram Stedman, a Bluegrass papermaker who came to Kentucky in 1816 at the age of eight. Writing in 1878, Stedman had this to say about whiskey rations for the men helping to rebuild a dam for his paper mill in 1834:

> The times i Speak of Ware the First year we Came down to Build the Mill dam. We woold work all the week then Jack woold haul us to Geotown. Some times we woold not get There till 12 oclock at night. What a Beginning of life, day, and night, and night, and day. On Monday Morning Before Breakfast, the Wagon woold Be on Main Street Geotown to lay in our Stock of Something to Eat for the week. The first thing was to have the Three gallon Stone Jug filled with Whiskey. It cost then Thirty seven Cents per gallon. We gave it to the Working Hands three times a day and to this day i am satisfide It Gave us more work to the hand than half more Wages. I wont pretend to Say What the poisend Whiskey woold do That is Made in Kentucky at this day. I dont think They woold work as well. But i Speak of the Good old time of the past, When there was no Yankee Skum defused into all we drink, Eat, Ware, or think about.

On another occasion, Stedman wrote:

> Them days the Bank officers and welthy men woold Come
> down and Fish, up the Creek a week at a time. They Came
> prepaired to Enjoy the Sport. They Brot the Best provisions
> and alwais The Best of old Burbon not to drink to Excess,
> But to Make one Feel Renewed after the toils of Fishing. The
> president of the Bank alwais Kept his Black Bottle in the Spring
> and the Mint grew Rank and Compleatly Hid the Bottle.
> I never saw one of them in the least affected by using What
> is now Called poison and the Reason was it was pure Whiskey.
> . . . Then the effects produced in drinking the pure Whiskey!
> In the Early days of Kentucky one Small drink woold Stimulate
> the Whole Sistom. One Could feel it in their feets, hands,
> and in Evry part. There was a warm Glow of Feeling, a
> Stimulus of Strength, of Beaurency [buoyancy] of feeling, a
> Something of Reaction of Joy in place of Sorrow. It Brot out
> Kind feelings of the Heart, Made men sociable. And in them
> days Evry Boddy invited Evry Boddy That came to their house
> to partake of this hosesome Beverage.

Concerning the variety of social occasions, public and private, on
which it was the custom to invite guests "to partake of this hosesome
Beverage," historians, biographers, novelists, essayists, and the folk
memory have handed down to the present their stories, their descrip-
tions, or their preachments. They tell us of the barrel of whiskey or
whiskey toddy at barbecues and political rallies, of the jug hidden
under the pile of corn to be shucked at a neighborhood corn shucking,
or of log rollings, house raisings, and other "workings" where the
men might expect a dram as well as a good dinner.

A folk custom called "running for the Bottle," which was a part
of wedding celebrations, intrigued writers of fact and fiction alike.
William Roscoe Thomas tells it this way:

> Another ceremony took place before the party reached the
> house of the bride. When the party arrived within a mile of
> the house, two young men would single out to run for the
> bottle. The worse the path the better, as obstacles afforded an
> opportunity for greater display in intrepidity and horseman-
> ship. The start was announced by an Indian yell; logs, brush,
> muddy hollows, hills and glens were speedily passed by the
> rival horses. The bottle was always filled for the occasion, and
> the first who reached the door was presented with the prize,
> with which he returned in triumph to the company. The con-
> tents of the bottle were distributed among the company.

Sometimes on the evening of the wedding, the young folk had rowdy fun with "Black Betty," the bottle of whiskey which added to the hilarity of the occasion. After the young women guests had stolen off the bride and put her to bed, the young men stole off the groom and placed him by the side of his bride—all of this with much suggestive banter. Later in the evening "Black Betty" was taken to the bridal couple, lest they need refreshment, and they were compelled to drink more or less of the whiskey offered them.

With the passing of the frontier, such customs have gone out of use. When they linger in the folk memory it is only as a colorful item of vocabulary which may bring to light a story of some wedding "way back before my time."

Among the "word hoard" of Kentuckians are numerous expressions meaning a drink of liquor, a good many of these terms a matter of current speech. Such terms as a *nip*, a *swallow*, a *drap*, a *wee drap* suggest an unmeasured and very small amount, which in practice may be quite otherwise than small. Other drinking words designate measured amounts, such as *jigger* or *finger*. The manner of drinking may be suggested, as with *sip*, *swig*, *snifter*. There is some special color of meaning in *shot, snort, whiff, night cap, phlegm cutter,* when applied to drinking. The term *hog-drover* for a drink of whiskey is rare today. The origin of the word is rather obvious, and those who know the expression can only "guess it wouldn't be no wee drap, for the men that followed hog droving never done things by littles."

Yarns about liquor and drinking—whatever the occasion—remain in the repertoire of Kentucky tale-tellers in "great plenty," and vary in degree of fact from "the God's truth" through "a little grain of truth" to tall tales "straight from the liars' bench." One of the favorite subjects is whiskey and politics, especially tales—both fiction and fact—of whiskey as a vote-getter. A rival product used to gain favor at election time was gingerbread, and in the 1930s a Letcher County woman was still following her practice of making large batches of gingerbread to sell to candidates. "That 'lasses cake of mine," she said, "it gets a mort of voters for them that's running for office. Folks are that fond of sweetening that it gets nigh as many votes as liquor, I claim. My brother John, he don't hold with that opinion, him always making a big run of liquor for politics and not wanting my trade to outdo hisn. They's them that claims John hadn't ought to make a run since he joined the meeting. But John holds that politics and religion don't do no hurt to each other iffen they don't get mixed."

"Religion's a right good thing," put in her husband, "but politics and liquor puts a heap more stir into living."

Moonshine lore in Kentucky ranges in mood from boisterous hilarity to dismal tragedy. Kentucky's traditions surrounding illicit liquor and resistance to revenue officers began in 1792, the year of admission to statehood, when federal officials attempted to enforce registration of distilleries and collection of the newly imposed tax. There was no Whiskey Rebellion in Kentucky, as in Pennsylvania in 1794. But the individual personal rebellion goes on to this day. Some whiskey distillers in those early days paid the tax, and their distilleries became the basis of Kentucky's legal whiskey industry. Those claiming the right to make whiskey without taxation felt that the government was not cognizant of pioneer conditions and did not take the right attitudes toward the maker of whiskey and his product. Pretty much the same reasons are expressed by those who make illegal whiskey today. They contend that "they's got to be liquor made" even if they have to "out the government" to do it.

The enforcement of laws relating to the manufacture and sale of whiskey is made more complex by the fact that a little over two-thirds of Kentucky's 120 counties are by local option legally dry. Being legally dry scarcely means, however, that the genuine bonded article or its backwoods cousin, moonshine, never flows. Even in dry counties, many a Kentuckian has been known to develop a thirst for "this hosesome Beverage."

Others have abandoned moonshine making to work in the legal distilleries, where, as one man said, he has "good pay and no risk of getting tangled up in the law. Like Granddaddy used to say, 'It's just in the generation of our family to make whiskey and whiskey making is as respectable as any other business if you stay inside the law.' I reckon you can leave the matter rest right there."

SOURCES

The quotations from Ebenezer Hiram Stedman are found in Frances L. S. Dugan and Jacqueline P. Bull, editors, *Blue-Grass Craftsman: Being the Reminiscences of Ebenezer Hiram Stedman, 1808–1885* (Lexington: University of Kentucky Press, 1959). "Running for the bottle" is quoted from William Roscoe Thomas, *Life among the Hills and Mountains of Kentucky* (Louisville: Standard Printing Company, 1930).

MINT JULEP

From the Kentuckians' taste for the "hosesome beverage" comes the famed mint julep. The Kentucky legend is that a boatman made the discovery when he left the Mississippi River in search of spring water to mix with his bourbon and, as a whim, added some of the mint growing beside the spring. The actual date of discovery is unknown but the drink was adopted by genteel Kentucky society in the nineteenth century.

The mixing of a mint julep—a concoction of bourbon, water, sugar, and mint—has become a more controversial subject than the curing and cooking of a country ham. Traditionally there seems to have been uniform agreement that the whiskey must be straight aged Kentucky bourbon and the water must be cold and fresh from a limestone spring. The controversy about the handling of the mint, whether to bruise the leaves or not, has been the subject of many newspaper columns and a few books.

The cup in which a mint julep is traditionally served is made of sterling silver (originally coin silver), about four inches tall and three inches in diameter. As early as 1816 such cups were being given as prizes at agricultural fairs. A specially designed julep cup has been presented to the owner of the Kentucky Derby winner for the past twenty-five years. A complete set, with the names of all the Derby winners, is in the director's room at Churchill Downs.

The reputation of the mint julep has now spread throughout the world, and it is known as the unofficial Kentucky Derby drink, enjoyed by thousands as the thoroughbreds canter to the starting gate at Churchill Downs to the strains of "My Old Kentucky Home."

Recipes for mint julep have been attributed to such noted Kentuckians as Henry Clay, Irvin S. Cobb, and Henry Watterson. Soule Smith (1848–1904), a Lexington attorney, in a monograph entitled *The Mint Julep*, gave the most eloquent and poetic description of its preparation. Henry Clay's recipe, which follows, was found in a diary.

"The mint leaves, fresh and tender, should be pressed against a coin-silver goblet with the back of a silver spoon. Only bruise the leaves gently and then remove them from the goblet. Half fill with cracked ice. Mellow bourbon, aged in oaken barrels, is poured from the jigger and allowed to slide slowly through the cracked ice.

"In another receptacle, granulated sugar is slowly mixed into chilled limestone water to make a silvery mixture as smooth as some rare Egyptian oil, then poured on top of the ice. While beads of moisture gather on the burnished exterior of the silver goblet, garnish the brim of the goblet with choicest sprigs of mint."

Henry Clay

Less romantic but perhaps more interesting to the contemporary taste is the following recipe for mint julep:

1 tsp. water	2 jiggers bourbon whiskey
1 tsp. sugar	1 sprig of mint
6 mint leaves	confectioners' sugar
crushed ice	

To a 12-ounce julep cup or glass which has been chilled in the freezer, add a syrup of water and sugar in which 6 mint leaves plucked from the stem have been bruised with a spoon and then removed. Fill the cup with crushed ice and add one jigger of whiskey. Stir vigorously until the ice level has dropped an inch or more, then again fill the cup with ice and pour in the remaining jigger of bourbon. Stir again until frost has formed on the outside of the cup. Garnish with a sprig of mint dusted with confectioners' sugar, insert two short straws, and serve immediately. If not served immediately, place in the freezing compartment for up to 25 minutes, then in the refrigerator until ready to serve, but do not add the sprig of mint until the last minute.

WHIPT CREAM

Take a Quart of thick cream, and the Whites of eight Eggs beaten with a half Pint of White wine; mix it together, and sweeten to your Taste with double refined Sugar; perfume it as you please with Musk; whip it up with a Whisk with a bit of lemon tied in the middle of the whisk; take the froth with a spoon and lay it in your glasses.

COMPLEAT HOUSEWIFE, *Williamsburg* (1742);
contributed by Mrs. Richard McClure, Crescent Hill Woman's Club

EGGNOG

12 eggs, separated
2 cups sugar
1 quart cream, whipped

1 quart milk
1 quart bourbon
2 oz. Jamaica rum

Beat egg yolks and whites separately, adding 1 cup sugar to each. Blend whites into yolks. Stir in whipped cream and milk. Add bourbon and rum; stir thoroughly. Serve with grated nutmeg sprinkled on top.

Mrs. Raymond Becht, Woman's Club of St. Matthews

While Kentucky's pioneers turned the surplus of the corn crop into bourbon, they also planted groves of honey locust trees so they could make metheglin from the pods, and peach and apple trees for making brandy and cider. Wild berries, fruits, vegetables, and even weeds were converted into wine.

GRAPE WINE

Stem 20 pounds of grapes. Crush slightly in a stone jar; add 6 quarts boiling water. Let stand 24 hours. Strain; add 10 pounds granulated sugar. Tie a cloth over jar; let stand 7 weeks to ferment. Skim carefully once a week for 4 weeks, then let stand for 6 weeks. Bottle tightly and keep in a cool place.

Mrs. H. H. Morgan, Maysville Woman's Club

GOOSEBERRY WINE

Pick and bruise the gooseberries and to every pound, put a quart of cold spring water, and let it stand three days, stirring it twice or thrice a day. Add to every gallon of juice three pounds of loaf sugar; fill the barrel and when it is done working, add to every twenty quarts of liquor, one quart of brandy and a little isinglass. The gooseberries must be picked when they are just changing color. The liquor ought to stand in the barrel six months. Taste it occasionally, and bottle when the sweetness has gone off. [These instructions were handwritten in July 1895.]

Mrs. Roy Roberts, Woman's Club of Richmond

NONALCOHOLIC BEVERAGES

MARTHA WASHINGTON'S COLONIAL CHOCOLATE

Mix to a paste in a saucepan four tablespoons cocoa and a little water. Stir in two cups water, one-third cup sugar, two cups milk. Bring to a boil and blend in two tablespoons cornstarch dissolved in a little cold milk. Boil three minutes longer. Remove from heat and set in a warm place. Beat until light and foamy one egg with one-half cup hot water. Pour half of the egg mixture into a pitcher and blend in one-half teaspoon vanilla. Add chocolate slowly. Pour remaining egg mixture over the top. Serve immediately.

Miss Edith Wood, Middletown Woman's Club

Miss Wood is author of *Middletown's Days and Deeds.*

SASSAFRAS TEA

Take a handful of bits of root for every ½ gallon of tea. Boil until the water turns darkish red. Sweeten to taste. Strain and save the roots for another cooking.

Morgan County Woman's Club

MAXWELL PLACE SPICED TEA

5 qt. water	3 sticks cinnamon
6 cups granulated sugar	2 tbsp. whole cloves
6 lemons	¼ pound Lipton's Orange
6 oranges	Pekoe tea

Boil water, sugar, lemon rinds, and orange rinds with cloves and cinnamon for 15 minutes. Remove from the stove. Add tea and let stand 3 minutes. Strain and dilute with 2 cups of water to 1 of tea. Add juice of lemons and oranges just before serving. Serve either hot or cold. Serves 120.

Recipe of Frances Jewell McVey (Mrs. Frank L.);
contributed by Miss Chloe Gifford

HOT TOMATO PUNCH

3 46-oz. cans tomato juice
3 10½-oz. cans beef broth
1 tsp. horseradish
few drops of Tabasco

3 tsp. Worcestershire sauce
lemons
whole cloves

Combine and heat all ingredients except lemons and cloves. Cut 1 lemon in thirds; stick with cloves; add to hot punch and simmer for a few minutes. Serve with a thin slice of lemon in each cup.

Mrs. Harold Collins, Lexington Woman's Club

CIDER TREAT

2 qt. apple cider
2 tsp. allspice berries
2 tsp. whole cloves

4 sticks cinnamon
12 thin lemon slices

In a large pot combine all ingredients except lemon slices. Cover; cook slowly for 20 minutes. Strain. Serve hot with lemon slices. Serves 6.

Mrs. Adron Doran, K.F.W.C. President, 1962–1964

QUICK APPLE PUNCH

2 qt. chilled apple cider
2 cups cranberry juice cocktail

2 tsp. lemon juice
1 qt. ginger ale

In a large pitcher combine cider and juices; add ginger ale just before serving. Pour over crushed ice. Makes 15 tall glasses.

Mrs. Adron Doran, K.F.W.C. President, 1962–1964

KENTUCKY SPARKLER

2½ cups lemon juice
⅔ cup crushed mint leaves
2 cups sugar

1 cup water
3 qt. ginger ale
sprigs of mint

Pour lemon juice over mint leaves. Add sugar and water; bring to a boil. Remove from heat; cool and strain. Add ginger ale. Pour over ice. Garnish each glass with a sprig of mint.

Mrs. Marvin Doyle, Park City Woman's Club

Vegetables

Vegetables have been an important element in Kentucky's foodways for the past two centuries. The Indians of the region were skilled in procuring and processing both wild and domesticated herbs and vegetables. Later the Scottish and English settlers drew on this knowledge and added a considerable store of their own. All three groups preferred well cooked vegetables stewed with meat, and the green bean and shucky bean recipes given here are examples of this tradition. Another recipe, in which the vegetable is baked with meat rather than stewed, is slow-baked beans. This dish has its origin in the north of England and is, of course, a favorite in New England. But the inclusion of jowl bacon and sorghum molasses gives it a distinctive Kentucky flavor. Another favorite Kentucky dish is poke sallet, customarily served with fried salt pork and corn pone. The Poke Sallet Festival in Harlan County is one of America's authentic folk festivals. Tater Day in Benton, over 125 years old, is another true folk festival, formerly focusing on the importance and popularity of sweet potatoes. The glazed sweet potatoes and sweet potato pudding recipes in this chapter are both fine examples.

But it is with corn that Kentuckians have really worked wonders. This vegetable is one of the world's most versatile foods. For two hundred years Kentucky cooks have been making the most of its potential. Corn is the basis for Kentucky's "hosesome beverage," sourmash bourbon whiskey. It has fattened innumerable country hams. It has been dried, ground into meal, and made into a variety of porridges, cakes, and breads. And it has been, and is, the primary ingredient in a number of staple vegetable dishes. The recipes in this chapter for corn pudding are traditional and highly economical, drawing on farm-produced ingredients such as honey, butter, milk, and eggs. As Harriette Arnow notes in her excellent study of early Kentucky life, *Seedtime on the Cumberland,* the settlers felt a craving for creamy vegetable dishes such as puddings. Perhaps the preponderance in their diet of salty and bitter foods set off a desire for the opposite tastes—sweet, bland foods. Another very old recipe here is for corn fritters, from the Old Stone Inn in Simpsonville.

But Kentucky foodways are not just an amalgam of old-time recipes, and this chapter reflects the trend toward national and international dishes: a broccoli casserole with Velveeta cheese and Ritz crackers, a cabbage-vegetable medley flavored with soy sauce, and an eggplant casserole garnished with Parmesan cheese. That these newer arrivals have found honored places beside such simpler and more traditional dishes as baked hominy and shucky beans is a testimony to the unique strength of Kentucky's heritage.

Jay Anderson

ARTICHOKE CASSEROLE

1 small onion, chopped	½ cup grated cheddar cheese
¾ cup chopped celery	1 3-oz. can mushrooms
1 tbsp. vegetable oil	½ cup sour cream
1 can cream of mushroom soup	salt and pepper to taste
1 can artichoke hearts	shredded wheat biscuit or crackers

Sauté onion and celery in vegetable oil. Remove from heat. Add soup, artichoke hearts, grated cheese, and drained mushrooms. Season to taste. Stir in sour cream. In a buttered casserole place a layer of crumbled shredded wheat or crackers. Cover with half the vegetable mixture. Dot with butter. Repeat layers. Bake at 350° for 30 minutes. Serves 6 to 8.

Mrs. Paul Wickliffe, K.F.W.C. President, 1935–1938

Mrs. Wickliffe's complete luncheon menu is molded chicken salad (page 175), artichoke casserole, nut bread, individual lemon meringues (page 207), and coffee.

MOTHER'S ASPARAGUS LOAF

8–10 crackers, crushed
1 cup hot cream
2 eggs, beaten
1 tsp. salt

2 tsp. butter
½ tsp. grated onion
2 cups cut asparagus

Combine ingredients and pour into a greased 1-quart mold. Set in a pan of hot water. Bake at 350° until set and lightly browned, 20 to 30 minutes. Serves 4 to 6.

Mrs. Thomas Shumate, Woman's Club of Richmond

OLD SOUTH ASPARAGUS
From the Old South Inn, Winchester

1 tbsp. chopped onion
3 tbsp. butter
3 tbsp. flour
1½ cups milk, light cream, or
   evaporated milk

1 4-oz. can of mushrooms
¼ cup slivered almonds
1 medium can asparagus
3 slices mild cheese

Sauté chopped onion in butter. Add flour and stir to make a thick paste. Gradually add milk. Cook, stirring constantly, until thickened. Add mushrooms and half of the almonds. Drain asparagus and place in a buttered casserole. Pour sauce over asparagus, lay cheese slices on top, and sprinkle with remaining almonds. Bake at 350° for 45 minutes. Serves 4 to 6.

Jane Ann Graham, Heritage Heights Woman's Club, Augusta

ASPARAGUS CASSEROLE

1½ cups Ritz cracker crumbs
½ cup butter
1 no. 2 can cut green
   asparagus
½ cup toasted slivered
   almonds

Sauce:
4 tsp. butter
1 tbsp. flour
1½ cups milk
1 jar Old English cheese
½ tsp. salt

Melt ½ cup butter and mix with cracker crumbs. Line a casserole with crumbs, reserving a few crumbs for the top. Add asparagus and almonds. Melt 4 tsp. butter, stir in flour, blend well, and add milk slowly, stirring constantly. Stir in cheese and salt. Pour sauce over asparagus. Sprinkle crumbs on top. Bake at 450° for 10 to 15 minutes. Serves 4 to 6.

Mrs. M. J. Cundiff, Bullitt County Woman's Club

BAKED BEANS

3 16-oz. cans pork and beans
½ cup catsup
1 large onion, chopped fine
2 tbsp. Worcestershire sauce
½ cup brown sugar
1 tsp. hot sauce
1 tbsp. mustard
3 tbsp. bacon drippings

Combine all ingredients and bake in a bean pot 1½ hours at 350°. Serves 8 to 10.

Mrs. Marvin Ray, Mayfield Woman's Club

SLOW-BAKED BEANS

2 lb. great northern beans
celery leaves
1 large onion, diced
1 tbsp. salt
1 small hot red pepper
rind from a 1-pound piece
   of jowl bacon
1 large clove garlic, peeled
1 tsp. dry mustard
1 tsp. ginger
1 cup brown sugar, packed
1 tbsp. Worcestershire sauce
½ cup molasses or sorghum
1 cup catsup
1 lb. jowl bacon, cubed

Wash beans and soak overnight in water to come 3 to 4 inches above the beans in an 8-quart kettle. Next morning add more water and a handful of celery leaves, diced onion, salt, red pepper, and the rind trimmed from the jowl bacon. Cover and simmer gently until beans are almost tender but before the skins pop—about 2 hours. Using a slotted spoon, transfer the beans to a bean pot. Add remaining ingredients, mixing gently. Add enough of the liquid in which the beans were cooked to fill the pot and completely cover the beans. Bake about 5 hours at 250°. Remove lid during the last hour of cooking. Serves 12.

Mrs. Ralph B. Cook, Sr., Erlanger Woman's Club

GREEN BEANS

Green beans are best if you cook them soon after they are picked. I usually pick about a gallon bucket full which will make about a quart and a half when you have them strung and broken. We like the young tender pole beans best or maybe the half-runners and break them into pieces about an inch long. Put them into a nice heavy kettle and barely cover them with water. Add a hunk of salt pork (at least a quarter of a pound, I'd reckon) or some left over ham fat and a ham bone if you have it, salt according to your liking, bring to a boil and cover your kettle. Let your fire go down to simmer and let your beans cook a while. We cook ours for most of the morning till most of the juice has cooked down. We don't do anything to them while they are cooking 'cept look at them every once in a while to be sure they aren't burning and maybe stir them a few times to be sure the seasoning is all through the beans. They won't be a bright green color when they are done, but a nice brownish green and I hope you have some left over for another day because they are better on the second day. Your Grandma has always added a bit of a red pepper pod to her beans but I don't like it much. You could add some if it is to your liking. Sometimes Grandma cooks some little new potatoes with her beans too, but I think plain beans is best.

Mrs. Charles Hembree, Lexington Woman's Club

These instructions were written by Mrs. Hembree's grandmother for her mother when she was a bride in 1921.

SHUCKY BEANS

Wash about 2 cups of dried green beans (page 301). Place them in a pan with 6 cups of water. Let stand overnight. Next day, pour off the water in which the beans were soaked and rinse them well. Put the beans into a large pot with a close fitting lid. Add 1½ tsp. salt, 4 cups of water, and a 3-inch square of salt pork. Cook over medium heat for about 3 hours, adding more water if needed.

Mrs. Oscar C. Sowards, K.F.W.C. President, 1968–1970

BROCCOLI CASSEROLE

2 10-oz. pkg. frozen chopped   ½ lb. Velveeta cheese
     broccoli   1   8-oz. pkg. Ritz crackers
1 tsp. salt   1   cup butter

Boil broccoli in salted water for 2 minutes. Drain. Alternate layers of broccoli and cheese in a greased 1½-quart casserole. Top with buttered cracker crumbs. Bake at 350° for 15 minutes, or until golden brown on top. Serves 8.

Mrs. Raymond Yelton, Covington Art Club

Mrs. Ralph Reasor, Corbin Woman's Club, uses only half the amount of crackers and butter.

BROCCOLI PUFF

1 10-oz. pkg. frozen broccoli   ¼ cup mayonnaise
1 can cream of mushroom   1   beaten egg
     soup   ¼ cup dry bread crumbs
½ cup grated sharp cheese   1   tbsp. margarine, melted
¼ cup milk

Cook broccoli in unsalted water. Drain and place in a baking dish. Combine soup and cheese; add milk, mayonnaise, and egg, and pour over broccoli. Combine bread crumbs and melted margarine, and sprinkle on top. Bake at 350° for 45 minutes. Let stand about 20 minutes before serving. Serves 6.

Mrs. Charles Schneider, Erlanger Woman's Club

CABBAGE-VEGETABLE MEDLEY

2 tbsp. margarine or bacon   ½ medium onion, diced
     drippings   2   medium tomatoes, chopped
2 cups shredded cabbage   1   tsp. soy sauce
1 cup celery, sliced thinly   1   tsp. salt
½ cup diced green pepper   dash of pepper

Melt the fat in a skillet or saucepan; add other ingredients. Cover and cook over low heat 10 to 12 minutes or until tender, stirring occasionally. Serves 6.

Alma Dickerson, Erlanger Woman's Club

CARROTS WITH WINE SAUCE

¼ cup minced onion	2 bouillon cubes, dissolved
1 tbsp. margarine	in ⅔ cup hot water
8 medium carrots	¼ cup sherry or other dry white wine

In a moderately hot skillet, sauté onion in margarine until golden brown. Meanwhile, scrape and quarter carrots and cut them into 1-inch lengths. Add carrots, bouillon, and wine to onion. Bring to a boil and cover. Simmer 20 minutes or until tender. Serves 6.

Mrs. E. G. Lamy, Crescent Hill Woman's Club

MARINATED CARROTS

2 lb. carrots	1 cup sugar
1 bell pepper, chopped	½ tsp. salt
1 medium onion, chopped	½ tsp. pepper
1 can tomato soup	1 tsp. prepared mustard
½ cup salad oil	1 tsp. Worcestershire sauce
⅔ cup vinegar	

Peel and slice the carrots; cook and drain. Combine other ingredients and pour over the warm carrots. Refrigerate overnight or longer. Drain before serving. The marinade is delicious also as a salad dressing.

Mrs. E. E. Sivis, Jessamine Woman's Club

CELERY CASSEROLE

2 bunches celery	1 can cream of chicken soup
8 slices white bread	½ cup or more slivered
1 cup margarine, melted	almonds
1 can water chestnuts, drained and sliced	salt and pepper to taste

Cut celery into small pieces and cook in boiling water until tender. Drain. Grate bread into a large bowl and pour melted margarine over the crumbs. Combine crumbs with celery. Add remaining ingredients, mix thoroughly, and put into a 1¾-quart or 2-quart casserole. Bake at 350° for 45 to 60 minutes. Serves 6 to 8.

Mrs. Veryl F. Frye, Jr., Somerset Junior Woman's Club

CORN FRITTERS

One of Kentucky's former stagecoach stops that has survived and has kept its reputation for good food is Old Stone Inn at Simpsonville, only 15 minutes from Louisville. The inn long ago ceased to provide overnight accommodations but when it was built in 1791 the bed or sleeping space was as appreciated as the food. The antique furnishings, the gracious service, and the good food do much to recapture the way of life of a century or more ago. Decisions are not too difficult. All you need do is tell the waiter your choice of meat; other food is served family style. If you are there on a day in July or August you may sample the corn fritters. If not, make them at home using the inn's recipe.

¾ cup sifted flour
2 tsp. baking powder
1 tsp. sugar
½ tsp. salt
1 beaten egg

½ cup milk
2 cups fresh corn or 1 16-oz.
 can whole kernel corn,
 drained
sifted confectioners' sugar

Sift together dry ingredients. Combine beaten egg, milk, and corn; add to dry ingredients. Mix just until flour is moistened. Drop batter by level tablespoonfuls into deep, hot fat (375°). Fry until golden brown, about 3 to 4 minutes. Drain on paper towels. Dust with confectioners' sugar. Serve warm. Makes about 1½ dozen fritters.

CORN PUDDING

¾ cup sugar
¼ tsp. salt
2 tbsp. flour
¼ tsp. cinnamon
¼ tsp. nutmeg
2 well-beaten eggs
½ cup milk

1 16-oz. can yellow cream-style
 corn
1 tsp. vanilla
2 tbsp. margarine
Topping:
3 tbsp. sugar
1 tsp. cinnamon-and-sugar

Combine sugar, salt, flour, cinnamon, and nutmeg. Add the eggs; cream until smooth. Add corn, milk, and vanilla, mixing well. Pour into a well-greased 1½-quart casserole and dot with margarine. Mix 3 tbsp. sugar with cinnamon-and-sugar and sprinkle on top. Cover and bake in a preheated oven at 325° until set, 45 to 55 minutes. Serves 8 to 10.

Mrs. Ruth T. Pohl, Horse Cave Woman's Club

CORN PUDDING

2 cups whole-kernel corn,   1 tbsp. sugar or honey
    drained   2 tbsp. melted butter
8 tbsp. flour   4 eggs
1 tsp. salt   4 cups milk

Place corn in a large bowl and stir in flour, salt, sugar, and butter. Beat eggs well, combine with milk, and stir into the corn mixture. Pour into a greased casserole and bake 30 minutes, or until firm, in a 350° oven, stirring from the bottom three times while baking. Serves 6.

Mrs. John A. Perkins, Carrollton Woman's Club
Mrs. Fred Basham, Leitchfield Woman's Club

Miss Mary Patrick, Morehead Woman's Club, uses twice the amount of corn and butter.

CORN PUDDING

4   eggs   6   ears corn, grated (2 cups),
2   cups light cream   or 1 16-oz. can cream-style
1   tsp. salt   corn
1¼ tsp. pepper

Beat eggs and stir in light cream, salt, pepper, and corn. Pour into a buttered deep 1½-quart baking dish. Set in a roasting pan with enough hot water to come about 2 inches up the side of the baking dish. Bake in a 350° oven 35 to 40 minutes or until the egg mixture sets. The corn will settle to the bottom. Serves 6 to 8.

Mrs. Clifford O. Hagan, Metropolitan Woman's Club of Lexington
Mrs. H. H. Morgan, Maysville Woman's Club
Mrs. S. Lee Rose, Sr., Beechmont Woman's Club, Louisville

GREEN CORN PUDDING

12 large ears green corn
5 eggs, separated
2 tbsp. butter, melted

4 cups milk
1 tbsp. sugar
½ tsp. salt

Grate the corn from the cob. Beat yolks and whites of eggs separately. Combine corn and yolks. Gradually add butter, then milk, mixing well. Add sugar and salt and fold in beaten egg whites. Pour the mixture into a buttered 1½-quart casserole. Bake covered in a 325° oven 1 hour. Remove the cover and brown. Serves 10.

Lucille E. Warren, Bullitt County Woman's Club

CHEESE GRITS

2½ cups milk
¾ cup grits
½ cup margarine

salt
1 jar Old English cheese
⅓ cup Parmesan cheese

Bring milk to a boil. Add grits and cook until thickened, stirring often. Stir in margarine, salt, and cheeses. Bake 20 minutes at 325°.

Mrs. Frank Hatfield, Bullitt County Woman's Club

GRITS CASSEROLE

1 cup grits
4½ cups boiling water
1 tsp. salt
½ cup butter
1 roll garlic cheese, chopped
2 eggs

milk
grated onion (optional)
garlic (optional)
crushed corn flakes
butter

Cook grits in boiling water with 1 tsp. salt. When thick, add butter and garlic cheese; stir until both are melted. Beat eggs in a teacup and finish filling the cup with milk. Blend egg mixture with grits. Add grated onion and garlic, if desired. Pour into a buttered casserole. Cover with crushed corn flakes and dot with butter. Bake 45 minutes at 350°. Serves 6.

Mrs. Ralph C. Edrington, Arlington Woman's Club
Mrs. Alline McGinnis, Beechmont Woman's Club

BAKED HOMINY

1 cup milk	2 eggs, beaten
2 tbsp. butter	½ tsp. salt
2 cups canned hominy, drained	¾ tsp. pepper

Heat milk and butter until butter is melted. Add hominy, eggs, and seasonings, and pour into a buttered baking dish. Bake at 350° until firm and top is browned, 30 to 40 minutes. Serves 6.

Mrs. J. R. English, Woman's Club of Elizabethtown

EGGPLANT AND TOMATO CASSEROLE

1 medium eggplant	1 tsp. sugar
1 clove garlic, minced	½ tsp. paprika
¼ cup oil	⅛ tsp. basil leaves
1 tbsp. flour	dash of pepper
1 can stewed tomatoes	¼ cup (or more) Parmesan cheese
½ tsp. salt	

Pare eggplant and cut into 2-inch cubes. Cook in salted water for 10 minutes. Drain. In a heavy skillet, sauté garlic in oil about 3 minutes or until golden. Stir in flour. Add tomatoes, salt, sugar, paprika, basil leaves, and pepper; cook until thickened. Add eggplant and pour into a buttered casserole. Top with Parmesan cheese. Bake at 300° for 20 minutes or until lightly browned. Serves 8 to 10.

Mrs. S. G. Hembree, Ossoli Woman's Club, Corbin

STUFFED EGGPLANT

1 medium eggplant	paprika
2 tbsp. butter	1 cup cream of mushroom soup
¼ cup chopped onion	
chopped parsley to taste	Worcestershire sauce
salt	buttered cracker crumbs
pepper	

Parboil the whole unpeeled eggplant 10 minutes. Cut in half lengthwise and scoop out pulp, leaving a 1-inch wall inside skin. Turn shell upside down in a pan to keep it from darkening. Melt butter in a skillet and sauté onion and parsley. Add undiluted mushroom soup and chopped eggplant pulp. Season to taste with salt, pepper, and Worcestershire sauce. Add cracker crumbs to make a firm but moist mixture. Stuff eggplant and place in a pan with a little water in the bottom. Bake at 375° about 25 minutes. Serves 6.

Mrs. Lillian Anderson, Carrollton Woman's Club

JERUSALEM ARTICHOKES

1½ pounds Jerusalem artichokes	3 tbsp. fresh lemon juice
	½ tsp. salt
⅓ cup melted butter	few sprigs parsley, chopped

Peel artichokes and cook in boiling salted water until tender. Test with a toothpick after 15 minutes—artichokes should not be over-cooked. Drain thoroughly. Dress with a mixture of butter, lemon juice, salt, and chopped parsley. Serves 4 to 6.

Mrs. H. C. Bohon, Harrodsburg Woman's Club

OKRA DELUXE

1 cup finely chopped okra	½ pound cooking cheese, grated
3 tbsp. butter	
3 tbsp. flour	1½ cups bread crumbs
1 cup milk	3 eggs, beaten
	salt and pepper

Cook ½ lb. okra in boiling salted water. Drain, chop fine, and measure. Melt butter and slowly blend in flour. Gradually add milk and stir over heat until thickened. Add grated cheese and remove from heat. Stir until cheese is melted. Add okra, crumbs, eggs, and seasonings. Pour into a buttered ring mold. Bake at 325° for 50 minutes, or until firm. Unmold onto a platter. If desired, fill center with hot mashed potatoes and garnish with tiny whole buttered beets and parsley. Serves 4.

Mrs. J. C. Wells, Lackey Garrett Wayland Woman's Club

ONIONS VIENNESE

The Stage Coach Inn was established some time in the early nineteenth century by Major John Gray, a veteran of the American Revolution. Formerly known as Old Graysville, the famous old landmark was built of handmade bricks by slave labor. Originally it was a stage stop and was located at the convergence of six roads. The Good Luck Well in the side yard was named Utok Anawaha, "The Well of Sweet Water," and was blessed by the Cherokee Indians in ancient ceremonial rites after one of their chieftains recovered from an illness when he drank water from the well.

The Stage Coach Inn was probably the birthplace of the American Blackface Minstrel Show. Thomas Dartmouth Rice, who stayed at the inn for several months following his release from the prisoner of war camp at Clarksville after the Civil War, is supposed to have written his famous minstrel song "Jim Crow" while there. He later wrote a show around the song, and produced it first in Louisville.

The inn is now a private residence but its Onions Viennese are still remembered.

2½ lbs. Bermuda onions
2 tbsp. sherry
½ cup chopped celery
¼ cup chopped pimientos
1 cup mushrooms
½ tsp. marjoram

pinch of thyme
1 tbsp. Alamo Zestful
   Seasoning
1 cup medium white sauce
cracker crumbs
cheddar cheese, grated

Peel and quarter the onions. Cover them with cold water, bring to a boil, and drain. Add sherry, celery, pimientos, mushrooms, marjoram, thyme, and seasoning. Combine the white sauce with the onion mixture. Place alternate layers of onion mixture, cracker crumbs, and cheese in a buttered casserole. Sprinkle the top with paprika and bake at 325° for 1 hour. Serves 10.

Contributed by Mrs. C. W. Gleaves, Lexington Woman's Club

ONION RINGS

6 large Spanish or Bermuda
   onions
1 egg
1⅓ cups milk
2 cups flour

2 tsp. salt
2 tsp. sugar
2 tsp. baking powder
2 tsp. melted butter
oil or shortening

Peel onions and slice them ⅛ inch to ¼ inch thick. Separate into rings and use larger ones for frying. Keep onion rings dry. Beat egg and add milk. Sift dry ingredients and gradually add to egg mixture, stirring until smooth. Add melted butter. Drop rings in batter to coat them. Heat fat to 360°. Gently drop rings into fat and let brown; turn once. Drain on absorbent paper. Serves 8.

Mrs. Joe W. Yarbrough, Jr., Marion Woman's Club

PEAS WITH MUSHROOM SOUP CASSEROLE

1 no. 2 can tiny peas, drained
1 can cream of mushroom
  soup

1 cup crushed crackers
½ cup butter, melted

Place peas in a 1½-quart casserole and pour undiluted mushroom soup over them. Combine crushed crackers and melted butter and use as a topping. Bake in a preheated 350° oven for 30 minutes, or until bubbly around the edge and crackers are slightly brown. Serves 6.

Mrs. Charles Meng, Ghent Woman's Club

POKE

Poke is an indigenous mountain green dating back to the days of the Indians. They and the early settlers relied on poke and sassafras tea to hone up the body in the spring after a long winter of sluggishness. Health then depended on the herbs from the land rather than on pharmaceutical houses. In addition to its medicinal properties, poke was a valuable food for those hardy pioneers. It saw them through the spring when the last of the old crop of potatoes was gone and the new garden had not yet come on. Poke was one of nature's bounties requiring no cultivation. The mountain men and boys were free to hunt and fish while the women and children gathered the bountiful natural poke crop.

The annual Poke Sallet Festival, held the last week in June at Stone Mountain Park in Harlan County, features Poke Eating Day. The menu for the day is poke sallet, fried salt pork, and corn pones (small, baked cornmeal cakes). An honorary poke warden protects the poke against greedy earlybirds who cut the poke too early or trim it too far beneath the ground, but the only punishment he can mete out is to shame the culprit.

Note: The roots and seeds of poke are poisonous.

POKE SALLET

1½ to 2 lb. poke greens and   ½ tsp. salt
     stalks   chopped onions
4   thick slices salt bacon

Select tender young poke greens; include some tender stalks not over 6 inches high. Cut the stalks in pieces. Clean the greens well, rinsing several times. Parboil and discard the water. Add fresh water and cook until barely tender. Fry bacon until crisp, remove from skillet, and set aside. Add greens, salt, and chopped onions to the drippings. Cook over low heat for about 20 minutes. Serve with fried salt pork (page 73) and corn pone. Serves 4.

Harlan Woman's Club

COTTAGE CHEESE POTATO BALLS

3 cups hot riced potatoes   3 eggs
1 tbsp. butter   2 cups cottage cheese
1 tsp. salt   4 tbsp. milk
few grains of pepper   fine dry bread crumbs

To potatoes add butter, salt, pepper, and 1 egg; beat until fluffy. Stir in cottage cheese; chill thoroughly. Blend 2 slightly beaten eggs and milk. Shape potato mixture into small balls. Dip balls into crumbs, then into eggs and milk, then into crumbs again. Refrigerate for a few minutes. Fry about 1 minute in deep hot fat (385°). Drain on absorbent paper. Serves 6.

Miss Margaret Carl, Erlanger Woman's Club

POTATOES AND ONIONS IN CHEESE SAUCE

6 medium potatoes   butter
1 to 2 onions   salt and pepper
2 cups medium cheese sauce   paprika
     or 1 can cheddar cheese
     soup

In a greased casserole place alternate layers of thinly sliced, seasoned potatoes, thinly sliced onions, and cheese sauce. Dot with butter, sprinkle with paprika, and bake at 350° for 2 hours or until potatoes are done. Serves 4. Serve with broiled lamb chops, green peas, pear and cottage cheese salad, and hot biscuits with jelly.

Mrs. C. C. Lowry, K.F.W.C. President, 1966–1968

SCALLOPED POTATOES

6 medium potatoes
4 tsp. butter
2 tsp. flour
3 cups milk

1 cup grated sharp cheddar
   cheese (optional)
1 tsp. salt
¼ tsp. pepper
2 tsp. chopped onion

Pare potatoes and slice thin. Melt butter, blend in flour, gradually add milk, and stir over heat until thickened. (If cheese is used it can be either added to the white sauce or sprinkled between the layers.) Place a layer of potatoes in a greased 2-quart casserole; cover with a layer of sauce and seasonings. Continue to build up in alternate layers, ending with a layer of sauce. Cover and bake at 400° for 20 to 30 minutes or until liquid begins to bubble up. Uncover and continue baking about 30 minutes or until potatoes are tender and top is brown. Serves 6.

Mrs. L. Wayne Cisney, Greenville Woman's Club

GOLDEN CHEESE AND RICE

2 cups cooked rice
3 cups shredded carrots
2 cups grated American
   cheese
2 eggs, beaten

1½ tsp. salt
¼ tsp. pepper
2 tbsp. minced onion
½ cup milk

Combine all ingredients, reserving ½ cup cheese. Pour into a greased 1-quart casserole. Sprinkle with remaining cheese. Bake at 350° for 35 to 40 minutes.

Mrs. R. W. Croft, Marion Woman's Club

BROWN RICE CASSEROLE

¼ cup butter
1 can onion soup
1 can beef bouillon

1 cup long grain white rice
1 8-oz. can sliced mushrooms

Melt butter. Add onion soup, bouillon, rice, and mushrooms. Stir to mix. Pour into a 2-quart casserole and bake 1 hour in a 325° oven. Serves 12.

Mrs. Herbert B. Steely, Williamsburg Woman's Club
Mrs. John Morgan, Lexington Woman's Club

MUSHROOMS AND RICE

2⅔ cups quick-cooking rice
6 tbsp. salad oil
2 small cans mushrooms,
   drained
green onions, chopped

2 cans beef consommé,
   undiluted
2 tbsp. soy sauce
½ tsp. salt

Combine all ingredients and bake, covered, at 350° until liquid is absorbed, no more than 30 to 45 minutes. Do not stir.

To prepare in advance, place dry ingredients in a casserole and add liquids just before baking. Serves 4 to 6.

Mae Burnett, Woman's Club of Elizabethtown

SQUASH CASSEROLE

2 lb. small summer squash
1 medium onion, chopped
1 tsp. salt
⅓ cup fine cracker crumbs

¼ cup butter
¼ cup milk
¼ tsp. pepper
2 eggs, well beaten

Place squash, onion, and salt in a saucepan; add water to half cover the squash. Cover and simmer until squash is tender, about 15 minutes. Drain well and mash. Add cracker crumbs, butter, milk, pepper, and eggs. Pour into a buttered baking dish and bake at 350° until golden brown, about 1 hour. Serves 4 to 6.

Mrs. James Baker, Madisonville Woman's Club

BUTTERNUT SQUASH AND APPLES

1 butternut squash
2 or 3 apples
brown sugar
salt and pepper

butter
½ cup maple syrup
cinnamon-and-sugar

Peel and cube the squash. Core and slice the apples. Place squash in a buttered casserole, sprinkle with brown sugar, salt, and pepper, and dot with butter. Cover with apples. Pour maple syrup over apples and dot with more butter. Bake covered at 350° for 30 minutes; uncover, sprinkle with cinnamon-and-sugar, and bake 15 minutes more. Serves 4 to 6.

Mrs. E. J. Lamy, Crescent Hill Woman's Club

CHICKEN-BAKED SQUASH

3 cups yellow squash, cubed	½ cup chopped nuts (optional)
1 cup Ritz crackers, crumbled	2 tbsp. chopped pimientos
2 tbsp. butter or margarine	2 tbsp. melted butter
1 can cream of chicken soup	

In a 1½-quart casserole, alternate layers of squash with half the crackers, bits of butter, soup, nuts, and pimientos. Top with remaining crackers mixed with melted butter. Bake in a preheated 375° oven for 50 minutes, or until bubbly and browned. Serves 6 to 8.

Mrs. S. Lee Rose, Sr., Beechmont Woman's Club

ZUCCHINI CASSEROLE

6 medium zucchini	salt
2 tbsp. bacon grease	pepper
1 medium tomato, peeled and chopped	pinch of oregano or Italian seasoning
1 small onion (or more if desired), chopped	buttered bread crumbs
1 rib celery, chopped	Parmesan cheese

Slice zucchini about ¼ inch thick but do not peel. Heat bacon grease in a heavy frying pan; add tomato, onion, celery, zucchini, and seasonings, in that order. Cover and steam until vegetables are tender crisp. (If you plan to freeze the dish, stop at this point and put the vegetables in a freezer container. Cool, then freeze.)

For immediate use, drain off excess liquid (it makes good broth), put vegetables in a greased casserole, and top with buttered crumbs. Sprinkle generously with Parmesan cheese. This recipe can be varied by using a good cheddar cheese instead of Parmesan, or by adding a sprinkling of paprika for color. Bake at 350° for 30 minutes or until top is browned and vegetables are bubbly. Serves 6.

Mrs. Austin R. Riede, Clinton Woman's Club

TATER DAY

Tater Day, held in Benton on the first Monday in April, was organized in 1843 and in recent years has been revitalized. Originally Tater Day was the time when farmers came to Benton to sell or buy "sweet tater" slips for planting and to visit with friends and relatives and maybe do a little mule swapping or knife trading. Nowadays you might have difficulty in finding a sweet tater but the crowds still come—an estimated 15,000 in 1974. In honor of the day you might want to try one of our sweet potato recipes.

GLAZED SWEET POTATOES

9 large sweet potatoes	1 tbsp. sugar
1 tbsp. water	4 tbsp. butter

Boil potatoes 50 minutes. Pare them, cut in halves lengthwise, and sprinkle both sides with salt. Place them cut side down in a dripping pan. Put sugar and water in a small pan; stir until sugar is dissolved. Add butter and stir over low heat until it melts. Baste the potatoes with this liquid and bake in a 400° oven 20 minutes. The potatoes should be glossy brown when they come from the oven. Serves 12.

Lummie Taylor, Beaver Dam Woman's Club

SWEET POTATO PUDDING

1 egg	1⅓ cups milk
½ cup sugar	¼ tsp. allspice
¼ cup melted butter	¼ tsp. nutmeg
1 cup grated sweet potatoes	pinch of salt

Beat egg and add remaining ingredients. Pour into a greased baking dish. Bake at 400° for 30 minutes or until thick, stirring occasionally. Serves 4.

Mrs. Carl James, Clinton Woman's Club

FRIED GREEN TOMATOES

6 green tomatoes
¾ cup cornmeal
2 tsp. salt

⅛ tsp. pepper
fat for frying (preferably
    bacon grease)

Wash tomatoes and slice them about ¼ inch thick. Mix cornmeal, salt, and pepper. Dip tomatoes in meal mixture. Fry them slowly until nicely browned, turning once. Drain on paper towels and serve hot. Serves 6.

Miss Patti Bolin, Clinton Woman's Club

TOMATO PUDDING

2 cups cubed white bread
    (4 slices)
¼ cup melted butter
1 cup brown sugar

1 10½-oz. can tomato puree
salt
pepper

Place bread cubes in a buttered casserole. Pour melted butter over them. Combine brown sugar with tomato puree; heat to a boil and continue to cook 15 minutes, stirring often. Season to taste and pour over cubed bread. Bake covered for 35 minutes at 350°. Remove cover and bake 10 minutes longer to form a crust. Serves 6.

Mrs. Harold Collins, Lexington Woman's Club

STUFFED TURNIPS

6 medium turnips
¼ tsp. salt
½ cup grated cheese
2 tbsp. butter

¼ tsp. white pepper
pinch of sugar
1 tsp. cornstarch

Peel turnips and shell out centers. Cook all in salted water until tender. Drain and mash the centers only, adding grated cheese, butter, pepper, and sugar. Thicken with cornstarch. Stuff the turnip shells and place in a baking dish. Bake at 375° for 20 to 30 minutes. Garnish with parsley. Serves 6 to 8.

Mrs. R. D. Carter, Crescent Hill Woman's Club

Salads

The Kentucky tradition in salads goes way back to Elizabethan England. Salads were then a popular dish on the tables of yeoman farmers. The first cookbook written for these ordinary farmers, many of whom emigrated to America and Kentucky, Gervase Markham's *The English Hous-Wife* (1615), opens with a four-page sections of salads. He first gives recipes for simple cold salads with such ingredients as chives, scallions, "radish roots," and sugar. He follows these with more elaborate salads containing "the young Buds and Knots of all manner of wholesome Herbs at their first springing . . . as Mint, Lettice, Violets, Marigolds, Spinage, and many other mixed together and then served up to the Table with Vinegar, Sallet-Oyle, and Sugar." His concluding recipes are for "excellent compound boyl'd Sallet." He suggests that the cook boil greens like spinach until they are "exceeding soft and tender as pap" and then season them with a garnish, such as currants or small pieces of toast and vinegar sweetened with a little sugar. In short, Markham anticipates virtually all the varied salads served up in this chapter, even the tropical fruit concoctions that Elizabethan Englishmen, had they known about them, would have thoroughly enjoyed.

Some of the older and more traditional Kentucky salad recipes contained here are for dandelion greens, wilted lettuce, and one that Markham would have been particularly pleased with, Spinach and Sprouts. These greens were especially important to early Kentuckians in spring, when, as Otis Rice points out in his essay, light foods were sought that would "thin the blood which had thickened during the winter." In fact, they did serve as preventives for scurvy and rickets—two diseases that plagued Appalachians.

Neither Markham nor the early settlers ever encountered Kentucky Bibb lettuce. It is a beautiful plant with crisp, deep green leaves that cluster like rose petals, only not so dense. It is said by gourmets to be the finest lettuce in the world. John B. Bibb, born in 1789 in Prince Edward County, Virginia, moved with his family to Russellville, Kentucky, as a young boy. Jack moved to Frankfort in 1845 and built Gray Gables, which still stands at the corner of Wapping Street and Watson Court. He was not interested in the social life of the city or in a career in public life. Instead he embarked on adventures in his lovely garden that rolled down to the Kentucky River. There he evolved the salad head that bears his name. In his eighties he began giving lettuce plants and seed to friends and neighbors. Otherwise it might have been lost. Bibb lettuce is now available throughout the world.

Two other modern salad ingredients, white potatoes and tomatoes, would not have been eaten in pioneer Kentucky. Potatoes became popular on the frontier only in the nineteenth century after the English and Scots would admit that this Irish invention had, indeed, some merit. Potato salad is a good example of Victorian Kentuckiana. Tomatoes were thought to be poison well into the nineteenth century and some country people still have an aversion to them. Sometimes they were eaten as a fruit with sugar; at other times they were used as the basis for a tomato aspic.

From the humble dandelion greens and the experimentation with lettuce, potatoes, and tomatoes, the contemporary salad chef moves on to Coke salad, made with strawberry gelatin, pecans, cream cheese, and Coca-Cola. That is the joy of Kentucky foodways—the old and the new harmonize.

Jay Anderson

DANDELION GREENS SALLET

2 qts. young dandelion leaves   ½ cup rich milk
    (or spinach)   1 tsp. finely chopped onion or
1 cup diced raw ham   onion juice
1 tbsp. vinegar   salt and pepper
1 egg, beaten

Wash greens thoroughly, dry, and shred coarsely. Fry ham lightly. Add vinegar. Stir beaten egg with milk; add to mixture in the skillet. Lastly add greens and seasoning. Cook, stirring constantly, until greens are wilted. Serves 6 to 8.

Mrs. Margaret Flanary, Marion Woman's Club

WILTED LETTUCE

6 slices bacon   1 tsp. sugar
¼ cup vinegar   ⅛ tsp. pepper
¼ tsp. salt   ¼ lb. leaf lettuce

Warm a large bowl by filling it with very hot water. Fry bacon, remove from pan, and set aside to crispen. Pour water from bowl and dry it. Put cut lettuce into the bowl. Add other ingredients to hot bacon grease and pour over lettuce immediately. Cover bowl and let lettuce wilt for 5 minutes. Uncover and sprinkle with crumbled bacon. Serve at once. Serves 4.

Mrs. Charles Hagan, Lexington Woman's Club

A similar recipe sent by Mrs. Roy Roberts, Richmond Woman's Club, calls for chopped green onion to be added to the lettuce and grated hard-boiled egg to be added with the bacon.

PEA SALAD

1 no. 2 can small peas   3 or 4 sweet pickles, chopped
1 cup shredded sharp cheese   ½ cup pecans, chopped
1 cup chopped celery   2 tbsp. salad dressing
½ cup chopped onion   salt to taste

Mix in order given. Serve on lettuce or from the bowl. Serves 8 to 10.

Mrs. Ralph Reasor, Corbin Woman's Club

POTATO SALAD

1 large Bermuda onion	¼ cup olive oil
3 lb. white potatoes	mayonnaise
1 lb. cottage cheese, small	½ tsp. cayenne pepper
curd	salt to taste

Peel onion and slice very thin. Place in ice water and refrigerate overnight. Boil potatoes in jackets; while warm, peel and slice. Place ingredients in layers in a dish in the following order: potatoes, cottage cheese, drained onion rings, olive oil, and mayonnaise to which cayenne and salt have been added. Repeat until all are used. Refrigerate several hours or overnight. Stir before serving. Serves 12.

Mrs. Theodore Aschman, Woman's Club of Elizabethtown

MASHED POTATO SALAD

6 medium potatoes	2 eggs
1 small onion, chopped	salt and pepper
¼ cup cider vinegar	hard-boiled eggs
¼ cup sugar	

Cook potatoes in salted water until tender; drain. Mash while hot. Add onion. Mix vinegar, sugar, and beaten eggs. Pour over potatoes and onion. Stir well. Add salt and pepper as needed. Garnish with hard-boiled eggs.

Mary Martina Scott, Beechmont Woman's Club

HOT MUSTARD SLAW

1 medium head cabbage	1 egg
2 tbsp. dry mustard	vinegar
½ cup sugar	2 tbsp. butter
1 tsp. salt	

Chop cabbage. Blend mustard, sugar, and salt in a 1-cup measure; add egg and beat well. Fill cup with vinegar. Cook, stirring constantly, until thick. Add butter; stir until melted. Pour over chopped cabbage; mix well. Return to pan and place over very low heat for about 10 minutes, stirring several times. Refrigerate, overnight if possible. Serves 7 to 8.

Mrs. J. H. Krusenklaus, Highland Woman's Club

COMBINATION SALAD

1 head cabbage	½ cup cider vinegar
1 green pepper	⅓ cup water
2 ribs celery	⅓ cup sugar
4 green onions, sliced	1 tsp. dry mustard
1 cucumber, seeded and diced	½ tsp. celery seed
2 tomatoes, diced	1 tsp. salt
2 eggs, hard boiled	⅛ tsp. pepper

Chop cabbage, green pepper, and celery in blender jar, following manufacturer's instructions. Drain. Place in a large bowl; add onions, cucumber, tomatoes, and chopped egg whites. Mash egg yolks in a small bowl; add remaining ingredients. Stir to dissolve sugar and pour over vegetables. Serves 8 to 10.

Mrs. Ralph M. Cooper, Lexington Woman's Club

RAW MUSHROOM SALAD

1 lb. raw mushrooms	2 pimientos, minced
1 bunch celery	salt and pepper to taste
2 eggs, hard boiled	French dressing, or oil and
2 tbsp. minced onion	vinegar dressing

Wash and dry mushrooms. Cut from rounded side through stems. Cut celery into bite-size pieces. Add chopped eggs, onion, pimientos, and salt and pepper. Combine with dressing to moisten. Mix well. Marinate in refrigerator several hours. Serves 6 to 8.

Mrs. Paul Lindsay, Lexington Woman's Club

SAUERKRAUT SALAD

2 cups sauerkraut	½ cup sliced green and sweet
½ cup sugar	red pepper
½ cup thinly sliced celery	¼ cup chopped onion
½ cup shredded carrot	

Cut sauerkraut into shorter strands with scissors. Stir in sugar and let stand for 30 minutes. Add remaining ingredients. Cover bowl tightly. Chill at least 12 hours. Serves 10 to 12.

This salad can be kept in the refrigerator for several weeks if tightly covered. It is especially good when used as a relish with pork.

Mrs. John McCubbin, Campbellsville Woman's Club

SPINACH AND SPROUT SALAD

1	10-oz. pkg. fresh spinach	¾ cup sugar
1	16-oz. can bean sprouts	⅓ cup catsup
8	slices bacon	¼ cup wine vinegar
3	eggs, hard boiled	1 medium onion
1	tsp. Worcestershire sauce	dash of salt
⅓ cup salad oil		

Wash and cut spinach. Drain bean sprouts. Fry bacon, drain on paper towel, and crumble. Slice eggs. Toss all together. Mix remaining ingredients in a blender. Pour dressing over spinach mixture and toss again. Serves 8.

Mrs. Louis Jaquith, Blue Grass Junior Woman's Club, Lexington

A similar recipe was contributed by Mrs. Fred Basham, Leitchfield Woman's Club.

FRUIT SALAD

1 20-oz. can sliced pineapple	3 tbsp. flour
3 or 4 bananas	butter the size of a walnut
3 large apples	(2 tbsp.)
Dressing:	2 eggs, beaten
½ cup sugar	1 tbsp. lemon juice

Drain pineapple, reserving juice; set fruit aside while making dressing. In the top of a double boiler mix sugar, flour, and eggs. Add 1 cup juice from pineapple. Cook until thick. Remove from heat and add butter. When cool, add lemon juice. Dice fruit and mix with dressing. Chill. Serve in a salad bowl or on crisp lettuce leaves. Garnish with nuts, grapes, or maraschino cherries, if desired. Serves 10 to 12.

Mrs. Roy Bondurant, Woman's Club of Frankfort

This is truly a family recipe. When Mrs. Bondurant was married 38 years ago her mother gave her this recipe. She in turn has passed it on to her daughters and daughter-in-law, and to anyone else who requested it.

48-HOUR SALAD

2 eggs
4 tbsp. vinegar
4 tbsp. sugar
4 tbsp. butter
1 cup heavy cream, whipped

2 cups Royal Anne cherries,
  seeded
2 cups pineapple chunks
2 cups marshmallows, cut or
  miniature

Cook eggs, vinegar, sugar, and butter in the top of a double boiler, stirring constantly, until thick. Cool. Add remaining ingredients. Refrigerate until ready to serve. Make at least one day ahead. Serve as a main luncheon dish with sandwiches or as a salad with dinner. Serves 8.

Mrs. Joseph C. Evans, K.F.W.C. President, 1970–1972

ORANGE, GRAPEFRUIT, AND ONION SALAD

4 large oranges
2 grapefruit

2 medium onions

Peel fruit. Slice oranges crosswise ¼ inch thick. Section grapefruit. Slice onions ⅛ inch thick. Arrange on greens and serve with grapefruit French dressing (page 177). Serves 8.

Mrs. Jo Ann Gardner, Cumberland County Woman's Club

FROZEN FRUIT SALAD

1 3-oz. pkg. cream cheese
1 cup mayonnaise
1 cup heavy cream, whipped
1 cup crushed pineapple

2 tbsp. confectioners' sugar
12 maraschino cherries, cut
  into quarters
8 marshmallows, cut into bits

Soften cream cheese and blend with mayonnaise. Fold in whipped cream. To well-drained pineapple add sugar, cherries, and marshmallows. Combine mixtures and pour into a freezing tray. If desired, additional cherries may be arranged on top before freezing. Remove from freezer a few minutes before serving.

Mrs. Aubrey Moorman, Leitchfield Woman's Club

A recipe for frozen fruit salad was also contributed by Mrs. Charles Meng, Ghent Woman's Club. She suggests freezing the salad in paper muffin cups that have been placed in a muffin pan. When frozen, remove from pan and store in a plastic bag until ready to use. Allow them to soften slightly for easy removal of the paper.

FROSTY SALAD LOAF

1 8-oz. pkg. cream cheese
1 cup dairy sour cream
¼ cup sugar
¼ tsp. salt
2 cups apricot halves, sliced

1½ cups dark sweet cherries,
   pitted
1 cup crushed pineapple
2 cups miniature
   marshmallows

Soften cream cheese and beat until fluffy. Stir in sour cream, sugar, salt, drained fruit, and marshmallows. Pour into an 8½- by 4½-inch loaf pan. Freeze 6 hours or overnight. To serve, let stand at room temperature for a few minutes, remove from pan, slice, and place on a bed of crisp greens. Garnish with additional fruit. Serves 10.

Mrs. Bill Sewell, Cumberland County Woman's Club

EMERALD SALAD

1 pkg. lime gelatin
¾ cup boiling water
¾ cup shredded cucumber
2 tsp. grated onion

1 cup creamed cottage cheese
1 cup mayonnaise
⅓ cup blanched almonds,
   slivered

Dissolve gelatin in boiling water; cool. When slightly jelled add remaining ingredients, pour into an oiled mold, and chill until firm. Serves 8.

Mrs. Robert Geer, Woman's Club of Elizabethtown

COKE SALAD

1 can Bing cherries
1 can crushed pineapple
1 pkg. strawberry gelatin
1 pkg. cherry gelatin

2 8-oz. bottles Coca-Cola
1 8-oz. pkg. cream cheese,
   diced
½ cup pecans

Drain juice from fruit; place in a saucepan and bring to a boil. Dissolve gelatin in hot juice. Add remaining ingredients. Mix well, pour into an oiled mold, and refrigerate. Serves 8.

Mrs. Fred Basham, Leitchfield Woman's Club

MANGO SALAD

1 large pkg. lemon gelatin   1 8-oz. pkg. cream cheese
2 cups boiling water   1 large can mangoes

Pour water over gelatin; stir to dissolve. Blend cream cheese and mangoes, including juice, in a blender. Add to gelatin. Pour into a large oiled mold. Refrigerate overnight. Serves 8.

Mrs. C. B. Morgan, K.F.W.C. President, 1960–1962

Mrs. Morgan suggests serving this salad with barbecued chicken, scalloped potatoes, lima beans, garlic bread, and hot fresh cherry cobbler with ice cream.

LIME SALAD

1 pkg. lime gelatin   1 cup crushed pineapple
1 cup boiling water   1 cup miniature marshmallows
1 8-oz. pkg. cream cheese   1 cup cream, whipped

Dissolve gelatin in boiling water. Soften cream cheese, and beat until smooth; add to gelatin with pineapple and marshmallows. Fold in whipped cream. Pour into an 8-inch square pan; chill several hours. Serves 12.

Mrs. Zack Church, Jr., Woman's Club of Frankfort

Mrs. Gene Murray, Morehead Woman's Club, adds ½ cup chopped pecans.

RHUBARB SALAD

1 box frozen rhubarb   2 boxes strawberry gelatin
¼ cup sugar   2 cups finely chopped apple
2 cups unsweetened pineapple   1 cup chopped pecans
   juice

Cook rhubarb as instructed on the box; sweeten with sugar. Add 1 cup pineapple juice; bring to a boil. Add gelatin; stir until dissolved. When cool, add remaining juice. Chill until partially set. Add apples and pecans. Mix well and pour into an oiled mold. Chill 24 hours. Serve with cream cheese dressing (page 176). Serves 8.

Mrs. Springer Hoskins, Ossoli Woman's Club, Corbin

HAWAIIAN AMBROSIA SALAD

1 pkg. lemon gelatin	1 13-oz. can pineapple tidbits
1 pkg. lime gelatin	1 cup dairy sour cream
1½ cups boiling water	½ cup flaked coconut
1 11-oz. can mandarin	¼ cup hulled sunflower seeds
oranges	or nuts
10 maraschino cherries	

Dissolve gelatins in boiling water. Add 1½ cups syrup drained from fruits; mix well. Arrange orange sections, cherries, and a few pineapple tidbits in an oiled 5-cup mold. Pour a thin layer of the gelatin over the fruit and chill until firm. Chill remaining gelatin until partially set; stir in sour cream, the rest of the pineapple, coconut, and sunflower seeds. Pour into the mold and chill until firm. Serves 8 to 10.

Mrs. William DeSpain, Woman's Club of Elizabethtown

A similar recipe was sent by Mrs. Marvin Ray, Mayfield Woman's Club.

TOMATO JELLY

Boil together two cupfuls of tomatoes, three cloves, one bayleaf, one slice of onion, one-half teaspoon of thyme, one teaspoon of salt, one teaspoon of sugar, one-fourth teaspoon of pepper, until the tomatoes are soft; strain, then add one-half cup of cold water, one tablespoon of isinglass* and stir until the isinglass is dissolved; pour into little moulds; when cold, unmould and serve with mayonnaise on lettuce leaves.

From an 1891 handwritten cookbook;
contributed by Mrs. Roy Roberts, Woman's Club of Richmond

* Isinglass is fish gelatine which is gradually going out of favor for animal gelatine. It is a hard translucent substance prepared from certain parts of the sturgeon and cod, principally used in refining liquors and in the manufacture of jellies and similar dessert sweets.

From The Master Dictionary of Food and Cookery
by Henry Smith (Bristol, England, 1950)

TOMATO SALAD

1 no. 303 can stewed tomatoes	1 cup diced celery
1 pkg. strawberry gelatin	½ cup sliced stuffed olives
1 tbsp. Worcestershire sauce	

Cut tomatoes into small pieces. Heat and add gelatin; stir to dissolve. Cool slightly. Add remaining ingredients and mix well. Pour into an oiled mold and chill until firm. Serves 4 to 6.

Mrs. C. E. Jones, Leitchfield Woman's Club

TOMATO ASPIC

1 large pkg. lemon gelatin	2 tbsp. vinegar
1 cup boiling water	juice of 1 lemon
2 small cans tomato paste	1 green pepper, chopped
1 cup water	1 rib celery, chopped
2 tsp. sugar	1 onion, chopped

Dissolve gelatin in boiling water; add tomato paste and cold water. Blend well and add remaining ingredients. Pour into 1 large or 8 individual molds. Refrigerate. Serves 8.

Mrs. H. S. Bowers, Sr., Nortonville Woman's Club

TOMATO ASPIC WITH CHICKEN SALAD

1 pkg. lemon gelatin	chopped celery
2 cups tomato juice	stuffed olives, sliced
1 dessertspoon Worcestershire	slivered almonds
sauce	capers
3 chicken breasts	mayonnaise

Heat 1 cup tomato juice; pour over gelatin and stir to dissolve. Add remaining juice and Worcestershire sauce. Pour into an oiled ring mold and refrigerate. To serve, unmold onto Bibb lettuce. Fill center with chicken salad made by stewing and boning chicken breasts, cutting meat into chunks, and adding remaining ingredients to taste. Refrigerate. Serves 6 to 8.

Mrs. R. G. Williams, K.F.W.C. President, 1941–1944

MOLDED CHICKEN SALAD

1 large hen	1 large avocado
4 envelopes unflavored gelatin	1 cup blanched almonds
	1 3-oz. pkg. cream cheese
1½ cups cold water	dairy sour cream
1 large cucumber	canned pears
1 cup celery	10 to 12 almonds

Simmer hen in at least 2 quarts of water until tender. Remove from stock and cool. Strain stock, return to stove, and keep hot. Soak gelatin in cold water for 5 minutes, add 7 cups of hot chicken stock, and stir until gelatin is dissolved. Salt to taste. Pour a 1-inch layer of clear gelatin into a large oiled ring mold. Chill until firm. Slice cucumber, soak in ice water 30 minutes, drain, and dry. Remove chicken from bones and cut meat into large pieces. Chop celery. Peel and slice avocado. Mix cucumbers, chicken, celery, and avocado with almonds. Fold into remaining gelatin mixture. Pour into mold and place in refrigerator for several hours. To serve, turn out onto a large chilled platter. Surround ring with lettuce and with pear halves stuffed with cream cheese that has been softened with sour cream. Garnish with almonds. Place spiced crab apples or ripe olives in the center of the ring. Serves 10 to 12.

Mrs. Paul Wickliffe, K.F.W.C. President, 1935–1938

LUNCHEON SALAD

1 pkg. lemon gelatin	2 cups chopped celery
1 envelope plain gelatin	1 12-oz. can corned beef
3 eggs, hard boiled	1 cup cooked macaroni
2 tbsp. chopped onion	1 cup mayonnaise
2 tbsp. chopped green pepper	salt and pepper

Mix and prepare gelatins as directed on packages. Combine and chill until partially thickened. Chop eggs, onion, green pepper, celery, and meat. Add macaroni, mayonnaise, and salt and pepper to taste. Fold into gelatin mixture. Turn into an oiled mold and chill overnight. Serves 6.

Mrs. O. L. Edwards, Woman's Club of Elizabethtown

AVOCADO SEAFOOD DELIGHT

4   avocados
lemon juice
1   lb. cooked shrimp, or shrimp
and crab meat, or lobster
½ cup diced onion
½ cup stuffed olives, sliced
½ cup diced green pepper
1   cup diced celery
1   can water chestnuts, sliced

½ cup slivered blanched
almonds
2   tbsp. lemon juice or wine
vinegar
½ cup dressing (mayonnaise or
sour cream or a mixture)
½ tsp. garlic salt
salt and pepper

Cut avocados in half lengthwise; do not peel. Spoon lemon juice over each cut edge to prevent darkening. Mix seafood, onion, olives, green pepper, celery, water chestnuts, and almonds. Blend 2 tbsp. lemon juice or vinegar with dressing. Season to taste. Fold dressing into seafood mixture. Spoon into avocados; serve on lettuce with toasted cheese rounds. Serves 8.

Mrs. Harold Mullins, K.F.W.C. President, 1972–1974

SALAD DRESSINGS

LEMON SESAME SALAD DRESSING

2   cups cottage cheese
1   tsp. grated lemon peel
2   tbsp. lemon juice

2   tbsp. milk
toasted sesame seeds

In a small mixing bowl beat cottage cheese until fairly smooth. Beat in lemon peel and juice. Gradually add milk. Chill. Serve over lettuce wedges and sprinkle with sesame seeds.

Mrs. Thomas Collins, Lexington Woman's Club

CREAM CHEESE DRESSING

1   3-oz. pkg. cream cheese
3   tbsp. mayonnaise

½ cup heavy cream, whipped
2   tbsp. lemon juice

Blend cream cheese and mayonnaise; fold in whipped cream. Add lemon juice; mix well. Chill several hours. Delicious with rhubarb salad (page 172).

Mrs. Springer Hoskins, Ossoli Woman's Club, Corbin

LORENZO DRESSING FOR BIBB LETTUCE

For 20 years Cissy Gregg's food articles were a first stop for many Kentucky housewives when reading the *Courier-Journal*. Cissy was a Kentuckian born, bred, and educated. A native of Cynthiana, she was graduated from the University of Kentucky with a degree in Home Economics and Agriculture. In 1942 she became "Home Consultant" with the newspaper. She was a tiny, nervous bundle of energy who radiated friendliness and was a frequent and popular speaker at women's gatherings. Some of her food columns were issued as two paperback cookbooks by the *Courier-Journal*. They are now out of print. This recipe comes from one of her columns.

Kentucky Bibb lettuce is the pride of a Kentuckian's heart. It enhances any salad as decoration, but we who know it best like it just as lettuce, served with a simple French dressing so the delicate flavor of the lettuce can shine through. Onion- or garlic-flavored croutons are often sprinkled over the lettuce to give it crunchiness. Lorenzo dressing is another favorite with Bibb lettuce:

½ cup well-seasoned French dressing	2 tbsp. snipped water cress
	2 tbsp. currant jelly
2 tsp. chili sauce	

Mix all ingredients and stir to blend.

GRAPEFRUIT FRENCH DRESSING

⅔ cup salad oil	1 tsp. salt
¼ cup vinegar	1 tsp. paprika
¼ cup grapefruit juice	1 tsp. tarragon or chopped
1 tsp. sugar	parsley

Combine ingredients; cover and store in refrigerator. Shake well before serving.

Mrs. Jo Ann Gardner, Cumberland County Woman's Club

WHITE HOUSE DRESSING

In 1917 Mr. and Mrs. Glave Goddard purchased the property of the former Daughters' College, later Beaumont College, in Harrodsburg, and converted it into Beaumont Inn. Fashioned in true colonial style, with spacious halls and broad galleries, it breathes welcome. For more than 50 years through four generations the inn has specialized in true Kentucky food. Country ham, fried chicken, corn pudding, corn bread, and chess pie are standards on the menu. During World War II when sugar was rationed many dessert favorites were dropped from the menu and at times the owners were not sure they would have a country ham for next week's guests.

Diners often become so engrossed in the heavy menu that they overlook the delicate extras like green salad with White House Dressing:

1 cup sugar	1 medium onion
1 cup white vinegar	3 tsp. prepared mustard
1 cup vegetable oil	3 tsp. coarse salt
1 green pepper, chopped	3 tsp. Worcestershire sauce
1 small can pimientos, chopped	

Stir sugar, vinegar, and oil together until sugar dissolves. Grind pepper, pimiento, and onion together; add to oil and vinegar. Stir in remaining ingredients; let stand for 3 hours. Makes 1 quart. Keeps indefinitely if kept cool.

Mrs. Pauline Goddard Dedman, BEAUMONT INN RECIPES;
used by permission of Mrs. T. C. Dedman, Jr.

COOKED SALAD DRESSING

3 egg yolks	1 tsp. salt
½ cup vinegar	½ tsp. prepared mustard
½ cup sugar	

Beat egg yolks. Gradually beat in other ingredients. Cook in top of double boiler until thick, stirring constantly. Add 1 tbsp. butter if dressing is to be used at once.

Mrs. Benjamin Landis, Eddyville Woman's Club

Mrs. David Patrick, Harrodsburg Woman's Club, uses the same ingredients in varying proportions and suggests using the dressing on potato salad, cole slaw, salmon salad, or banana croquettes.

COOKED DRESSING

½ cup flour

6 tbsp. sugar

1 tsp. salt

2 tsp. dry mustard

dash of cayenne pepper

dash of paprika

1 cup milk

3 eggs

1 cup mild vinegar

½ cup salad oil

Mix dry ingredients in a saucepan. Slowly stir in milk, add eggs, and beat well. Blend vinegar in gradually. Cook over medium heat until thick and smooth, stirring constantly. Remove from heat; stir in oil.

Mary Wilson Eldred, Cadiz Woman's Club

Appetizers and Soups

The tradition of gradually "working" into a meal with a light appetizer or soup is not a particularly old one. The French introduced it to the world in the early nineteenth century. Before that, the English custom of serving all dishes together, buffet style, prevailed in most countries, and large meals in Colonial America followed the English tradition. The French idea of having several courses, however, made sense to most people, including Americans, especially when the meal was going to be a sumptuous one. For appetizers stimulate the senses and prepare the stomach for the heavier courses that are to follow.

The test of a good appetizer is its sensory appeal. Does it look, smell, feel, taste, and even sound good? Is it light and nonfilling? Does it harmonize with the other appetizers? If it meets these criteria, it will accomplish its purpose.

Most of the appetizers in this section are not particularly rooted in Kentucky's past. Rather they reflect the nationalization, even internationalization of the Commonwealth's foodways since World War II.

There is nothing wrong in this—just a fact of history. In fact, at least three of the recipes—chopped liver, hot clam dip, and crab spread—are veritable American institutions. And cheese thins ought to be; it is a superb dish.

But the pride of this section is, without doubt, Derby Spread. Its blending of butter, Roquefort cheese, and bourbon whiskey captures elements in Kentucky's past, both folk and elegant. When served on beaten biscuits or hoe cakes, Derby Spread is as close to the spirit of traditional Kentucky as we can get in an appetizer.

While there is no strong appetizer tradition in early Kentucky history, soups have long been of great importance in the diets of the Commonwealth's many peoples and regions. The Indians and Scottish settlers were both good soup makers. The Indians used a variety of meats and vegetables in their concoctions. Their pumpkin, corn, and bean soups were especially satisfying. The Scots were masters of meat-based vegetable soups. Both types have been popular throughout Kentucky's history,

The soup section of this chapter offers a good cross-section of historic recipes. The bean soups represent the Indian tradition that was happily borrowed by both Scots, English, and black Kentuckians. Burgoo, the crowning glory of Kentucky's soups, is more difficult to trace. The Indians certainly enjoyed soups with a variety of wild meats stewed together with herbs and vegetables. But so did the Scots. The question of origin aside, burgoo is as Kentucky as bluegrass and bourbon. Burton Milward's notes on the dish (pp. 53–54), and especially on Gus Jaubert, the "Burgoo King," are must reading. The recipe for turtle soup also represents the rich tradition of wild game soups. The originator of this dish was obviously a gifted cook from a well-established tradition who was not afraid to improve an already excellent recipe.

Jay Anderson

APPETIZERS

DERBY SPREAD

1 lb. butter	½ cup bourbon
1 lb. Roquefort or bleu cheese	

Cream butter and cheese; add bourbon slowly. Shape into a ball. Refrigerate 24 hours. Serve with crackers.

Mrs. Raymond Becht, Woman's Club of St. Matthews

CREAMY TUNA DIP

1	7-oz. can tuna	1	tbsp. horseradish
1½	tsp. onion salt	1	cup dairy sour cream
1	tsp. Worcestershire sauce	2	tsp. chopped parsley

Drain and flake tuna. Combine with other ingredients except parsley. Cover and chill. Garnish with parsley and surround with potato chips. Yields 1½ cups.

Mrs. Adron Doran, K.F.W.C. President, 1962–1964

HOT CLAM DIP

3	tbsp. butter	1	cup minced clams, drained
½	lb. Velveeta cheese	1	tbsp. Worcestershire sauce
4	tbsp. catsup	1	tbsp. sherry
1	small onion, chopped	¼	tsp. red pepper
½	green pepper, chopped		salt to taste

Melt butter and cheese in top of a double boiler. Add remaining ingredients and heat thoroughly. Serve in a chafing dish with crackers.

Mrs. E. Wilson Yates, Metropolitian Woman's Club of Lexington

CRAB SPREAD

1 8-oz. pkg. cream cheese	cocktail sauce (hot)
1 7- or 8-oz. can crab meat	

Soften cream cheese and spread along sides and bottom of a serving dish. Flake crab meat and sprinkle on top of cheese. Spread cocktail sauce over crab meat. Serve with crackers.

Mrs. Michael Stanifer, Richmond Younger Woman's Club

CHOPPED LIVER

1 lb. chicken livers	salt and coarse black pepper
4 eggs, hard boiled	rendered chicken fat
1 large sweet onion	

Soak livers in cold water until blood is extracted. Simmer in fresh water until cooked thoroughly. Grind livers, eggs, and onion. Season to taste with salt and pepper. Add sufficient chicken fat to moisten mixture to a paste. Mix well. Refrigerate several hours. Serve on crackers or use as filling for celery.

Mrs. Frank Tanner, Eddyville Woman's Club

CHICKEN ALMOND HASH

3 tbsp. butter	1 cup cooked diced chicken
2 tbsp. flour	½ cup sautéed mushrooms
1 tsp. salt	½ cup toasted slivered
¼ tsp. pepper	almonds
2 cups dairy sour cream	bread
1½ tbsp. lemon juice	deviled ham

Melt butter; add flour, salt, and pepper. Stir until well blended. Remove from heat. Gradually stir in sour cream and return to heat. Cook, stirring constantly, until thick. Add lemon juice and stir well; add chicken, mushrooms, and almonds. Heat thoroughly. Serve on rounds of oven-toasted buttered bread that have been spread with a thin layer of deviled ham. Enough for 25 to 30 toast rounds.

Mrs. Rufus Brandenburg, Woman's Club of Elizabethtown

CHICKEN-STUFFED EGGS

12 eggs, hard boiled	⅓ tsp. salt
¾ cup flaked cooked chicken	¼ cup mayonnaise
½ cup chopped celery	paprika
½ tsp. dry mustard	

Cut eggs in half lengthwise; remove and mash yolks. Combine with other ingredients, except paprika. Mix well. Stuff whites with mixture. Sprinkle with paprika.

Mrs. Adron Doran, K.F.W.C. President, 1962–1964

SAUSAGE BALLS

1 lb. lean bulk sausage	½ lb. sharp cheese, shredded
2 cups biscuit mix	

Mix uncooked sausage, biscuit mix, and cheese. Chill. Shape into small balls and place on an ungreased cookie sheet. Bake at 375° for 15 minutes.

Mrs. George Ridings, Jr., Richmond Younger Woman's Club

PEANUT BUTTER SNACKS

1 20-oz. loaf of sandwich   1 lb. peanut butter
   bread   ⅔ cup Wesson oil

Freeze the bread. Remove from the freezer 1 or 2 slices at a time and cut crusts from them; return trimmed slices to the freezer. Dry the crusts in a slow oven (250°), then roll into fine crumbs. Thoroughly mix peanut butter and Wesson oil, adding more oil if it is needed to make the mixture of coating consistency. Working with 1 or 2 slices at a time, cut frozen bread into four "fingers" per slice. With a fork dip each piece in the peanut butter, hold until dripping stops, then place on a cookie sheet. When cookie sheet is full bake at 200° for 2 hours. Place prepared crumbs in a cake or pie pan and put in the oven at the same time. Remove crumbs about 15 minutes before the snacks are done. Roll the snacks in the cooled crumbs. These will keep for several days and are delicious with salad or as a snack.

Mrs. T. D. Winstead, Woman's Club of Elizabethtown

CHEESE STRAWS

¼ lb. butter   ¼ tsp. salt
½ lb. sharp cheese   ½ tsp. baking powder
2 cups flour   cayenne pepper, good sized
1 tsp. dry mustard   sprinkle

Mix together, roll thin, cut and bake at 400° for 11 minutes.

Mrs. Pauline Goddard Dedman, BEAUMONT INN RECIPES;
used by permission of Mrs. T. C. Dedman, Jr.

CHEESE THINS

2 5-oz. jars Old English sharp   1 tsp. cayenne pepper
   cheese   2½ cups sifted flour
½ lb. butter or margarine   1 cup finely chopped pecans
1 tsp. salt

Cream the cheese and margarine. Add salt, cayenne, and flour; mix well. Add finely chopped pecans; mix again. On lightly floured waxed paper shape into four 1-inch-thick rolls. Refrigerate or freeze until firm. Slice thin; bake at 350° for 10 to 12 minutes. Makes 70 to 80 thins.

Mrs. T. J. Hill, Stanford Woman's Club

SOUPS

BEAN SOUP

1 lb. navy beans	2 ribs celery
1 ham hock	1 medium onion
1 medium potato	1 tsp. salt or more to taste
1 carrot	pinch of soda

Wash beans and soak overnight in cold water, or quick-soak them in water kept just below the boiling point for 2 or 3 hours. Cook cleaned ham hock in 2 cups water in a pressure cooker at 10 pounds pressure for 30 minutes. Reduce pressure normally. Remove ham. Clean and peel vegetables; cut into large chunks. Place them in a blender, cover with water, and blend at shredding speed for a few seconds. Pour into the pressure cooker, add beans, salt, and soda. Set pressure gauge at 15 pounds and cook for 30 minutes. Reduce pressure instantly. Remove lid and add lean meat from the ham hock and more water if needed. Adjust heat to keep the soup very hot until ready to serve. Serves 6 to 8.

Mrs. Ralph M. Cooper, Lexington Woman's Club

BLACK BEAN SOUP

2 cups black turtle beans	1 tbsp. salt
1 large onion	black pepper
1 doz. whole cloves	cayenne pepper
knuckle or shank of veal	flour

Soak beans in ½ gallon of water. Boil them in the same water, with onion and cloves, until beans are tender. Remove cloves. Put beans and onion through a food mill or colander. Boil veal in 1 gallon of water until tender; add salt. Strain broth into another kettle; add beans and onion. Season with pepper and thicken with flour. Remove meat from bone; grind and shape into meat balls while warm. Serve with soup garnished with a slice of lemon and a slice of hard-cooked egg. Serves 6 to 8.

Mrs. Ben Clement, Marion Woman's Club

BOUILLON

10¢ beef bone   10¢ veal bone

Put 2 spoons full of butter in kettle to brown and add 1 onion chopped fine. Add soup vegetables, bay leaves, and onion stuffed with cloves, (celery, carrot) then put in meat and cover with water. Let it come to a boil and put back on stove to simmer for 4 to 5 hours. Then strain into bowl and let stand overnight. Next day, take off grease and put on stove, when hot add beaten white of egg and season. Strain carefully and put aside to jell.

This recipe was handwritten in an old BLUE GRASS COOK BOOK by an unknown owner.

POCKET SOUP

The Long Hunters and other early travellers in the wilderness often carried with them "pocket soup." This was made by cooking bouillon to a gluelike consistency, then drying it on cloth in the same manner as apples and beans. On journeys it was used as we use bouillon cubes today, or it could be dissolved in the mouth for quick energy. One pound was said to be enough to keep a man healthy for a month.

BURGOO

1 lb. pork shank	2 onions
1 lb. beef shank	2 potatoes
1 lb. breast of lamb	1 pt. tomatoes
1 lb. veal shank	1 cup corn
half of a 4-lb. fat hen	1 pod red pepper
4 qt. water	½ cup lima beans
½ bunch parsley	2 tsp. Worcestershire sauce
1 cup cabbage	cayenne pepper and salt to
1 green pepper	taste
2 carrots	

Boil meats in water until tender. Remove from broth. Cool. Remove meat from bones, and dice. Chop parsley, cabbage, and green pepper. Peel and dice carrots, onions, and potatoes. Put all ingredients in meat stock and cook until thick. Serves 12.

Mrs. Walter Kimbell, Woman's Club of Frankfort

BURGOO

Mr. J. E. Wuersch, whose daughter contributed this recipe, used it for his annual burgoo dinners over 50 years ago.

To prepare this you will need a large iron kettle, 12- to 15-gallon capacity. It should be placed outside over a wood fire—hickory wood, if possible.

5 large soup bones with meat
several marrow bones
3 lb. bacon
2 large chickens
10 lb. potatoes
3 lb. onions
4 lb. navy or great northern
   beans, soaked overnight
2 lb. dried lima beans, soaked
   overnight
1 lb. dried split peas, soaked
   overnight
2 cans peas
3 lb. apples
2 bunches celery

1 lb. green beans
1 medium head cabbage
3 or 4 bunches carrots
1 doz. ears corn or 3 large
   cans corn
1 bunch turnips
2 gal. tomatoes or 14 no. 2
   cans
4 green peppers
4 red peppers
1 or 2 cups okra
parsley
salt, pepper, cayenne pepper,
   chili pepper

Cook meat and bones for 3 to 4 hours in water. While meat is cooking, cut up the vegetables. Remove meat and bones from water. Cut meat and chicken from bones and put back in kettle. Add vegetables and seasonings. Cook, stirring often to prevent sticking, for 4 or 5 hours. If it thickens too much, add more hot water. The longer it cooks the better the flavor. Serves 144.

Mrs. Evelyne Thomas, Woman's Club of Henderson

OYSTER STEW

½ pt. oysters and liquid
2 tbsp. butter
½ tsp. celery salt

¼ tsp. pepper
¼ tsp. paprika
2 cups milk

Simmer oysters, liquid, and butter for 3 minutes until edges curl. Scald milk in a separate saucepan. Add oysters and seasoning. Heat but do not allow to boil. Serves 2.

Recipe of the late Mrs. John Rodman of Versailles;
contributed by Mrs. Richard Crutcher

REAL TURTLE SOUP

4 to 5 lb. cooked turtle meat	6 lemons
3 bay leaves	1 cup parsley, chopped
1 small pod red pepper	1 30-oz. can tomatoes
1 tsp. whole cloves	1 20-oz. bottle catsup
1 tsp. salt	½ cup Worcestershire sauce
2 bunches carrots	2 cups flour
1 large bunch celery	6 eggs, hard boiled
3 large onions	sauterne

To cook turtle meat, put it in a large kettle with bay leaves, red pepper pod, whole cloves, chopped celery tops, and salt. Cover with water and simmer until meat is tender. Strain and reserve liquid.

To prepare soup, grind turtle meat, carrots, celery, onions, and whole seeded lemons. Put all ingredients except flour, eggs, and sauterne into the strained broth. Simmer until tender. Brown flour in a heavy skillet, stirring often. Add about 1 qt. water, all at once; stir until smooth. Stir browned flour paste into soup, adding more salt if needed. Simmer a few minutes more; add chopped eggs. Before serving put 1 tbsp. sauterne in each bowl and pour hot soup over it. Serves 16 to 20.

Mrs. Ralph B. Cook, Sr., Erlanger Woman's Club

This recipe originated with Mrs. Cook's father, Wm. H. Maynard.

VEGETABLE SOUP

2 medium onions	soup bone (knuckle—no
2 large potatoes	meat)
2 or 3 carrots	1 qt. water
2 ribs celery	½ tsp. black pepper
¼ medium head of cabbage	1 tbsp. salt
1 pt. tomatoes or tomato juice	

Cut up vegetables. Combine ingredients in a large pot with a lid. Bring to a boil, reduce heat, cover, and simmer for 2 hours. Cool and refrigerate. Remove soup bone and skim unwanted fat before reheating.

Leftovers, such as lima beans, green beans, peas, corn, and noodles, can be saved in the freezer and added to the soup. Serves 4 to 6.

Mrs. Patch Woolfolk, Lexington Woman's Club

GREEN SOUP

½ cup chopped yellow onion
2 cups diced potatoes
½ lb. pepperoni, cut in ¼-inch
   slices
2 tbsp. olive oil
2 qt. boiling water

4 cups cabbage, shredded, or
   half cabbage and half
   spinach
3 tsp. salt
pepper to taste

Cook onion, potatoes, pepperoni, and olive oil in boiling water over medium heat until potatoes are done. Remove pepperoni and set aside. Remove potatoes and onions; force through a coarse sieve; return to liquid in the kettle. Add green vegetables, pepperoni, salt, and pepper. Cook about 10 more minutes. Serve with crusty dark bread or corn bread. Serves 4.

Maude S. Hancock, Horse Cave Woman's Club

TOMATO CELERY SOUP

A modern version of a Shaker recipe from Pleasant Hill.

1 small onion, chopped
½ cup finely chopped celery
2 tbsp. butter
1 10½-oz. can tomato soup
1 soup can of water

1 tsp. minced parsley
1 tbsp. lemon juice
1 tsp. sugar
¼ tsp. salt
⅛ tsp. pepper

Sauté onion and celery in butter; do not brown. Add remaining ingredients and simmer for 5 minutes. Celery will remain crisp. Serve topped with unsweetened whipped cream and chopped parsley. Serves 3 to 4.

Elizabeth C. Kremer, WE MAKE YOU KINDLY WELCOME (1970)

Desserts

Kentuckians have always been especially fond of desserts. When someone from this state is asked to remember a favorite family recipe, chances are that memory will be a pound cake that was baked for every Sunday dinner during the years spent at the "homeplace," or an apple pie that grandmother baked while she was doing the washing, feeding the coal stove in the kitchen, baking the bread, and perhaps making apple butter for the winter.

Baking desserts was not an easy task for Kentuckians in the past. There were no supermarkets with their convenient cake mixes and prepared pie shells. Good cooks had to be knowledgeable about their craft. Baking was somewhat dependent on guesswork. Recipes obtained from friends did not list the time or temperature for baking an item because each home had variations in its cooking devices and the homemaker had to learn the capabilities of her system. Early Kentuckians used the fireplace and then the brick oven. It was not until about 1870 that the stove, invented much earlier, was adapted to the needs of the cook. Each time the cooking device changed, recipes had to be revised or abandoned. Cakes, pies, puddings have all had their zeniths in popularity and at other times have fallen into disfavor; frequently the reason for the change was advancement in technology.

The ingredients used for desserts in early Kentucky were those that were widely available, once the original supplies of flour and sugar were used. Settlers produced their own food, and their diet was, of necessity, seasonal. People had to "make do" with whatever ingredients were at hand.

Corn was a staple which was prepared in many different ways. Indian pudding, for example, was made with corn, sorghum molasses, and milk, and was baked slowly in the fireplace of the pioneer cabins. Puddings like this would not be pleasing to today's palate because the long cooking period in a slow oven dried them out. Nevertheless, they were a treat for those dessert-starved early Kentuckians.

Pumpkins, or "pompions," as they were called, were cultivated by our first settlers and used in pies and other desserts. The dessert eaten at the first Christmas celebration in Louisville in 1778 was pumpkin pie. Apple and peach seeds were planted the first year Kentucky was settled, and their first fruits were a welcome addition to the wild fruits and berries. Later, fruit trees and berry bushes were planted near farmhouses so the women and children could gather the fruits quickly and safely for desserts, jams, and jellies. Apples, pears, and peaches were used in season and frequently sun-dried for winter use. Many kinds of berries were cultivated—raspberries, dewberries, gooseberries, elderberries, and strawberries—but the Kentucky favorite, blackberries, grew wild. Some berries would be eaten fresh with cream or in such desserts as blackberry stack pie or strawberry shortcake. When sugar was unavailable the surplus crop was dried in the sun or on racks above the fireplace and stored, along with crocks of mincemeat, in the fruit cellar for use in winter desserts.

Milk and eggs were available year-round, although the quantity varied. In summer eggs were plentiful and cheap; in winter they were scarce, and dessert recipes had to be adjusted accordingly. Fresh eggs were kept in brine or heavy lime water for winter use.

Many early cookbooks scorned the use of rising agents for cakes and stressed the importance of fresh eggs. Unless the cook had a good strong arm, the cake might be underbeaten and quite heavy. The earliest leavenings used were ale-yeast and pearlash, which was refined from potash. Later, baking ammonia was used; when heated it released two gases, ammonia and carbon dioxide, which increased the volume of the cake and gave it a porous texture. Some early recipes called for "Sub Cor" plus tartaric acid as leavening agents. Tartaric acid was obtained from the tartar of wine casks. (Cream of tartar is a refined form of this substance.) It was often used when the recipe called for sweet milk instead of sour, to get the gas bubbles started.

Saleratus (baking soda) was used in combination with fruit juice, molasses, or sour milk (the last readily available in the days before refrigeration). Baking powder was not introduced to the homemaker until the middle of the nineteenth century. The next step was the addition of baking powder and salt to flour for one of the first convenience products, self-rising flour.

The major sources of shortening for Kentucky's pioneers were lard, rendered at hog-butchering time in the fall, and butter churned by the homemaker. When milk was plentiful, the excess was often made into butter and sold.

Flour was an uncertain product for early Kentuckians. Grain was at first ground with a mortar and pestle at home or in a local stone mill until commercial mills developed. Today both hard and soft wheats are blended to achieve an all-purpose flour, but in former times a homemaker would have to make do with either hard or soft flour, depending upon which was grown in her area. Hard flour contains more protein and makes more successful breads, while soft flour is better for cakes.

For sweetening their desserts, Kentuckians used sorghum, honey, or Southern cane sugar rather than the maple sugar New Englanders favored. Early recipes for cakes frequently called for powdered sugar. During most of the nineteenth century commercially processed sugar came in blocks. For ordinary use the cook had to pound the sugar into small pieces and then sieve it. For use in cakes she would pulverize it in a mortar to make the crystals fine enough to cream with the butter.

Many recipes from Virginia called for brandy for flavoring. Wealthier Kentucky families used brandy, but those less affluent frequently substituted apple jack (fermented cider) or raisin jack (raisins fermented in fruit juice). Spices were imported into Kentucky as early as 1800 but were quite costly. Many homes had special chests with locks to hold the treasured cinnamon, nutmeg, and pepper.

Rosewater flavored many cakes and other desserts, but eighteenth- and nineteenth-century recipe books often called for musk, obtained from the male musk deer, and "amber grease" (ambergris), a fragrant substance obtained from the sperm whale and widely used in colonial days. Vanilla came to the United States from France in 1789, when Thomas Jefferson brought the first vanilla beans to America, but sorghum and fruit and berry syrups remained the most common flavoring ingredients in Kentucky.

Chocolate first came to America before the Revolution, and Kentucky cookbooks began mentioning chocolate about 1800. It was very bitter and was used primarily in beverages, but a process for removing the fat from the cocoa beans was patented in 1828 and shortly thereafter sweet chocolate became popular as a coating for candies and cookies or for eating. *The Housekeeper's Companion,* published in 1889, contains a recipe for a chocolate beverage with a whipped cream topping. Natural-process chocolate had no alkali added, but "Dutching" agents containing this additive made the chocolate darker and more flavorful and allowed it to dissolve more freely. Some early chocolate recipes were for *pots de creme,* demon's cake, and chocolate trifle. The Depression years of the 1930s brought chocolate into new prominence with such treats as devil's food cake, chocolate pie, and fudge, many of the recipes coming from a brand new cookbook distributed in 1934 by a chocolate manufacturer. Limited budgets and more time than money encouraged homemakers to spend long hours in the kitchen making special but inexpensive treats to brighten dreary times.

Cooks have not always had what we would consider accurate ways to measure ingredients for the desserts they made. Sorghum was measured by the number of "blurps" which came from the jug. Recipes often called for a wine glass of liquid, which might be one-fourth cup in today's measurements. Butter was measured to "the size of a walnut" or "the size of a goose egg." Flour was measured by the handful. Often the cookbook reminded the user that a cupful was a tea cup, not a coffee cup. Cooking was done much more by look and feel than by exact measurement. While old methods may seem incomprehensible to us, future cooks who use the metric system may be just as mystified when they read our cookbooks and wonder how today's homemaker was able to make a cake without a scale in her kitchen to measure the grams.

Desserts in the kitchens of our grandmothers ranged from heavy steamed puddings to light refreshing ice creams and sherbets. None was more versatile than custard. Boiled, baked, or molded, it appeared often, either alone or in combination with leftover cake. Floating Island, often sweetened with rose water, was the gem of the puddings. Tipsy cake and trifle, made by pouring custard over wine-soaked cake and topping it with meringue, were also very popular. Flummeries, molded custards, were the ultimate test for the cook.

One nineteenth-century dessert seldom remembered today is tomatoes. Once our ancestors discovered these fruits weren't poisonous, they served them in many ways. As dessert, tomatoes were sprinkled with sugar and often cream was poured over them. A few older Kentuckians still enjoy them served this way.

During the late nineteenth century, recipes for calf's-foot jelly appeared in many cookbooks. Although the name sounds unappealing today, it was merely the forerunner of the many gelatin recipes found in modern cookbooks. Not many homemakers today would take the time to boil calves' feet until three tablespoonfuls of gelatin were extracted. Housewives of that era had then to tint the gelatin green with "spinage" or red with cochineal, a red dye made from dried insects. Isinglass, or fish glue, was another popular form of gelatin. Commercial packages of gelatin can be seen today in the Kentucky Historical Museum with other post-Civil War products, but cookbooks in widespread use did not call for flavored colored gelatin until 1928's *Frigidaire Recipes.*

Kentuckians have always regarded certain types of dessert and certain ingredients with special favor. Apples, for example, have always had an honored place in the baking of Kentuckians. Either fresh or dried, they were made into pies, sometimes in combination with other fruits, with a top crust or a sugar topping. They also appeared in dumplings, puddings, and cookies, or candied as a sweet-meat. An early recipe from Eastern Kentucky, originally brought "by memory" across the mountains from the Shenandoah Valley of Virginia, is for apple stack cake. It consists of thinly sliced biscuits made without baking powder, layered with apple butter or freshly made applesauce flavored with cinnamon and nutmeg, and topped with milk and honey. Layered cakes and pies have had wide acceptance in Kentucky throughout the years. Other versions of the much-loved stack cake from Eastern Kentucky call for sauce made from dried apples between the layers. A stackable combination found in a nineteenth-century Bluegrass cookbook is gingerbread layers filled with applesauce sweetened with sorghum. In Western Kentucky, the pleasing stacked combination contains pecans in a chess pie type of filling.

The origin of the stack cake may lie in the inventiveness of a baker whose thriftiness resulted in thin layers of cake. Putting filling between these layers made a more attractive dessert. Some believe the stack cake came about because of "dinners on the ground." It took many cakes to feed large gatherings, and the best way to transport them was to stack them and place filling between the layers.

Cakes have long been a part of Kentucky's heritage and reflect the ingenuity of the cook. Substitutions for unavailable ingredients in the early days developed new cakes that have become favorites as the years have passed. Some.ingredients used in old cake recipes may seem extravagant to us today, but in the days when most Kentuckians raised their own food the dozen eggs required for an angel food cake were a low-cost ingredient. Pork cake, a recipe dating back more than a hundred years, is made with salt pork, which was plentiful and inexpensive for the family that raised its own hogs. When placed in a stone crock, pork cake improved in flavor, even when kept a month or more (provided the family didn't discover it).

Scripture cake, for which the ingredients were named in specified Bible verses, undoubtedly owed its widespread popularity to the circuit-riding ministers, who enjoyed the cake on Sundays and spread the recipe from household to household. Black cake, which appears in some family recipe books, was a traditional molasses and spice cake with fruit and nuts added, but in Kentucky this rich cake would not have been complete without the addition of bourbon. Spice cake was also the basis for applesauce cake or the Kentucky favorite, jam cake.

Pies, a uniquely American dessert, often had cornmeal crusts when there was no flour in the pioneer kitchen. Early fillings included mincemeat, pumpkin, and fruits. The state of the economy and the availability of ingredients is evident in the use of vinegar, butter, jam, cornmeal, or sorghum as flavoring for pies. Dried apple pies—rounds of crust filled, folded in half, and fried to a crispy golden brown—are an old favorite with Kentuckians. Chess pie has long been made in Kentucky and throughout the South. According to the authors of *Virginia Cookery Past and Present,* this pie may have been the product of an inventive housewife who left out the cheese and misspelled the name. No matter what the origin of this delightful pie, Western Kentuckians make a pecan-filled version for their culinary claim to fame. Other flavors—orange, lemon, and vanilla—are served throughout the state. In the days when the men were busy discussing the relative merits of the mint julep, the ladies discussed whether chess pie was authentic without that spoonful of cornmeal.

Events, especially wars, have always influenced the foods appearing on Kentuckians' tables, just as foods have played a role in shaping history. Today for many people the reasons for not serving a rich dessert are probably either calorie restrictions or high cost, but this has not always been the case, as many Kentuckians know. Wartime shortages of certain ingredients have often determined the type of dessert appearing on the family menu.

During the Civil War, desserts had to be made from home-grown products, for imported spices and flavorings were in short supply because of shipping restrictions. Cake and pie recipes often had to be revised. Butter was one of the major flavorings but when passing soldiers conscripted the family cow for duty, even this ingredient disappeared. In spite of hardships, recipes from that era reflect a valiant effort on the part of those at home.

World War I again brought short supplies, and once again the country found it difficult to supply both guns and butter. With eggs selling for the unheard-of price of a dollar a dozen, one-egg cakes temporarily replaced twelve-egg angel food cakes. In World War II meat, butter, and sugar were scarce, and ration coupons issued by the government attempted to prevent hoarding and divide supplies fairly. Newspaper columnists told housewives that their role was as important as that of the munitions factory workers. Books with such titles as *Thrifty Cooking for Wartime* detailed the ways in which housewives could tighten their families' belts. Many suggestions dated from previous wars when deprivation was the order of the day. Homemakers were encouraged to use honey and molasses for sweetening, fruit for flavoring, and grains for stretchers because these products were home-grown and plentiful. Oatmeal became the nutritious extender which appeared in everything from meatloaf to cookies. Many Kentuckians used bacon drippings for seasoning and frying and saved the shortening for baking. A sugar-saving trick was to sweeten fruits to taste at the end of the cooking period, since fruits release some sweetness during cooking.

When sugar was decreased in cake recipes, certain problems developed. Since sugar is a bulking agent, cakes did not rise as well. Some were less brown because sugar contributes to the browning process, and they did not retain moisture so well, since sugar aids in this process, too. One of the cakes which achieved popularity in this sugarless era was pineapple upside-down cake, since the canned pineapple provided the sweet taste and the cake needed only a small amount of sugar. Frostings were deemed unpatriotic because of the quantity of sugar required, so bakers reinstituted the powdered sugar topping.

Because meat was rationed, protein foods such as eggs and cheese were incorporated into desserts whenever possible to raise the nutritional level. Carrot cake was developed because it used ingredients from the victory garden and supplied needed nutrients.

Cookies of the day also reflected the spirit of wartime. Honey- or molasses-flavored cookies were frequently baked to be sent to servicemen. Other items often sent to our fighting men abroad were fruit cake and country ham. Most Kentucky soldiers would not feel far from home with these two favorite dishes close at hand.

Since the war, supermarkets have emerged, and with them innumerable convenience products which have become popular with Kentuckians, as with most Americans. Many of today's popular desserts begin with a mix and are adapted to make a completely different dessert than the original package intended, showing the continuing ingenuity and originality of Kentucky cooks. Many delicious desserts which were baked in the gas or electric range are now being revised for use in the energy-saving microwave oven, which speeds the baking process.

What does the future hold for Kentuckians? Chances are that we will be seeing many interesting new products on the market. These products will be based on the traditional favorites but they will speed the process of cooking and baking while retaining the favorite Kentucky flavors. They will probably use freeze-dried fruits, dried eggs, irradiated milk which can be stored at room temperature, and spun soybean fibers for additional protein. Hopefully these technological advances will not destroy the tradition of serving delicious desserts, a legacy from our Kentucky grandmothers.

Shirley Snarr

GREAT GRANDMOTHER SPEIDEN'S
APPLE AND RAISIN PUDDING

½ cup butter	1 cup sugar (a little less if
1 tsp. soda	the apples are sweet)
1½ cups stewed apples or	1 tsp. ground cloves
applesauce	1 tsp. cinnamon
2 cups bread crumbs	½ cup pecans
1 cup raisins	1 tsp. salt

Melt butter in a pudding pan. Stir soda into apples. Combine all ingredients (including melted butter) in a large bowl and mix well. Pour mixture into the pudding pan. Bake at 350° for 15 to 20 minutes, or until slightly brown. Serve with a hard sauce made with brown sugar (page 215). Serves 8.

Mrs. Fillison L. Speiden, Jr., Woman's Club of St. Matthews

DEEP DISH BANANA PUDDING

The idea of a banana festival in Kentucky seems odd, since bananas aren't grown anywhere in the state. The Fulton Banana Festival is actually an international friendship gesture. It was begun in the early 1960s, when railroads still carried a major portion of the freight in the United States. Illinois Central trains from New Orleans would roll into South Fulton, Tennessee, and Fulton, Kentucky, carrying bananas from Central and South America. No matter what the destination, more than half the banana trains in this country came through Fulton. The trains stopped about ten years ago; trucks now pick up the cargo in New Orleans.

The festival is attended by Latin American students and dignitaries, the governors of both states, and thousands of visitors. There are exhibits of local and Latin American crafts, and entertainment is from both south and north of the border. Following the parade, the world's largest banana pudding is served. To make the pudding, take a bowl 3 feet high and 5 feet across. Slice 3,000 bananas. Place them in the bowl in alternating layers with 250 pounds of vanilla wafers and 950 pounds of boiled custard. This will serve 10,000.

If you don't have 10,000 to be served, try the following recipe:

¼ cup sugar
2 tbsp. flour
¼ tsp. salt
2 egg yolks
1½ cups milk
1½ tsp. vanilla extract

1 pkg. graham crackers or
   1 4-oz. pkg. vanilla
   wafers
1 lb. bananas
Vanilla meringue:
2 egg whites
3 tbsp. sugar
2 tsp. vanilla extract

Combine sugar, flour, and salt in the top of a double boiler. Add egg yolks and ¼ cup of the milk. Heat remaining milk and gradually stir it into egg and sugar mixture. Cook over hot water, stirring constantly, until mixture coats a metal spoon. Add vanilla extract. Arrange graham crackers or vanilla wafers and sliced bananas in alternating layers in a 1-quart casserole, with crackers as the bottom layer and bananas as the top. Pour custard over all.

For the meringue, beat egg whites until they stand in soft peaks. Gradually beat in sugar and vanilla extract and continue beating until stiff. Spread over the pudding. Bake in a preheated 325° oven 10 minutes, or until brown. Serves 6.

Mrs. H. E. Richardson, Louisville

CHOCOLATE PUDDING

3 tbsp. cocoa   pinch of salt
4 tbsp. cornstarch   1 qt. milk
8 tbsp. sugar   1 tsp. vanilla

Mix all dry ingredients in the top of a double boiler. Add milk gradually and beat with an egg beater until free of lumps. Cook over hot water until thickened. Add vanilla and pour into 6 dessert cups. Cool, covering each cup with plastic wrap to prevent a crust forming. Serve with a dollop of whipped cream. Serves 6.

Mrs. George Bauer, Woman's Club of Elizabethtown

FOOD FOR THE GODS
(Date Pudding)

¾ cup nuts, finely chopped   4 tbsp. crushed Ritz crackers
¼ lb. dates, finely chopped   1 tsp. baking powder
1 cup sugar   3 eggs, separated

Mix nuts, dates, sugar, crackers, and baking powder with egg yolks. Fold into stiffly beaten egg whites. Bake in a buttered 9-inch square pan at 350° about 30 minutes. Serve with whipped cream.

Dorothy Grider, Bowling Green

Miss Grider is a descendant of one of Bowling Green's early families. A native Kentuckian, she is an illustrator of children's books and now lives in Pennsylvania.

OZARK PUDDING

½ cup sifted flour   2 tsp. vanilla
2 tsp. baking powder   3 tbsp. melted butter
½ tsp. salt   1 cup chopped walnuts
2 eggs   1 cup chopped apples
1 cup brown sugar

Sift together flour, baking powder, and salt. Beat eggs well; add sugar and beat with a rotary beater until creamy. Stir in dry ingredients and mix well. Add vanilla, melted butter, nuts, and apples. Pour mixture into a greased 9-inch pie plate and bake at 350° for 35 minutes. Serve warm or cold with ice cream or whipped cream. Serves 6.

Mrs. Charles Schneider, Erlanger Woman's Club

FIG PUDDING

1 cup sugar
1 cup butter
3 eggs, beaten
1 cup milk
2 cups fine dry bread crumbs

1 lb. dried figs, finely chopped
2 oz. sherry or maraschino
   cherry juice
2 tbsp. flour
2 tsp. baking powder

Cream sugar and butter; add beaten eggs. Add milk and bread crumbs alternately. Add figs and sherry. Sift flour and baking powder together and add them to the mixture. Pour into a greased mold and steam 3 hours. (See instructions for steaming, page 130.) Serve with hard sauce. Serves 16.

Mrs. Frances H. Cook, Ghent Woman's Club

PORE MAN'S PUDDIN'

2 cups cold boiled rice
3 cups hot milk
¼ cup molasses
¼ cup raisins

1 tbsp. margarine
1 tsp. salt
½ tsp. nutmeg

Mix rice and milk. Add remaining ingredients. Mix well and pour into a buttered baking dish. Bake at 350° for 1 hour, stirring after the first 30 minutes. Serves 5 to 6.

Mrs. Garey Hawn, Richmond Younger Woman's Club

WOODFORD PUDDING

½ cup butter
1 cup sugar
3 eggs
1 cup blackberry jam
1 tsp. soda

3 tsp. sour milk
1½ cups sifted flour
cinnamon and nutmeg to
   taste

Cream butter and sugar. Add eggs and jam; then add soda which has been dissolved in milk, and flour which has been sifted with spices. Bake in a lightly greased 8- by 8-inch cake pan at 325° for 45 minutes or until pudding is firm but soft. Cut into squares and serve with caramel sauce (page 216). Serves 8.

Mrs. I. D. Thompson, K.F.W.C. President, 1952-1954

Mrs. George Wilson, Horse Cave Woman's Club, uses only ½ cup flour and bakes the pudding in a tube pan.

ENGLISH PUDDING

Mix this pudding 3 days before it is to be cooked. Beat nine eggs to a froth, add enough flour to make a thick batter free from lumps. Add one pint of new milk and beat well. Add ¾ pound brown sugar, when it looks quite light put in ¾ pound beef suet, chopped fine, one nutmeg grated and one teaspoon each, allspice, mace and cinnamon. Mix with it two pounds stoned and floured raisins, two pounds currants, washed, picked and dried, one pound of citron, sliced, and ¼ pound almonds, divided. Put the pudding in a cloth or sock and steam. Steam 6 or 7 hours if made into one pudding, two puddings steam 4 hours. Be sure the water is boiling when you start cooking, suspend the cloth so it does not touch the water, turn the pudding often. When done, put it in a pan of cold water and the cloth can be easily removed. Add your favorite sauce.

Mrs. Wayland Rhoads, Greenville Woman's Club

This recipe was sent to Mrs. Rhoads's grandfather from England in the 1850s.

APPLE DUMPLINGS

pastry for 2 crusts
1 tsp. cinnamon
sugar

1 pint fresh applesauce, sweetened, or 1 16-oz. can applesauce

Roll pie dough thin; cut into 4- or 5-inch squares. Mix cinnamon with applesauce and place 2 or 3 tablespoonfuls on each square. Bring the corners of the dough to the center, overlapping edges slightly so the applesauce won't leak while cooking. Secure with a toothpick. Sprinkle with sugar and with a spatula place on a slightly greased cookie sheet. Bake at 350° for 15 to 20 minutes, or until crust is a light golden brown. Serve warm with dessert sauce (page 216). Serves 6.

Shirley C. Greene, Eddyville Woman's Club

Mrs. John W. Stevens, Metropolitan Woman's Club of Lexington, makes her apple dumplings with 6 fresh tart apples that have been peeled, cored, and sprinkled with a spoonful of sugar and a pinch of cinnamon. She serves them with cinnamon sauce (page 216).

SULFURED APPLE-MAPLE DUMPLINGS

Syrup:

¼ lb. sulfur-dried apple
   pieces
3 cups water
⅛ tsp. salt
1 tbsp. margarine
2 2-inch maple sugar
   "muffins," crushed, or ¾
   cup dark brown sugar
   with 5 drops maple
   flavor
2 tsp. cornstarch
⅛ tsp. powdered cinnamon
⅛ tsp. grated nutmeg
1 tsp. cider vinegar or lemon
   juice

¼ tsp. vanilla extract
½ cup seedless raisins
¼ cup chopped black walnuts
   (optional)

Dumpling dough:

1½ cups all-purpose flour,
   unsifted
1 tsp. baking powder
2 tbsp. crushed maple sugar
   or 2 tbsp. granulated
   sugar with 2 drops
   maple flavor
¼ tsp. salt
3 tbsp. cold, firm margarine,
   snipped BB size
1 cup milk

In an 11-inch stainless steel skillet, combine all ingredients for syrup. Bring to a boil, uncovered. Boil for 4 minutes. With a fork, lightly toss together dumpling dough ingredients in a mixing bowl. Do not beat. Drop by well-rounded teaspoonfuls (about 30) onto the hot liquid. Cover pan, lower heat to simmer, and cook 30 minutes without lifting the cover. Serve promptly in shallow individual bowls with apple syrup spooned over dumplings. Add a dollop of unsweetened whipped cream if desired. Serves 6.

Mrs. T. Richard Swearingen, Lexington

KENTUCKY BLACKBERRY DUMPLING WITH MILK DIP

A guest entering the Boone Tavern Hotel in Berea immediately feels that he is a guest in a Southern home. Part of the inn's charm derives from the fresh naturalness of the young people, students at Berea College, who serve as desk clerks, bellmen, housemen, hosts, cashiers, waitresses, and traymen. They all work together with enthusiasm and courtesy toward visitors. In the Appalachian culture, a strong loyalty to home and family is a dominant characteristic, and a welcome from an Appalachian youth is sincere and open.

Food at the inn is prepared in small quantities and from the fresh stage; great care in checking procedures and reproduction makes possible the tavern's excellent food. Everyone loves the spoonbread, cornsticks, and relish trays. Other favorites are Boone Tavern chicken pie, Kentucky lamb, and blackberry dumpling with milk dip (below).

Mr. Richard T. Hougen, a graduate of Cornell University's Hotel Management School, recently retired as manager of the inn and associate professor in hotel management at Berea College. He has published three cookbooks, and from his latest, *More Hougen Favorites,* comes the following:

Crust:

2 cups flour
¾ tsp. baking powder
½ tsp. salt
⅔ cup lard
4 tbsp. cold water

Filling:

1 15-oz. can blackberries
2 tbsp. cornstarch
½ cup sugar

pinch of salt
1 tbsp. butter
1 tsp. lemon juice

Milk dip:

3 cups milk
¾ cup sugar
2½ tbsp. cornstarch
6 tbsp. butter
1½ tsp. vanilla

Sift flour for crust before measuring. Sift again with baking powder and salt. Work lard into flour, using finger tips. Add water and mix. Divide dough into 2 parts. Place on a floured pastry board and roll into 2 9-inch circles. Cut each circle into 4 wedges.

Drain the blackberries, reserving liquid. Combine juice, cornstarch, sugar, and salt in the top of a double boiler, and cook to thicken. Remove from heat and add butter, lemon juice, and berries. Place a generous tablespoonful of berry mixture in the center of each wedge and bring edges together, pinching to close the dumpling. Bake at 450° for 15 minutes. Serve warm with milk dip, made by mixing sugar and cornstarch and adding to milk that has been heated in the top of a double boiler. Cook until thickened, stirring to prevent lumping. Add butter and vanilla. Serves 8.

FLOAT

3 eggs, separated   ½ gallon milk
2 tbsp. cornstarch or flour   1 tbsp. vanilla
2 cups sugar

Beat egg yolks. Add cornstarch or flour and sugar; blend in milk a small amount at a time. Cook over medium heat in the top of a double boiler until mixture is medium thick. Beat egg whites until stiff; drop by spoonfuls on top of custard so they will float. Continue to cook for 3 minutes. Remove from heat, stir in vanilla, and allow to cool to room temperature. Serve immediately or refrigerate for later use. Serve in small glasses with coconut cake or pound cake. Serves 12.

Mrs. A. Baxter Riley, LaCenter Woman's Club

BOILED CUSTARD

1 gallon milk   12 eggs
peel of 2 lemons   1½ to 2 cups sugar

Scald 3 quarts of milk in a double boiler and add lemon peel. Beat eggs well and add 1 quart of milk to them. Stir the egg mixture into the scalded milk. Cook just until it begins to thicken, or until it will coat a silver spoon. Remove from heat, add sugar, and stir well. If cooked too long after sugar is added, it will curdle. The custard will thicken some as it cools. When cooled, place in the refrigerator. Serve very cold. It is especially good served almost frozen. Serves 24.

Mrs. S. W. Lykins, Metropolitan Woman's Club of Lexington

CUSTARD OR ICE CREAM

2 cups sugar   1 tsp. vanilla (for custard)
2 heaping tbsp. flour   6 mashed bananas or 2 cups
3 qt. whole milk   mashed peaches or straw-
1 cup cream   berries with 1 cup sugar
6 eggs, well beaten   (for ice cream)

Mix sugar and flour. Add milk, cream, and eggs. Cook in the top of a double boiler, stirring until the mixture coats a silver spoon or until it just begins to thicken. Remove from heat and cool. For boiled custard, add vanilla and serve in glasses. For ice cream, add fruit and additional sugar; freeze.

Mrs. Ezra H. Webb, Bardwell Woman's Club

BAKED CUSTARD

1 qt. milk   ½ cup sugar
5 eggs   1 tsp. vanilla
pinch of salt

Scald milk in the top of a double boiler. Cool slightly. Beat eggs thoroughly, add salt, sugar, and vanilla. Pour slowly into the hot milk, stirring constantly. Pour into a 10- by 5- by 3-inch glass baking dish. Set the dish in a slightly larger pan with an inch of water in the bottom. Bake at 350° for 30 minutes, or until a silver knife inserted in the center comes out clean. Serves 8.

Mrs. Frances B. Berkshire, Florence Woman's Club

"MOONSHINE"

6 egg whites   1 tbsp. peach preserves,
6 tbsp. powdered sugar   chopped fine

Beat egg whites for 30 minutes, gradually adding powdered sugar. Then beat in chopped peach preserves. Set on ice until cold. Serve with thick cream flavored to suit taste.

Mrs. Joseph Hines, Somerset Woman's Club

A similar recipe called Angel's Food was found in *Housekeeping in the Blue Grass* (1874). It instructed the cook to pour thick custard into a serving bowl and spoon this topping over it. The beating time was, of course, without an electric beater.

CHARLOTTE RUSSE

Make a custard with the yolks of three eggs, a pint of morning's milk in which a vanilla bean has been boiled; sweeten to taste. Dissolve one half ounce of isinglass in one half pint of warm water and stir it into custard. When the custard is cool enough, stir in a quart of rich cream that has been well whipped, and seasoned with wine and sugar. Put into a glass bowl before it is congealed; lay on the top lady-fingers, and just before serving beat the whites of three eggs to a froth, mix with whipped cream, and pile on top. In summer use more isinglass.

Mrs. William Marsh, Maysville Woman's Club

This was one of Mrs. Marsh's grandmother's favorite recipes from *Housekeeping in the Blue Grass* (1874).

ORANGE CHARLOTTE

1⅓ tbsp. gelatin	3 tbsp. lemon juice
⅓ cup cold water	1 cup orange juice and pulp
⅓ cup boiling water	3 egg whites, beaten
1 cup sugar	½ cup cream, whipped

Soak gelatin in cold water, then dissolve in hot water. Add sugar, lemon juice, and orange juice and pulp. Chill. When thick and syrupy, beat until fluffy. Add beaten egg whites and fold in whipped cream.

Mrs. Dyer J. Lockwood, Highland Woman's Club, Louisville

If you want a more decorative dish, line a mold with orange slices, turn in the charlotte, smooth the top, and chill.

TRIFLE

Pastry cream:	sponge cake, pound cake,
⅔ cup sugar	or ladyfingers
⅓ cup flour	rum, sherry, or bourbon
5 egg yolks, slightly beaten	strawberry or raspberry
2 cups milk	jam
1 tbsp. butter	chopped walnuts
1½ tsp. vanilla	fruit (for decoration)

To make pastry cream, add sugar and flour to egg yolks. Heat milk slightly and add egg mixture. Return to heat and cook until thickened, stirring constantly. Remove from heat. Add butter and vanilla. Cool.

Line a suitable serving dish with slices of cake or ladyfingers. Moisten them well with the rum, sherry, or bourbon, and spread with jam. Spread half the pastry cream over the cake. Sprinkle with chopped walnuts. Repeat layers. Refrigerate 3-4 hours or longer. Before serving cover with whipped cream and decorate with fruit.

Mrs. A. W. Fullerton, Jr., Florence Woman's Club

OLD FASHIONED STRAWBERRY SHORTCAKE

The Muhlenberg County Strawberry Festival was begun in 1939 to direct attention to and stimulate interest in strawberry production. It was interrupted by World War II and was not resumed until 1959. Since then it has changed from a strawberry festival to a strawberry and coal festival, and more recently to a coal festival. In the early years there was judging of fresh strawberries, strawberry preserves, and canned strawberries. Contests for festival visitors included hog calling, greased pig relays, greased pole climbing, and husband and wife calling. Food served at the festival included old fashioned strawberry shortcake, strawberry ice, and strawberry pie.

2 cups flour	⅔ cup milk
1½ tsp. baking powder	½ tsp. vanilla extract
½ tsp. salt	butter
¾ cup sugar	1 qt. strawberries
5 tsp. lard	sugar

Sift dry ingredients together and blend in lard. Add milk and vanilla extract; stir well. Pat into a 10- by 12-inch pan. Bake at 425° for 15 minutes. Remove from oven, split, and butter generously. Serve at once with chilled sweetened strawberries between the layers and on top.

From THE GREENVILLE WOMAN'S CLUB COOKBOOK

INDIVIDUAL LEMON MERINGUES

Meringues:	¼ tsp. salt
3 egg whites	1 cup sugar
1¼ cups sifted sugar	2 cups water
2 tsp. baking powder	3 egg yolks
¼ tsp. vanilla	2 tbsp. butter
Lemon filling:	2 tsp. lemon rind, grated
6 tbsp. cornstarch	6 tbsp. lemon juice

Beat egg whites until stiff, gradually adding ¾ cup sugar. Sift remaining sugar with baking powder; fold into egg whites. Add vanilla. Cover a cookie sheet with unglazed paper. Spoon and shape six or eight meringues on the paper. Bake at 275° for 45 minutes. Remove from oven and let cool before filling.

Combine cornstarch, salt, and ½ cup sugar in the top of a double boiler; add water. Cook, stirring constantly, until thick. Beat egg yolks with remaining ½ cup sugar. Spoon a little of the hot mixture into egg yolks until all is added, return to double boiler, and cook for 5 minutes. Remove from heat and add butter, lemon rind, and lemon juice. Cool and pour into meringues. Serve with chocolate sauce if desired. Serves 6 to 8.

Mrs. Paul Wickliffe, K.F.W.C. President, 1935–1938

CHEESE CAKE

2   tbsp. finely chopped nuts
2   lb. cream cheese
1½ cups sugar

2   tbsp. lemon juice
6   large eggs

Butter the bottom and sides of a 9-inch springform pan and sprinkle nuts over the bottom. Beat cream cheese (at room temperature), gradually adding sugar and lemon juice. Then add eggs, one at a time, beating constantly. Pour into the prepared pan. Bake at 350° until the top cracks and browns slightly (45 minutes to 1 hour). The cake will puff up and then collapse. Keep refrigerated. Serves 12.

Jan Stewart, Bullitt County Woman's Club

UNCOOKED PERSIMMON PUDDING

1   cup persimmon pulp
½ cup sugar
1   cup chopped nuts

2½ cups graham cracker
     crumbs
12   marshmallows, cut fine

Mix all ingredients thoroughly and shape into a roll. Wrap in foil or plastic wrap and refrigerate 12 hours or longer. Slice and serve with whipped cream.

Mrs. Charles Dobbins, Crescent Hill Woman's Club

INDIA'S MERINGUE

7   egg whites
2   cups sugar
1   tsp. vinegar

1   tbsp. vanilla
½ pint whipped cream

Beat egg whites until quite stiff. Gradually fold in sugar, then vinegar and vanilla. Put the meringue in 2 ungreased 9-inch square pans. Bake at 275° for 1 hour. Turn off heat and allow meringue to dry in the oven another hour or more.

When completely cooled, spread one layer (still in its pan) with the whipped cream and invert the other pan over it, so that they form a closed container. Place in the refrigerator and leave 5 hours or more. When ready to serve, remove the top pan and you will have a 2-layered meringue. Cut it into squares and serve with ice cream and fresh strawberries or raspberries. It is a beautiful and delicious dessert.

Theresa E. Slavosky, Covington Art Club

COCONUT SNOWBALL CAKE

2 envelopes unflavored gelatin	3 envelopes dessert topping
4 tbsp. cold water	mix
1 cup boiling water	1 no. 2 can crushed
¾ cup sugar	pineapple, undrained
¾ tsp. salt	1 large angel food cake
juice of 1 lemon	1 can flaked coconut

Soften gelatin in cold water; add boiling water, sugar, salt, and lemon juice. Stir until gelatin is dissolved. Let cool. Prepare topping mix as directed on the package. Fold pineapple and half of topping into gelatin; chill until syrupy. Break cake into bite-size pieces. Line a large mixing bowl with waxed paper. Alternate layers of gelatin and cake in the bowl. Press down with a spoon after each layer of cake. Chill overnight. To serve, turn cake onto a cake plate, remove paper, and spread with remaining topping; sprinkle with coconut.

Miss Katherine Russell, Carrollton Woman's Club
Mrs. Joe Shields, Woman's Club of Frankfort
Mrs. John T. Tully, Radcliff Woman's Club

PINEAPPLE MACAROON ICEBOX DESSERT

This recipe was a favorite of the first Mrs. Alben Barkley, who often used it during her years in Washington.

1 cup butter	½ cup nuts
1 cup sugar	2 doz. ladyfingers
4 eggs	1 doz. macaroons
½ cup drained crushed	½ pint whipping cream
pineapple	

Cream butter and sugar thoroughly. Add eggs, one at a time, beating 5 minutes after each addition. Add pineapple and nuts. Cut ladyfingers in half lengthwise. Line the bottom of an 8- by 8-inch dish with half the ladyfingers. Spread with half the creamed mixture. Cover with crumbled macaroons. Spread with the rest of the creamed mixture. Cover with remaining ladyfingers. Refrigerate 48 hours. Serve with whipped cream. Serves 12.

Mrs. M. F. Osting, Woman's Club of Paducah

PINEAPPLE DESSERT

½ cup butter
1¼ cups sugar
2 egg yolks, slightly beaten
1 cup drained crushed
    pineapple

20 graham crackers
½ cup ground nut meats
   (optional)

Cream butter and sugar. Add egg yolks and pineapple. Roll graham crackers to make crumbs. In an 8- or 9-inch square pan, put a layer of crumbs, then half the pineapple mixture. Repeat layers. Top with crumbs. Leave covered in the refrigerator for 24 hours before serving.

Mrs. C. E. Kouts, Eddyville Woman's Club

Mrs. Kouts contributed this recipe at a World Service Guild recipe exchange in the 1930s. Forty years later, after moving to Kentucky, she saw the menu for an antiques show luncheon in Evansville, Indiana. The dessert was "Florence Kouts's Pineapple Dessert."

FRENCH PUDDING

½ cup butter
1½ cups confectioners' sugar
2 eggs
2 cups crushed vanilla wafers

1 no. 2 can crushed
   pineapple, drained
1 cup sweetened whipped
   cream
1 cup pecans, chopped

Beat together butter, sugar, and eggs. In a buttered pan place a layer of wafer crumbs. Add successive layers of butter mixture, pineapple, whipped cream, and nuts. Repeat layers until all ingredients are used. Refrigerate 24 hours. Top each serving with whipped cream, nuts, and half a maraschino cherry, if desired.

Mrs. Ida Murray, Horse Cave Woman's Club

ENGLISH TOFFEE PUDDING

½ cup butter
2 cups confectioners' sugar
2 tbsp. cocoa
¼ tsp. salt
2 eggs, separated

1 cup finely chopped nuts
1 tsp. vanilla
1¾ cups finely rolled vanilla
   wafer crumbs

Cream butter with sugar, cocoa, and salt. Add unbeaten egg yolks one at a time. Add nuts and vanilla. Beat egg whites until stiff and fold into the mixture. Put ¾ of the rolled wafers in the bottom of a greased oblong pan (about 7 by 9 inches). Add chocolate filling and top with remaining crumbs, patting them down. Refrigerate 24 hours or more. Cut into squares and serve with whipped cream.

Mildred A. Campbell, Caby M. Froman Woman's Club

CRUNCHY PIE

3 egg whites	1 cup finely chopped nuts
1 cup sugar	¾ cup graham cracker crumbs
1 tsp. baking powder	1 cup whipping cream

Beat egg whites until stiff; add sugar and baking powder gradually and continue beating. Fold in nuts and crumbs. Pour into a well-greased 9-inch pie tin. Bake at 350° for 30 minutes. Cool, cover with whipped cream, and refrigerate for at least 4 hours. Add additional whipped cream just before serving.

Mrs. Lyman Hall, Carrollton Woman's Club
Mrs. Thomas McCardwell, Falmouth Woman's Club

FROZEN CHEESE DESSERT

1 8-oz. pkg. cream cheese	pinch of salt
1 cup sugar	1 cup whipping cream, whipped
3 eggs, separated	vanilla wafer crumbs

With an electric mixer cream the cheese; beat in sugar, egg yolks, and salt. Beat egg whites separately. Fold whipped cream and then beaten egg whites into the cheese mixture. Line 2 buttered 9-inch pans with vanilla wafer crumbs. Pour in filling and cover with additional crumbs. Freeze. This dessert may be prepared 2 or 3 days ahead; it keeps well in the freezer. It is delicious when served with fresh strawberries or fresh peaches. Serves 12.

Mrs. Frank Straub, Woman's Club of Frankfort

SHERBET ICEBOX CAKE

2 envelopes dessert topping
        mix
12 coconut bar cookies, crushed

½ cup finely chopped nuts
3 pints sherbet, different
        flavors

Line a loaf pan with foil. Prepare topping mix according to package directions; fold in cookie crumbs and nuts. Allow sherbets to soften slightly. Alternate layers of whipped topping and sherbet in prepared pan, beginning and ending with whipped mixture. Freeze. Slice to serve.

Mrs. Fred Smith, Lexington Woman's Club

STRAWBERRY FROZEN DESSERT

1 cup flour
¼ cup brown sugar
½ cup nuts
½ cup melted butter
2 egg whites
1 cup sugar

1 pint strawberries or 1 10-oz.
        pkg. frozen berries
2 tbsp. lemon juice
1 pint prepared whipped
        topping

Combine flour, brown sugar, nuts, and melted butter. Bake at 350° for 20 minutes, stirring occasionally. Sprinkle ⅔ of this mixture in a 9-inch square pan. In a large bowl, beat egg whites to the soft peak stage, gradually beating in sugar. (If using frozen berries, reduce sugar to ½ cup.) Add strawberries and lemon juice; beat at least 10 minutes longer. Fold in whipped topping and spread over the nut mixture in the pan. Top with remaining nut mixture. Freeze until ready to serve. Serves 12.

Mrs. Alline McGinnis, Beechmont Woman's Club

OLD FASHIONED BLACKBERRY ICE CREAM

4 cups blackberries
2 cups sugar

4 cups heavy cream
4 tbsp. lemon juice

Crush the blackberries and force the pulp through a fine sieve to remove the seeds. Combine sugar and cream; stir until sugar is dissolved. Stir in berry puree and lemon juice. Freeze. Makes 2½ quarts.

Mrs. David Zachary, Carlisle Junior Woman's Club

CRANBERRY ICE

4 cups cranberries	1 tbsp. plain gelatin softened
4 cups water	in 2 tbsp. cold water
2 cups sugar	2 beaten egg whites (optional)
½ cup lemon juice	

Cook cranberries in 2 cups water in a 2-quart pan until soft. Run through a sieve and set aside. Boil together 2 cups water and the sugar for 10 minutes. Add softened gelatin to the hot syrup. Fold in cranberries and lemon juice. Cool. Freeze in two ice trays until mushy. Beat with an egg beater or at low speed with an electric mixer. Stiffly beaten egg whites may be added, if desired. Refreeze until ready to use. Serves 12.

Mrs. John R. Reid, Lawrenceburg Woman's Club

GRAPEFRUIT SHERBET

1 cup sugar	1 can grapefruit sections,
1 cup water	mashed
juice of 3 oranges	juice of 1 lemon

Dissolve sugar in water and boil 2 minutes. Let cool. Add remaining ingredients. Pour into a refrigerator tray immediately and freeze, stirring occasionally. This is delightful for a light dessert in hot weather. It is also good in drinks such as iced tea and ginger ale.

Mrs. Courtland F. Pollard, K.F.W.C. President, 1944–1946

STRAWBERRY ICE

2 qt. strawberries, crushed	2 egg whites, beaten
2 lb. sugar	

Mix strawberries and sugar; let stand for at least an hour to draw the juice. Strain. Measure the strained juice and add an equal amount of water. Pour into a freezer container. When partially frozen, add the stiffly beaten egg whites and continue freezing.

From THE GREENVILLE WOMAN'S CLUB COOKBOOK (1957)

KENTUCKY CREAM

2 quarts new milk
8 eggs, separated
1½ pounds sugar
2 tbsp. gelatine, dissolved
   in ½ cup milk
2 tbsp. vanilla

1 lb. raisins
1 pint strawberry preserves
1 quart rich cream, whipped
almonds, cocoanut, chopped
   citron (optional)

Take two quarts new milk, put on three pints to boil in a custard kettle, beat yolks and whites of eggs separately, mix the yolks with the remaining pint and stir slowly into the boiling milk, boil two minutes. Remove from stove, immediately add sugar, let it dissolve, strain while hot through a towel and add dissolved gelatine. Let custard cool, add vanilla and egg whites, put in freezer and as soon as it begins to freeze, add raisins, strawberry preserves, and whipped cream; stir and beat well like ice cream. Blanched almonds or grated cocoanut are additions. Some prefer currants to raisins, and some also add citron chopped fine.

Recipe of Mrs. J. B. McCreary, wife of Kentucky's governor (1875–1879);
contributed by Mrs. James Anderson, Carlisle Junior Woman's Club

VANILLA ICE CREAM

4 eggs
2½ cups sugar
4 cups light cream

6 cups milk
2 tbsp. vanilla
½ tsp. salt

Beat eggs until light. Add sugar gradually and beat until thickened. Add remaining ingredients and mix well. Freeze in a churn packed in 8 parts crushed ice to 1 part ice cream salt. (If no churn is available, this may be frozen in a hand-cranked freezer.) When mixture is frozen to a mush, remove the dasher. Cover and pack the churn in 4 parts ice to 1 part salt and allow the ice cream to harden for 3 hours. Makes 1 gallon.

Mrs. Victor Sams, Somerset Woman's Club

QUICK VANILLA ICE CREAM

2 cans sweetened condensed milk
6 cups fresh milk

2 tbsp. vanilla extract
fresh fruit (optional)

Place condensed milk in a large bowl; gradually stir in fresh milk. Add extract and fruit if you are using it; stir until smooth. Chill. Pour into a chilled 1-gallon ice cream freezer can. The mixture will not fill the can, but while freezing the ice cream will double in volume. Follow the operating instructions for your type of freezer.

Mrs. Herbert R. Ledford, Somerset Literary Club

INDIVIDUAL BROWNIE ALASKAS

1 pkg. fudge brownie mix
1 pint pink peppermint or strawberry ice cream

4 egg whites
½ cup sugar

Prepare and bake brownies according to package instructions. When cool, cut into 12 3-inch squares. Place on a baking sheet and top each with a small scoop of ice cream. Freeze 1 hour or longer. Heat the oven to 500°. Beat egg whites until foamy; add sugar, 1 tablespoonful at a time. Continue beating until the egg whites are stiff and glossy. Cover brownies and ice cream with meringue, sealing the edges thoroughly. Bake 3 to 4 minutes, or until meringue is light brown. Serves 12.

Carolyn Bradbury, Heritage Heights Woman's Club, Augusta

DESSERT TOPPINGS

KENTUCKY DELIGHT

½ lb. miniature marshmallows
½ cup bourbon

2 doz. almond macaroons, crumbled
1 pint heavy cream, whipped

Soak marshmallows in bourbon for 1 hour. Add macaroons and whipped cream. Chill slightly or serve immediately over angel food cake or ice cream. It can be kept refrigerated for 2 to 3 days or can be frozen. Serves 12 to 16.

Mrs. James A. Miner, Sr., Woman's Club of Madisonville

CARAMEL SAUCE

1 cup brown sugar   1½ cups boiling water
2 tbsp. butter

Combine all ingredients; stir until sugar is melted. Bring to a full boil. Remove from heat and serve hot over Woodford Pudding or any steamed pudding.

Mrs. I. D. Thompson, K.F.W.C. President, 1952–1954

CINNAMON SAUCE

1 tbsp. cornstarch   3 tbsp. butter
1 cup sugar   1 tsp. cinnamon
2 cups boiling water   1 tsp. lemon juice (optional)

Mix cornstarch with sugar. Add to boiling water and boil for 3 minutes. Remove from heat; add butter and cinnamon. When cool, add lemon juice if desired.

Mrs. John W. Stevens, Metropolitan Woman's Club of Lexington

DESSERT SAUCE

1 cup sugar   1 tbsp. butter
4 tbsp. flour   1 tbsp. nutmeg
1 cup hot water

Mix sugar and flour in a small pan, add hot water, and stir until sugar is dissolved. Add butter. Cook over low heat, stirring constantly, until sauce is thickened. Remove from heat and stir in nutmeg. Serve warm.

Shirley C. Greene, Eddyville Woman's Club

PUDDING SAUCE

1 egg   ½ cup cream
1 cup sugar   1 tbsp. whiskey

Combine egg, sugar, and cream in the top of a double boiler and cook for 10 minutes. When ready to serve, pour it over the whiskey in a serving dish. Serve over baked or steamed pudding or any kind of cake.

Mrs. Mamie Haycraft, Brandenburg Woman's Civic Club

HARD SAUCE I

2 cups confectioners' sugar   brandy or bourbon
1 cup butter

Cream sugar and butter. Add brandy or bourbon to tase. Serve
with baked or steamed pudding.

Mrs. Frances Cook, Ghent Woman's Club

HARD SAUCE II

1 cup light brown sugar   1 tsp. whiskey
½ cup butter

Sift sugar and beat it into the softened butter. Add whiskey. Serve
with baked or steamed pudding.

Mrs. Fillison L. Speiden, Jr., Woman's Club of St. Matthews

FRIENDSHIP CUP

2 cups sugar   2 cups fruit
1 cup brandy

Place sugar and brandy in a wide-mouth decanter with a tight fitting
stopper. Stir until sugar is dissolved. Add fruit. (Any well-drained
canned fruit, or any cut-up fresh fruit except apples, bananas, or
grapes, is usable.) Let stand untouched for 2 weeks. Serve over ice
cream. Replenish supply by adding 1 cup sugar and 1 cup fruit every
two weeks. Unless it is fed regularly it will spoil. As time passes you
will, by necessity, give a cup of the mixture to some friend as your
family's taste for the sauce wanes.

Eva Conner, Clinton County Woman's Club

Cakes

HICKORY NUT CAKE

Irvin Shrewsbury Cobb, journalist, author, and humorist, was born in Paducah on June 23, 1876. His first newspaper story appeared in the Paducah *Daily News* in 1893. His magazine career began in 1911 when he joined the staff of the *Saturday Evening Post*. His famous Judge Priest stories were published in several books, whose characters were easily recognizable as people he had known in Paducah.

Cobb made annual trips back home to see his mother and to hunt, fish, play poker, and swap stories with his cronies. He was inordinately fond of hickory nuts and each fall his mother picked out pounds of Scaly Barks and sent them to New York to be used in his favorite recipes, one of which was the hickory nut cake recipe that follows.

After his death in 1944, Cobb's ashes were placed at the roots of a dogwood tree in Oak Grove Cemetery, Paducah. The inscription on his marker reads: "Here in Paducah one encounters, I claim, an agreeable blend of western kindliness, northern enterprise superimposed on a southern background. Here, I claim, more chickens are fried, more hot biscuits eaten, more cornpone is consumed and more genuine hospitality is offered than in any town its size in the Commonwealth."

1   cup butter
3   cups sugar
1   cup dairy sour cream
4   cups flour
½ tsp. soda
1   tsp. cream of tartar

1   tsp. mace
½ tsp. freshly grated nutmeg
4   tbsp. bourbon
7   egg whites
1   cup white raisins
1   cup chopped hickory nuts

Cream butter with sugar; add sour cream and beat well. Sift the flour, measure, and sift again with soda, cream of tartar, and spices. Add to creamed mixture. Add bourbon and fold in the well-beaten egg whites. Fold in raisins and chopped nuts. Pour the batter into a greased and floured tube pan and bake at 300° for 2 hours or until done. When cake is completely cool, wrap in a cloth, pour a little whiskey over it, and store.

Mrs. M. F. Osting, Woman's Club of Paducah

PECAN CAKE

4   cups flour
1½ tsp. baking powder
2½ tsp. nutmeg
⅔ cup butter
2½ cups white sugar
1   cup brown sugar

6   eggs, separated
½ tsp. soda
½ cup buttermilk
1   cup bourbon
2   lb. pecans

Sift flour and measure. Set aside ½ cup for dredging nuts. Sift remaining flour with baking powder and nutmeg. Cream butter, add sugars gradually, and cream until light and fluffy. Add well-beaten egg yolks; beat well. Dissolve soda in buttermilk. Add buttermilk and bourbon to creamed mixture; blend thoroughly. Add pecans, either whole or broken, that have been dredged in flour. Fold in dry ingredients, adding about one-third at a time. Beat egg whites until stiff; fold into batter. Turn into a tube pan that has been greased and lined with waxed paper cut to fit smoothly. Cover with heavy parchment or waxed paper to extend about 1 inch over the edge of the pan; tie tightly. Steam 3 to 3½ hours. Remove from steamer and uncover. Brush with brown sugar glaze (page 248). Bake at 250° about 1½ hours. While still warm, brush again with glaze and wrap in a clean cloth that has been saturated with whiskey. Store in an airtight container.

Mrs. Dean Caton, Florence Woman's Club

MARTHA WASHINGTON'S CAKE

10 eggs, separated	1 tsp. mace
1 lb. butter	half a nutmeg, grated (1½ tsp.)
1 lb. confectioners' sugar	gill of wine (½ cup)
(3½ cups)	some good brandy
5 cups flour	1¼ lb. mixed candied fruit

Beat egg whites to a froth. Work butter to a cream; mix egg whites into the creamed butter, a spoonful at a time. Add confectioners' sugar, a few spoonfuls at a time. Add egg yolks, two at a time, beating well after each addition. Mix flour, mace, and nutmeg, and gradually add to the creamed mixture alternately with wine and brandy. Fold in candied fruit. Pour into a well greased and floured 10-inch tube pan and bake at 300° for 1½ hours.

Mrs. William C. Richards, Harlan Woman's Club

CHRISTMAS FRUIT CAKE

1 cup butter	2 tbsp. cloves
2 cups sugar	2 tbsp. cinnamon
4 eggs	1 cup jam
1 cup buttermilk	2 cups raisins
4 cups flour	2 cups currants
2 tsp. soda	1 cup nuts
2 tbsp. nutmeg	

Cream butter and sugar; add eggs one at a time, beating each in well. Add remaining ingredients in order given, beating well after each addition. Bake in 2 greased and floured 9-inch square pans at 375° for 25 minutes. Frost with fruit cake icing (page 246). The cake will be well seasoned if baked at Thanksgiving and stored in a tin with quartered apples until Christmas.

Mrs. J. B. Helm, Smith's Grove Woman's Club

Applesauce Cake: Omit buttermilk, fruits, and nuts. Reduce the spices to 1 tsp. each cloves and nutmeg, 1 tbsp. cinnamon. Add 1 more cup sugar, 2 cups unsweetened applesauce, and 1 tsp. vinegar. Bake at 350° for 45 minutes. Frost with caramel icing (page 245).

Mrs. Michael Ellis, Harrodsburg Woman's Club

CHRISTMAS CAKE

1 lb. butter	4 cups flour
5 cups sugar	1 tsp. cinnamon
12 eggs, separated	½ tsp. allspice
1 cup sorghum molasses	1 tsp. cloves
1 lb. raisins	1 cup buttermilk
1 box mincemeat	1 tsp. soda
1 lb. pecans	1 cup strong coffee

Cream butter with sugar; add beaten egg yolks and molasses. Clean raisins, crumble mincemeat, break pecans, and sift over them the flour to which the spices have been added. Dredge thoroughly before adding to creamed mixture. Stir in buttermilk and coffee. Finally, fold in stiffly beaten egg whites. Fill a well-greased tube pan, which has been lined with greased brown paper, two-thirds full. Bake at 300° for 3 to 4 hours with a pan of hot water on the lower shelf.

Mrs. Edna Jones, Bardwell Woman's Club

WHITE FRUIT CAKE

1 cup butter	1 lb. shelled almonds,
2¼ cups sugar	blanched and slivered
1 large fresh coconut, grated	¼ lb. citron, diced
12 egg whites	4 slices candied pineapple,
4 cups flour	cut in small wedges
2 heaping tsp. baking powder	¼ lb. candied red cherries

Cream butter and sugar until light and fluffy; add coconut and mix well. Beat egg whites until stiff but not dry. Sift flour and add to creamed mixture alternately with egg whites, beginning and ending with flour. Mix baking powder into the last ½ cup of flour before adding it. Stir in almonds, citron, and pineapple. Pour half the batter into a tube pan that has been lined with well-greased heavy brown paper. Carefully place cherries on the batter, but do not mix, or they will bleed and discolor the batter. Cover with remaining batter. Bake at 325° for 2 hours with a pan of hot water on the lower rack of the oven. Lightly cover with foil when cake begins to brown. Makes a 6-pound cake.

Mrs. Talmage Rogers, Greenville Woman's Club

OLD HARTFORD ELECTION CAKE

Five pounds sifted flour, two of butter, two of sugar, three gills distillery yeast or twice the quantity of home brewed, four eggs, gill of wine, gill of brandy, one quart sweet milk, half an ounce of nutmeg, two pounds raisins, one of citron; rub the butter and flour together very fine, add half the sugar, then the yeast and half the milk (hot in winter, blood-warm in summer), then add the eggs, then remainder of the milk, and the wine; beat well and let rise in a warm place all night; in the morning beat a long time, adding brandy, sugar, spice, and fruit well floured, and allow to rise again very light, after which put in cake pans and let rise ten or fifteen minutes; have the oven about as hot as for bread. This cake will keep any length of time. For raised cakes use potato yeast if fresh made; it is always a perfect success. This recipe is over one hundred years old.

From PRACTICAL HOUSEKEEPING (1886);
contributed by Miss Marie Gore, Clinton Woman's Club

BAKELESS FRUIT CAKE

1½ lb. graham crackers	½ cup candied pineapple
32 marshmallows	¾ cup candied cherries
1½ pints whipping cream	¼ cup chopped citron
¼ cup wine	¼ cup chopped figs
1 cup currants	2 tbsp. shredded orange peel
1 cup raisins	1 cup chopped dates
½ tsp. cinnamon	1 cup pecans
½ tsp. nutmeg	

Roll graham crackers to very fine crumbs. Cut marshmallows into small pieces. Whip the cream; add marshmallows and wine. Set aside. Wash currants and raisins; pour boiling water over them to cover; let soak. Place crumbs and spices in a large mixing bowl, mix thoroughly; add pineapple, cherries, and citron. Drain raisins and currants and roll in a towel to absorb moisture. Add to crumb mixture. With a wooden spoon stir in the whipped cream mixture. Add remaining fruits and nuts; if necessary, knead with your hands. When thoroughly mixed, pack into a loaf pan lined with 2 sheets of waxed paper. If desired, reserve some pineapple, cherries, and pecan halves for decoration. Refrigerate at least 24 hours before serving.

Mrs. William E. DeSpain, Woman's Club of Elizabethtown

BEER CAKE

3 cups flour	2 tsp. soda
1 tsp. salt	1 cup shortening
1 tsp. cinnamon	2 eggs
1 tsp. cloves	2 cups dates, chopped
1 tsp. allspice	1½ cups nuts, chopped
2 cups dark brown sugar, firmly packed	2 cups beer, at room temperature

Sift flour with salt and spices; set aside. Sprinkle soda over sugar and cream with shortening until light. Add eggs; beat until smooth. Add dates and nuts alternately with beer. Stir in sifted dry ingredients. Mix well and pour into a well-greased and floured 9-inch tube pan. Bake at 300° for 1½ hours.

Mrs. Pat Wilson, Danville Woman's Club

KENTUCKY POOR MAN'S CAKE

1 cup hog lard	2 tsp. cinnamon
2 cups sugar	1 tsp. cloves
4 cups flour	1 tsp. nutmeg
2 tsp. soda	2 cups buttermilk

Cream lard and sugar. Sift together dry ingredients and add to creamed mixture alternately with buttermilk. Bake in a greased tube pan at 350° for 1 hour.

Mrs. George Koppel, Pleasure Ridge Woman's Club, Louisville

For those not so poor, Mrs. M. L. Buckingham, Paducah, uses 1 pound of finely chopped salt pork with 2 cups boiling water poured over it in place of the lard, and 1 cup sorghum for the liquid. She adds 1 pound raisins and ¼ pound citron. The amount of flour is increased to 6 or 7 cups.

Mrs. Lena Holt, Maysville Woman's Club, uses the same ingredients as Mrs. Koppel, except that she substitutes brown sugar and adds currants, dates, figs, cherries, and English walnuts. Neither of these pork cakes uses butter, milk, or eggs, an economy measure of a hundred years ago.

LAUREL MOUNTAIN APPLESAUCE CAKE

3 cups unsweetened applesauce	1 or 2 cups raisins
2 cups sugar	1 or 2 cups walnuts
1 scant cup butter	1 cup jam or preserves
4 tsp. soda	4 cups flour
3 tsp. cinnamon	4 tsp. baking powder
2 tsp. cloves	2 tsp. vanilla

Combine first 9 ingredients and bring to a boil. Cook 5 minutes, stirring constantly. Let cool overnight. Add flour, baking powder, and vanilla. Bake in a large, well-greased tube pan at 350° for about 2 hours, with a pan of hot water on the lower shelf. After removing from pan, place a lace doily on top of cake. Sprinkle powdered sugar over doily, then carefully remove doily.

Mrs. Marianne Kiser, Lexington

Mrs. Lucian Hornsby, Highland Heights Woman's Club, omits the baking powder and vanilla; she uses the larger amount of nuts and raisins, and adds 2 cups dates and ¼ pound each candied cherries, pineapple, and citron. Bake in 4 loaf pans at 250° for 2 hours.

DRIED APPLE CAKE

3 cups dried apples	1 tsp. soda
3 cups molasses	1 tsp. cinnamon
1 cup butter	¼ tsp. cloves
1 cup raisins	½ tsp. nutmeg
3 cups flour	3 eggs

Soak apples overnight; drain and chop. Stew in molasses over medium heat until tender, about 30 minutes. Add butter and raisins; set aside to cool. Sift together dry ingredients; add to the cooled apple mixture and mix well. Beat in eggs. Pour into a well greased and floured tube pan. Bake at 325° for 1 hour.

Mrs. W. C. Richards, Harlan Woman's Club

Mrs. Carl Blackwell, Woman's Club of Madisonville, makes a similar cake using 2 cups sugar and 1 cup blackberry jam instead of molasses. All the dry ingredients, including the sugar, are creamed with the butter. Then the apples, jam, nuts, and raisins are added. Omit eggs.

BLACKBERRY CAKE

Blackberries are one of Kentucky's most common shrubs and are often considered a weed, especially by farmers. But a great many people find the fruits delicious and look forward to July, when they ripen. In 1948, Carlisle and Nicholas counties started a Homecoming Festival which evolved into the Blackberry Festival, held the first weekend in July. There is always a patriotic parade with bands and floats, a festival queen, and a fireworks display. On sale are blackberry jam, jelly, pies, and cakes, and homemade blackberry ice cream is sold by a local service club. The following blackberry cake is always a favorite:

1	cup shortening	2½	cups flour
2	cups sugar	2	tsp. soda
2	eggs	1	tsp. cloves
2	cups canned blackberries, undrained	1	tsp. cinnamon
		1	tsp. allspice

Cream shortening and sugar until light and fluffy; add eggs one at a time, beating well after each addition. Sift flour and measure; add soda and spices, and sift twice more. Add to creamed mixture alternately with blackberries. Pour into 2 well-greased and floured 9-inch cake pans. Bake at 350° for 25 to 30 minutes.

Mrs. George Powers, Williamstown Woman's Club

Mrs. Susie See, Louisa Woman's Club, uses drained blackberries and adds 2 tbsp. blackberry jelly.

Mrs. Anthony Walters, Elizabethtown Junior Woman's Club, adds 1 cup nuts and 1 cup raisins.

Mrs. David Zachary, Carlisle Junior Woman's Club, uses fresh blackberries, increases eggs to 3 and flour to 3 cups, and adds 3 tbsp. cocoa.

All cautioned the cook to fold, not beat, the blackberries into the batter.

ORANGE CAKE

1 cup butter	cream
2 cups sugar	4 cups flour
6 eggs	2 tsp. baking powder
2 large oranges	

Cream butter; add sugar gradually. Separate 3 of the eggs and set whites aside for icing. Add the 3 yolks and 3 remaining eggs to the creamed mixture. Grate the rind and squeeze the juice from the oranges. Measure the juice. In a separate cup measure enough cream for both to equal 1 cup. Sift flour; measure and sift again with baking powder. Add to creamed mixture alternately with liquids. Fold in grated rind. Pour into two greased and floured 9-inch round pans. Bake at 350° for 25 to 30 minutes.

Mrs. T. C. Carroll, K.F.W.C. President, 1938–1940

JAM CAKE

1 cup butter	3 tsp. cinnamon
2 cups sugar	1 cup buttermilk
4 eggs, beaten	1 cup blackberry jam
3 cups flour	1/4 cup orange juice
1 tsp. soda	1 cup raisins
1 tsp. allspice	1 cup chopped nuts

Cream butter and sugar until light and fluffy; add beaten eggs. Sift flour and measure; reserve 1/4 cup for dredging. Sift remaining flour with soda and spices. Add to creamed mixture alternately with buttermilk. Stir in jam and orange juice. Fold in raisins and nuts that have been dredged in reserved flour. Turn into a well-greased, lightly floured tube pan and bake at 350° for 1½ hours.

Joyce Williams, Ashland

Mrs. Jim Gates, Danville Woman's Club, makes the same basic cake, omitting the orange juice and adding 2 tbsp. cocoa.

Mrs. Ruth Scott, Eddyville Woman's Club, adds an additional egg, 1 cup black walnuts, 2 tsp. baking powder, and 1 more cup of jam. She also omits the orange juice. She separates the eggs and folds the beaten whites into the batter last.

JAM CAKE

1½ cups butter
2 cups sugar
6 eggs
¼ tsp. salt
4 cups flour
2 tbsp. cinnamon
2 tbsp. allspice
1 tsp. nutmeg

1 tsp. cloves
½ cup sour milk
1 cup blackberry jam
½ cup seedless raisins
½ cup chopped dates
1 cup cherry preserves, chopped

Cream butter and sugar until light and fluffy. Add eggs which have been beaten with salt; mix well. Sift flour with spices; add to creamed mixture alternately with milk, beating well after each addition. Fold in remaining ingredients and mix thoroughly. Turn into 3 well-greased and floured 9-inch round cake pans. Bake at 350° for 40 minutes. When layers are cooled, put fig filling (page 249) between layers; frost with caramel icing.

Mrs. W. Ed Hamilton, K.F.W.C. President, 1964–1966

Mrs. Malcolm Cross, Calvert City Woman's Club, uses the same basic recipe, decreasing the butter to 1 cup and increasing the milk to 1 cup and the jam to 2 cups. She also adds 2 tsp. soda.

Mrs. Hubert Fulks, Woman's Club of Elizabethtown, makes the same changes and uses 2 tsp. of each of the spices.

Mrs. Eugenia Bassett, Clinton County Woman's Club, makes a cake half the size of Mrs. Hamilton's and omits all spices except 1 tsp. cinnamon.

Mrs. George Martin, Greenville Woman's Club, substitutes 2 cups strawberry jam for blackberry jam and 1 cup milk for sour milk. She reduces the spices to ½ tsp. each and adds 2 tsp. soda. The eggs are beaten separately.

All omit the raisins, dates, and cherry preserves.

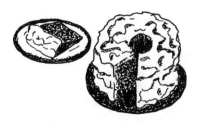

SPICED JAM CAKE

1½ cups butter	1 tsp. nutmeg
2 cups sugar	1 cup buttermilk
6 eggs, beaten separately	2 cups jam
4 cups flour	1 cup nuts, broken
2 tsp. soda	*Filling:*
2 tsp. cinnamon	1 cup sugar
2 tsp. allspice	½ cup milk
2 tsp. cloves	2 tbsp. butter

Cream butter and sugar until light and fluffy; add beaten egg yolks and mix thoroughly. Sift together flour, soda, and spices; add to creamed mixture alternately with buttermilk. Add jam and nuts; mix well. Fold in beaten egg whites. Remove 1½ cups of the batter and place in a saucepan. Turn remaining batter into 3 well-greased 8-inch round cake pans. Bake at 375° for 25 minutes. To the batter in the saucepan add filling ingredients. Cook until smooth and thick; spread between cooled layers and on top and sides of cake. It will keep the cake moist until ready to be frosted.

Mrs. Will Callison, Campbellsville Woman's Club

Mrs. Robert West, Florence Woman's Club, doubles the amount of jam and adds 2 tsp. cocoa. Her cake is baked in a tube pan at 300° for 1 hour and 15 minutes. She uses the filling as frosting.

Mrs. Deloris G. Sallengs, Radcliff Woman's Club, adds 1 cup raisins to batter. She bakes the cake in 3 layers at 325° for 40 minutes. Her recipe for filling is as follows:

¾ cup sugar	½ tsp. vanilla
½ cup flour	1 cup boiling water
1 tbsp. cocoa	2 tbsp. cake batter
1 tbsp. jam	¼ cup chopped dates
dash of cinnamon	⅓ cup chopped walnuts
dash of nutmeg	

Mix sugar, flour, cocoa, jam, spices, and flavoring; gradually add water; stir until smooth. Add remaining ingredients. Cook in the top of a double boiler until smooth and thick, stirring constantly. Let cool before spreading between cake layers. Frost with caramel icing (page 245).

WARTIME JAM CAKE

1½ cups buttermilk	1 tbsp. allspice
1½ tsp. soda	1 tbsp. cinnamon
2 cups flour	3 tbsp. butter
1 tsp. baking powder	1 cup sugar
1½ tbsp. cocoa	1 cup blackberry jam
1 tbsp. nutmeg	

Dissolve soda in buttermilk. Sift together flour, baking powder, cocoa, and spices. Cream butter and sugar; add jam, buttermilk, then dry ingredients. Turn into a well-greased 9- by 12-inch pan. Bake at 350° for 35 to 40 minutes.

During World War I eggs were scarce and none were used in this cake. For the same reason, sugar and butter were used sparingly.

Mrs. Lawrence Callaway, Younger Woman's Club of St. Matthews

KENTUCKY BLACKBERRY JAM CAKE

1 cup brown sugar	¼ tsp. cloves
½ cup butter	1 tsp. soda
1 cup blackberry jam	½ cup buttermilk
2 cups flour	2 eggs, well beaten
¼ tsp. cinnamon	1 cup nuts
¼ tsp. nutmeg	1½ cups seedless raisins

Cream sugar and butter; add jam and mix well. Sift flour with spices and soda; add to creamed mixture alternately with buttermilk. Blend well after each addition. Add eggs and nuts; mix well. Fold in raisins just before pouring into 2 greased and lightly floured 8-inch round cake pans. Bake at 350° for 45 to 50 minutes.

Mrs. Donald Thomas, Erlanger Junior Woman's Club

Mrs. Aubrey Moorman, Leitchfield Woman's Club, uses white sugar and increases the spices to ½ tsp. each.

Mrs. Charles Parks, Carlisle Junior Woman's Club, uses ¼ cup butter, 1 cup white sugar, and ½ cup brown sugar. She omits all spices except 1 tsp. cinnamon and adds 1 square melted unsweetened chocolate.

CELEBRATION CHOCOLATE CAKE

2⅓ cups sifted flour
1   4-oz. pkg. chocolate
    pudding mix
1   tsp. salt
1   tsp. soda
1½ cups firmly packed brown
    sugar

⅔ cup butter, softened
1   cup buttermilk
3   eggs
1   tsp. vanilla extract
¼   cup chopped walnuts
1   cup semisweet chocolate
    morsels

Sift together flour, pudding mix, salt, and soda in a large mixing bowl. Mix well. Add brown sugar, softened butter, and buttermilk. Beat with mixer on low speed for 1½ minutes. Add eggs and vanilla. Beat 1½ minutes longer. Stir in nuts. Spread in a well-greased and floured 9½- by 13-inch pan. Sprinkle chocolate morsels evenly over the batter. Bake at 350° for 30 to 35 minutes. Place the pan on a wire rack and allow to cool completely before frosting.

Mrs. Durie Chaney, Woman's Club of Elizabethtown

CHOCOLATE SYRUP CAKE

½ cup butter
1   cup sugar
4   eggs
½   tsp. vanilla

1   cup sifted flour
1   tsp. baking powder
1-lb. can chocolate syrup

Cream butter and sugar; add eggs and vanilla. Blend well. Sift together flour and baking powder and gradually add to creamed mixture. Stir in chocolate syrup. Bake in a greased 9- by 12-inch pan at 350° for 35 to 45 minutes. Do not overbake. Remove from oven and frost while hot.

Joyce Mae Hoskins, Berea Woman's Club

CHOCOLATE COOKIE SHEET CAKE

2   cups flour
2   cups sugar
½   cup shortening
1   cup water
4   tbsp. cocoa

2   eggs, beaten
1   cup buttermilk
1   tsp. soda
2   tsp. vanilla extract

Sift together flour and sugar. Combine and bring to a boil shortening, water, and cocoa. Pour over dry ingredients and beat well. Add eggs, buttermilk, soda, and vanilla extract; beat well again. Bake 20 minutes at 400° in a jelly roll pan. This cake will stay moist for days.

Mrs. Charles W. Jackson, Woman's Club of Elizabethtown

AUNT BESS T. C. CHERRY'S MAHOGANY CAKE

1 tsp. soda	½ cup butter
1 cup milk	1½ cups sugar
4 squares unsweetened	3 eggs
chocolate	2½ cups sifted flour

Dissolve soda in half the milk. Melt chocolate in the other half over low heat; set aside to cool. Cream butter and sugar until no longer grainy. Add one egg and beat well. Add flour alternately with milk and soda. Add remaining eggs, one at a time, beating thoroughly after each addition. Stir in melted chocolate. Pour batter into a lightly greased 9- by 12-inch pan or three 9-inch round pans. Bake at 350° for 20 to 30 minutes.

From THE HAND-ME-DOWN COOKBOOK,
by permission of Mrs. Frances Bradshear;
contributed by Mrs. Joseph Mayfield, Bowling Green Woman's Club

CHOCOLATE NUT CAKE

4 squares unsweetened	2 tsp. baking powder
chocolate	½ tsp. salt
½ cup butter	2 cups cake flour
2 cups sugar	1½ cups milk
2 eggs, separated	1 cup pecans, broken
1 tsp. vanilla	

Melt chocolate over hot water and allow to cool. Prepare two 9-inch round cake pans by greasing well and flouring lightly. Cream butter; add sugar and chocolate, then beaten egg yolks and vanilla. Sift dry ingredients together and add to creamed mixture alternately with milk. Add nuts and fold in stiffly beaten egg whites. Bake at 350° for 35 minutes.

Mrs. Gratton Varner, Woman's Club of Harrison County

SORGHUM CAKE

1 cup butter	2 tsp. soda
2 cups sorghum	2 cups sour milk
6 cups flour	4 eggs
2 tbsp. ginger	

Cream butter and sorghum. Sift flour with soda and ginger, add to creamed mixture alternately with sour milk. Beat in eggs. Bake in 2 greased 9- by 5-inch loaf pans at 350° for 50 to 60 minutes.

Mrs. Douglas Banks, Lewisport Woman's Club

GRANDMA'S MOLASSES CAKE

1 tbsp. shortening	½ tsp. nutmeg
1 cup sugar	1 tsp. soda
1 egg	1 cup hot black coffee
¾ cup molasses	1 cup raisins
2½ cups flour	1 cup chopped walnuts
pinch of salt	

Cream shortening, sugar, and egg; add molasses. Sift together flour, salt, and nutmeg. Put soda into coffee and add to creamed mixture alternately with flour. Fold in raisins and nuts; mix well. Pour into a well-greased, paper-lined 9-inch square pan. Bake at 325° for 45 to 50 minutes.

Mrs. S. C. Ross, Maysville Woman's Club

GINGERBREAD

½ cup shortening	1 tsp. soda
1 cup brown sugar	¼ tsp. salt
1 cup molasses	1½ tsp. ginger
2 eggs, well beaten	1 tsp. cloves
3 cups flour	1 tsp. cinnamon
2 tsp. baking powder	1 cup buttermilk

Cream shortening and sugar until light and fluffy; add molasses and beaten eggs. Sift dry ingredients together; add to creamed mixture alternately with buttermilk, beating thoroughly after each addition. Bake in greased and floured 10- by 14-inch pan at 350° for 30 to 40 minutes. When cool, serve with your favorite sauce or dip.

Mrs. Iva Duvall, Clinton County Woman's Club

LAFAYETTE GINGERBREAD

This gingerbread is supposed to have been served to the Marquis de LaFayette by George Washington's mother.

Cut in a pan ½ cup butter and ½ cup brown sugar. Beat these to a cream with paddle. Add 1 cup of West India molasses, 1 cup warm milk, 2 tablespoons of powdered ginger, 1 tablespoon cinnamon, nutmeg, and of mace mixed (not one of each), 1 wine glass coffee, 3 eggs beaten separately until light, 3 cups of flour, sift and stir alternately with beaten eggs into batter. Last mix the juice and rind of 1 orange. Dissolve one level teaspoon of soda in a little warm water and stir in. Beat until very light. 1 cup of raisins is a good addition. Bake in a moderate oven [350°, in a 9- by 13-inch pan].

Mrs. V. P. Henry, Columbia Woman's Club

For the same flavor and much less effort, add 1 tsp. instant coffee, 1 tsp. mace, and 1 tsp. grated orange rind to a package of gingerbread mix. Make and bake according to package instructions, substituting ½ cup orange juice for part of the liquid.

WHITE CAKE

1 cup butter	1 cup milk
2 cups sugar	1 tsp. vanilla
4 cups flour	8 egg whites
2 heaping tsp. baking powder	

Grease and lightly flour three 8-inch round pans. Preheat oven to 375°. Have all ingredients at room temperature. Cream butter well; add sifted sugar gradually, creaming until very light. Sift flour, measure, and sift again with baking powder. Add flour to creamed mixture alternately with milk, about one-third at a time. Beat in vanilla. Beat egg whites until stiff but not dry. Fold lightly into batter. Pour into prepared pans and bake for 25 minutes.

Mrs. Joseph Buchanan, Prestonsburg Woman's Club

Mrs. W. L. Greenup, Florence Woman's Club, reduces the butter to ⅔ cup and uses only 6 egg whites.

At Christmastime, Mrs. Carl Evans, LaCenter Woman's Club, fills and frosts her white cake with 3 cups sweetened whipped cream and the meat of a freshly grated coconut.

COCONUT CAKE

2 cups sugar	1 tsp. salt
1 cup shortening	1 can grated coconut
5 eggs	*Glaze:*
1 tsp. coconut extract	1 cup sugar
1 cup buttermilk	½ cup water
2 cups flour	1 tsp. coconut extract
½ tsp. baking powder	

Cream sugar and shortening. Add eggs, one at a time, beating 2 minutes after each addition. Add coconut extract, buttermilk, and flour which has been sifted with baking powder and salt. Add coconut. Stir until well mixed, then beat 2 to 2½ minutes with an electric mixer. Bake in a 10-inch tube pan at 350° for 1 hour.

For glaze, mix sugar and water. Boil 1 minute. Stir in coconut extract. Pour over hot cake while still in the pan. Let cool completely before removing from pan.

Mrs. Charlene O'Daniel, Louisa Woman's Club

SPONGE CAKE

6 egg yolks	*Custard:*
1 cup sugar	1 cup sugar
½ cup boiling water	⅓ cup flour
1½ cups cake flour	3 egg yolks
2 tsp. baking powder	2 cups milk, scalded
½ tsp. salt	1 tsp. vanilla or lemon
1 tsp. vanilla or lemon extract	extract

Beat egg yolks with a rotary beater; add sugar gradually, then add boiling water, beating after each addition. Add flour, baking powder and salt which have been sifted together. Beat thoroughly. Beat in flavoring. Pour into two ungreased 8- or 9-inch round pans and bake at 325° for 25 minutes.

To make the custard, mix sugar and flour; add beaten egg yolks and stir into scalded milk. Cook over medium heat, stirring constantly, until thick. Remove from heat, add flavoring, and allow to cool. Spread over cooled layers, using as both filling and frosting.

Mrs. W. M. Bright, Stanford Woman's Club

PINEAPPLE SPONGE CAKE

1 cup brown sugar	1½ cups flour
3 tbsp. butter	1½ tsp. baking powder
1 cup crushed pineapple	pinch of salt
3 eggs	1 tsp. vanilla
1½ cups sugar	

Drain pineapple; reserve juice. Heat brown sugar and butter in an iron skillet until it foams; remove from heat and spread pineapple evenly over the mixture. Set aside while preparing batter.

Separate eggs. Beat yolks with sugar. Sift flour with baking powder and salt; add to yolks and sugar alternately with ½ cup of reserved pineapple juice. Stir in vanilla. Fold in stiffly beaten egg whites. Pour over pineapple. Bake at 350° for 1 hour. Take from oven and allow to cool 1 minute; then invert onto a cake plate.

Mrs. Donald W. Dammert, K.F.W.C. President, 1974–1976

MOSS ROSE CAKE

2 cups cake flour	2 cups sugar
2 tsp. baking powder	1 cup scalded milk
½ tsp. salt	½ tsp. almond extract
4 eggs	

Sift flour, measure, and sift again with baking powder and salt. Beat eggs, adding sugar gradually; continue beating until mixture holds soft peaks. Fold in flour. Add hot milk gradually, mixing quickly. Add extract and beat until smooth. Batter will be thin. Turn into two 8-inch square pans lined with waxed paper and lightly greased. Bake at 350° for 25 to 30 minutes. Frost with moss rose icing (page 244).

Mrs. David Rippetoe, Valley Woman's Club, Louisville

ANGEL FOOD CAKE

1 cup cake flour	1½ tsp. cream of tartar
1½ cups plus 2 tbsp. sugar	¼ tsp. salt
1½ cups egg whites	1 tsp. vanilla

Sift flour; measure; sift again with ¾ cup plus 2 tbsp. sugar. Sift 3 more times. If egg whites are cold let them stand until they have warmed to room temperature. Then beat them until frothy; sprinkle over them cream of tartar and salt. Continue beating, gradually adding remaining ¾ cup sugar, 2 tablespoonfuls at a time. Beat until meringue is stiff enough to form peaks. Fold in vanilla. Fold in flour and sugar mixture with a wire whip, sifting about ¼ cup at a time over the surface. Turn into an ungreased 10-inch tube pan. Gently cut through batter with a knife. Bake in a preheated oven at 375° for 30 to 35 minutes. Invert pan and leave until cool, about 2 hours.

Mrs. Levona Bradford, Butler Woman's Club

Mrs. Joe R. Hines, Somerset Woman's Club, adds a few drops of almond extract and frosts her cake with pink fondant icing (page 244).

YELLOW ANGEL FOOD CAKE

1½ cups sugar	pinch of salt
½ cup water	1 cup flour
6 eggs, separated	¾ tsp. cream of tartar

Cook sugar and water together until it spins a thread (230° to 234°). Beat egg whites with salt until stiff. Pour syrup in a fine stream over egg whites, beating constantly until mixture is cool. Add well-beaten egg yolks. Fold in flour that has been sifted with cream of tartar. Pour into an ungreased 10-inch tube pan. Bake at 250° for 55 minutes. Invert pan until completely cooled.

Mrs. Harry Carl, Sr., Erlanger Woman's Club

CHOCOLATE POUND CAKE

3 cups flour	½ cup shortening
¼ tsp. salt	3 cups sugar
½ tsp. baking powder	5 eggs
½ cup cocoa	1 cup milk
1 cup butter	1 tsp. vanilla extract

Sift flour; measure and sift again with salt, baking powder, and cocoa. Cream butter and shortening; add sugar and beat thoroughly. Add eggs, one at a time, beating well after each addition. Add sifted dry ingredients alternately with milk. Stir in vanilla. Bake in a greased and lightly floured tube pan at 325° for 1½ hours.

Mrs. Wallace Shockley, Fountain Run Woman's Club

Brown Sugar Pound Cake: Omit cocoa, increase baking powder to 2 tsp., and substitute 2 cups brown sugar for 2 cups white sugar. Bake as above; while still warm, punch holes in cake and pour over it uncooked rum glaze (page 248).

Mrs. Romanza O. Johnson, Bowling Green Woman's Club

Mrs. J. Robert West, Florence Woman's Club, uses 6 eggs in her brown sugar pound cake and frosts it with caramel icing (page 245).

OLD FASHIONED POUND CAKE

1 cup butter	2 tsp. baking powder
2 cups sugar	1 cup milk
3 eggs	2 tsp. vanilla extract
3 cups flour	1 tsp. almond extract

Cream butter; add sugar gradually, beating at least 10 minutes. Add eggs, one at a time, beating thoroughly after each addition. Sift flour; measure and sift again. Mix ½ cup flour with baking powder and set aside. Add remaining flour to creamed mixture alternately with milk. Add flavorings. Sift reserved flour over batter and stir, do not beat, until smooth. Pour into a well-greased and floured tube pan. Bake at 325° for 1 hour or until golden brown.

Eleanor H. Bruce, Woman's Club of St. Matthews

Mrs. Jesse Brewer, Twentieth Century Woman's Club, Smithland, substitutes buttermilk with ½ tsp. soda for milk, and 1 tsp. lemon extract for flavorings. She increases eggs to 5 and decreases baking powder to 1 tsp.

Mrs. Mary Alice Jayne, Morehead Woman's Club, varies the flavor by using 1 tsp. vanilla plus ½ tsp. nutmeg, or 1 tsp. rum extract plus ½ tsp. mace.

Mrs. Marow Cox, Ossoli Woman's Club, Corbin, beats the egg yolks and whites separately, adding 6 tbsp. of the sugar to the whites and folding them in last.

GRANDMA'S POUND CAKE

1 lb. flour (4 cups)	1 lb. sugar (2 cups)
1 lb. butter (2 cups)	10 eggs, separated

Sift flour; measure and sift again. Cream butter, add sugar gradually, and continue beating until light and fluffy. Add egg yolks that have been beaten until thick and lemon-colored. Beat thoroughly. Beat egg whites until stiff but not dry. Add to the creamed mixture alternately with the flour. Beat until smooth. Long beating of air into the batter is necessary for success in making this cake. Pour into a greased tube pan; bake at 325° for 2 hours.

Mrs. Minnie H. Dobbs, Monticello Woman's Club

MOLASSES POUND CAKE

½ cup seeded raisins	¼ tsp. mace
⅓ cup citron	⅔ cup butter
2 cups plus 2 tbsp. flour	¾ cup sugar
¾ tsp. soda	2 eggs
1 tsp. cinnamon	⅔ cup milk
½ tsp. allspice	⅔ cup molasses
¼ tsp. cloves	

Chop raisins and citron into small pieces; dredge in 2 tbsp. flour. Sift remaining flour with soda and spices. Cream butter; add sugar gradually, beating vigorously. Add well-beaten eggs, milk, and molasses. Stir in dry ingredients, then fold in fruit. Turn into a well-greased 10-inch tube pan. Bake at 350° for 50 minutes.

Mrs. George Bauer, Woman's Club of Elizabethtown

APPLE BUTTER STACK CAKE

4 cups flour	1 cup sugar
1 tsp. salt	1 cup sorghum
½ tsp. soda	3 eggs
2 tsp. baking powder	1 cup milk
¾ cup lard or margarine	

Sift together dry ingredients. Cream lard and add sugar gradually, beating well. Add sorghum and beat vigorously. Add eggs, one at a time, beating after each addition. Stir in dry ingredients alternately with milk. Beat until smooth. This makes six 9-inch layers. If you are using three pans divide the batter in half; if you have only two pans divide it in thirds. Pour the batter into greased and floured pans and bake at 350° for 15 to 20 minutes. Refrigerate remaining batter while waiting to reuse the pans. When all layers are baked and cooled, stack them, using ½ cup homemade apple butter between layers and on top.

Mrs. S. H. Buckley, Westwood Woman's Club, Ashland

Mrs. Oscar C. Sowards, K.F.W.C. President, 1968–1970, makes a similar stack cake but uses boiling water instead of milk. She measures her batter by placing 8 tbsp. (½ cup) batter in each pan.

MOLASSES STACK CAKE

1½ tsp. soda	⅔ cup shortening
1 cup Kentucky sorghum	1 tsp. cinnamon
½ tsp. salt	1 tsp. ginger
1 cup brown sugar, firmly	½ tsp. nutmeg
packed	½ tsp. allspice or cloves
2 eggs	3 to 4 cups flour, as needed
1 cup buttermilk	

Stir soda into sorghum; add salt. Then add all other ingredients except flour. Mix well. Add just enough sifted flour to make the batter stiff enough to roll. Knead as little as possible. Divide dough into 6 parts. Roll each to ¼ inch thickness to fit 9-inch pans. Bake in well-greased and floured pans at 350° for 25 minutes. Stack, using dried apple filling (page 248) between the layers.

Mrs. Gladys Osborne, Stanford Woman's Club

Mrs. Elizabeth Tipton, Erlanger Woman's Club, bakes her stack cake in cast iron skillets.

Mrs. Arnold Beard, Bardwell Woman's Club, cuts hers using a plate for a pattern and bakes the layers on cookie sheets.

Mrs. Daisy Cross, Clinton County Woman's Club, advises letting both filling and cake cool completely before stacking to avoid a soggy cake.

Mrs. James D. Bolen, Ashland Junior Woman's Club, suggests trimming the cake to form a pentagon. Pieces then are cut alternately from the five sides so it will retain its shape.

All who contributed stack cake recipes agree that it tastes better on the second day but should be kept in the refrigerator or other cool place after the first day.

RUM CAKE

½ cup chopped pecans	½ cup light rum
1 pkg. butter cake mix	½ cup water
1 3¾-oz. pkg. vanilla instant	½ cup oil
pudding mix	4 eggs

Sprinkle nuts in the bottom of a well-oiled bundt pan. In a large mixing bowl blend cake mix and pudding mix. Add rum, water, oil, and eggs; beat at medium speed for 2 minutes. Pour into prepared pan and bake at 325° for 50 to 60 minutes. With an icepick or 2-tined fork, punch holes in the cake, then pour hot rum glaze (page 247) over the hot cake. Let stand 30 minutes before serving.

Mrs. Melvin Hart, Falmouth Woman's Club

Mrs. C. W. Gleaves, Lexington Woman's Club, makes a similar cake using sherry or orange juice instead of rum. She also adds ¼ cup sugar and 2 tsp. cinnamon to the nuts, and uses vanilla glaze (page 248).

APPLE CAKE

1½ cups oil	1 tsp. soda
2 cups sugar	2 tsp. baking powder
2 large eggs	1 cup chopped pecans
2½ cups flour	3 cups chopped raw apples
1 tsp. salt	1 tsp. vanilla

Pour oil into a large mixing bowl. Add sugar and eggs; beat until creamy. Sift flour and measure; sift again with salt, soda, and baking powder. Add to creamed mixture, about ¼ cup at a time, beating well after each addition. Batter will be stiff. Fold in nuts, apples, and vanilla. Spread evenly in a greased and floured 9- by 13-inch pan. Bake at 350° for 55 minutes.

Topping:

2½ cups miniature	1 no. 2½ can crushed
marshmallows	pineapple, undrained
	1 cup coconut
	1 pint whipping cream

Combine marshmallows and pineapple; let stand in refrigerator overnight. Next day, beat until smooth. Add coconut. Whip the cream and fold into mixture. Serve on individual pieces of cake.

Mrs. Sue Stivers, Columbia Woman's Club

CARROT CAKE

3 cups flour	1½ cups chopped pecans
2 tsp. soda	1 8-oz. can crushed
2 tsp. cinnamon	pineapple, undrained
1 tsp. salt	½ cup chopped dates
1¼ cups oil	3 eggs, well beaten
2 cups sugar	2 tsp. vanilla
2 cups grated carrots	

Sift together dry ingredients. Beat together oil and sugar; add half the dry ingredients and beat well. Beat in carrots, pecans, pineapple, and dates. Add remaining dry ingredients; beat until well blended. Add eggs and beat well. Add vanilla. Line the bottom of two 9- by 5-inch loaf pans with brown paper; lightly grease and flour the pans. Pour batter in pans; bake in a preheated 350° oven 1 hour. Cool 10 minutes before removing from pans. Frost with cream cheese frosting (page 247).

Mrs. Charles Hembree, Lexington Woman's Club

PUMPKIN WALNUT CAKE

3 cups flour	2 cups sugar
2 tsp. baking powder	1½ cups corn oil
2 tsp. soda	2 cups mashed pumpkin
1 tsp. salt	1 cup coarsely chopped
3½ tsp. cinnamon	walnuts
4 large eggs	

Sift flour and measure. Add baking powder, soda, salt, and cinnamon; sift again. In a large mixing bowl, beat eggs with electric mixer until yolks and whites are combined. Gradually add sugar, beating until thick and lemon-colored. Pour in oil, beating constantly. With mixer at low speed, blend in dry ingredients alternately with pumpkin; beat until smooth after each addition. Stir in walnuts. Turn into an ungreased 10-inch tube pan. Bake in a preheated oven at 350° for 1 hour and 10 minutes. Place on a wire rack and allow to cool completely before removing from pan. If desired, sprinkle with confectioners' sugar.

Mrs. Janet Chambers, Cave City Younger Woman's Club

PRUNE CAKE WITH BUTTERMILK SAUCE

2   cups sugar
1   cup oil
3   eggs
1   cup buttermilk
1   tsp. cinnamon
1   tsp. cloves
1   tsp. allspice

1   tsp. soda
½   tsp. salt
2   cups flour
1   tsp. vanilla extract
1   cup nuts
2   jars strained baby prunes

Cream sugar and oil. Add eggs, then buttermilk. Beat well. Sift together dry ingredients and add to creamed mixture. Stir in extract, nuts, and prunes. Pour into a well-greased bundt pan. Bake at 350° for 50 to 60 minutes. When cake has baked for 50 minutes begin making the sauce.

Sauce:
1   cup sugar
½   cup margarine

1   tbsp. light corn syrup
1   tsp. soda
½   cup buttermilk

Combine ingredients and cook in an iron skillet over low heat, stirring constantly for 5 minutes or until a soft ball forms when tested in water (234° to 240°). Pour over hot cake.

Mrs. William H. Layne, Morehead Woman's Club

Mrs. Lyman Hall, Carrollton Woman's Club, cooks and purees 20 prunes.

Mrs. C. E. Kouts, Eddyville Woman's Club, substitutes baby plums.

RING-OF-COCONUT FUDGE CAKE

Filling:
¼   cup sugar
1   tsp. vanilla
1   8-oz. pkg. cream cheese
1   egg
½   cup flaked coconut
1   6-oz. pkg. milk chocolate
     morsels
Cake:
2   cups sugar
1   cup oil

2   eggs
3   cups flour
¾   cup unsweetened cocoa
2   tsp. soda
2   tsp. baking powder
1½ tsp. salt
1   cup hot coffee or hot water
1   cup buttermilk
1   tsp. vanilla
½   cup chopped nuts

Generously grease and flour a 10-inch tube pan.

Prepare filling: In a small mixer bowl, beat sugar, vanilla, cream cheese, and egg until smooth. Stir in coconut and chocolate morsels. Set aside while making cake.

In the large mixer bowl, combine sugar, oil, and eggs; beat 1 minute at high speed. Add remaining cake ingredients except nuts; beat 3 minutes at medium speed, scraping bowl occasionally. Stir in nuts. Pour half of batter into prepared pan. Carefully spoon prepared filling over batter; top with remaining batter. Bake at 350° for 70 to 75 minutes, or until top springs back when lightly touched in center. Cool upright in pan for 15 minutes. Remove from pan, place on a cake rack, and cool completely. Drizzle with chocolate glaze (page 248).

Mrs. Jimmie Maupin, Clinton County Woman's Club

AUNT MYRTLE'S SWEET MUFFINS

⅓ cup shortening	1 4/5 cups self-rising flour,
1 cup sugar	sifted
1 egg	1 tsp. vanilla
½ cup buttermilk	

Cream shortening and sugar; add egg and beat well. Add buttermilk, flour, and vanilla. Beat again. Fill muffin cups and bake at 350° until light brown, about 20 to 25 minutes. Makes 18 average size muffins.

Mrs. Jewell Thomas, Cumberland County Woman's Club

CUP CAKES

¼ cup shortening	½ tsp. salt
1 cup cake flour	6 tbsp. milk
½ cup sugar	2 egg yolks
1¼ tsp. baking powder	½ tsp. vanilla

Stir shortening to soften. Add flour, sugar, baking powder, and salt which have been sifted together. Add 3 tbsp. milk and egg yolks; stir until flour is dampened, then beat at slow speed with electric mixer for 2 minutes. Add remaining milk; beat 1 minute longer. Fill greased muffin cups half full and bake at 375° for 18 to 20 minutes. Makes 12.

Mrs. Malcolm Cross, Calvert City Woman's Club

FROSTINGS AND FILLINGS

FONDANT ICING

3 cups sugar   1 cup cream

Boil sugar and cream over low heat until a soft ball forms when dropped in cold water (234° to 240°). Remove from heat, let cool, then beat until creamy. If desired, add a few drops of food coloring. When icing small cakes or angel food cake, place over a pan of boiling water and stir until melted. Dip small cakes with a fork; pour over angel food.

Mrs. Joe R. Hines, Somerset Woman's Club

To frost Mrs. Cherry's mahogany cake (page 231) use a half recipe. If using milk instead of cream, add butter the size of an egg, about 4 tbsp.

BOILED ICING

2 cups sugar   2 egg whites
⅔ cup water   4 marshmallows
¼ tsp. cream of tartar   1 tsp. vanilla

Mix thoroughly in a saucepan the sugar, water, and cream of tartar. Boil slowly without stirring until syrup spins a thread (230° to 234°). While syrup is cooking, beat egg whites until stiff enough to hold a point. Pour all but 2 tbsp. hot syrup into egg whites very slowly in a thin stream, beating constantly. Add marshmallows and vanilla. While beating continues, return pan to heat and scorch remaining syrup to a golden brown. Quickly add it to the frosting.

Mrs. H. R. White, Williamsburg Woman's Club

Sea Foam Icing: Substitute 1 cup brown sugar for 1 cup white sugar, and 1 tbsp. white corn syrup for cream of tartar. Omit marshmallows and scorching step.

Mrs. Susie D. See, Louisa Woman's Club

Moss Rose Icing: Make boiled icing, omitting marshmallows and scorching step. Mix 1½ cups moist shredded coconut, 3 tbsp. orange juice, ¼ tsp. grated orange rind, and 1 tsp. sugar. Let soak while frosting the cake. Then squeeze moisture from the coconut and pat onto set but not hard frosting.

Mrs. David Rippetoe, Valley Woman's Club

CARAMEL ICING

½ cup butter
1 cup brown sugar

¼ cup milk
1½ cups confectioners' sugar

Cook butter, brown sugar, and milk until slightly thickened, about 1 minute. Remove from heat and let cool. Add confectioners' sugar and beat until smooth and thick.

Mrs. Michael Ellis, Harrodsburg Woman's Club

Mrs. Deloris Sallengs, Radcliff Woman's Club, increases the milk to ⅓ cup and boils the mixture for 2 minutes, then immediately stirs in 2 cups confectioners' sugar.

Mrs. Donald Thomas, Erlanger Junior Woman's Club, reduces the butter to ¼ cup, increases the milk to 6 tbsp., the confectioners' sugar to 2 cups. She adds 1 cup of sugar to the boiled mixture immediately, and the second cup when it has cooled slightly.

Mrs. J. Robert West, Florence Woman's Club, boils the brown sugar and butter for 1 minute, adds ½ cup milk, and boils for 2 minutes longer. She adds 2 cups confectioners' sugar to the cooled mixture.

NEVER FAIL CARAMEL ICING

6 tbsp. brown sugar
6 tbsp. white sugar
3 tbsp. butter
½ cup evaporated milk

9 large marshmallows
1½ tsp. vanilla
1½ cups confectioners' sugar

Mix the brown and white sugar; add butter and milk. Bring to a boil and cook 2 minutes. Remove from heat; add marshmallows and beat until they are melted. Add vanilla and confectioners' sugar; beat until frosting is of a good spreading consistency.

Mrs. William Dudderar, Stanford Woman's Club

CARAMEL BUTTERMILK FROSTING

½ cup butter
2 cups white sugar
1 cup brown sugar

1 cup buttermilk
1 tsp. soda

Combine all ingredients and cook over low heat to very soft ball stage (234°). Cool, then beat until thick enough to spread.

Mrs. Shelley Caulder, Buechel Woman's Club

CARAMEL FILLING

3 cups sugar   ⅓ cup butter
½ cup milk

In a heavy skillet caramelize the sugar; very slowly add milk and butter. Cook until syrup reaches the soft ball stage (234° to 240°). Remove from heat; cool before beating. Use to "dress" a layered jam cake.

Mrs. Thomas Shumate, Woman's Club of Richmond

FRUIT CAKE ICING

5 cups brown sugar   ½ lb. citron
2 tbsp. butter   2 lb. figs
1 cup water   1 lb. English walnuts (before
2 tsp. vanilla   shelling)
1 lb. raisins   1 lb. almonds (before shelling)

Boil brown sugar, butter, and water for 2 to 3 minutes. Remove from heat; add vanilla, fruits, and nuts. Beat well. Spread between layers and on sides and top of fruit cake.

Mrs. J. B. Helm, Smith's Grove Woman's Club

FLUFFY CHOCOLATE FROSTING

½ cup butter   2 egg whites
⅛ tsp. salt   3 squares unsweetened
1 tsp. vanilla   chocolate, melted
1 lb. confectioners' sugar,   2 to 3 tbsp. milk
      sifted

Cream butter with salt and vanilla. Add sugar and egg whites alternately, beating well after each addition. Add chocolate and beat well; gradually beat in milk until frosting is smooth.

Mrs. Morris Miller, Woman's Club of Elizabethtown

Mrs. Wallace Shockley, Fountain Run Woman's Club, uses 2 egg yolks instead of egg whites.

Mrs. Gratton Varner, Woman's Club of Harrison County, uses 1 whole egg, reduces the chocolate to 2 squares, and adds 1 tsp. lemon juice and 1 cup chopped nuts.

CHOCOLATE FROSTING

½ cup butter
6 tbsp. milk
3 tbsp. cocoa

1 lb. confectioners' sugar
1 tsp. vanilla

Place butter, milk, and cocoa in a saucepan; bring to a rapid boil. Remove from heat and add sugar and vanilla. Beat until smooth.

Mrs. Charles Jackson, Woman's Club of Elizabethtown

Mrs. Durie Chaney from the same club substitutes 1 6-oz. package semisweet chocolate morsels and reduces the butter to ¼ cup. She only heats the mixture enough to melt the chocolate.

Mrs. Talmage Rogers, Greenville Woman's Club, substitutes strong coffee for the milk and adds one egg to make a mocha frosting. She mixes everything at room temperature.

CREAM CHEESE FROSTING

1 3-oz. pkg. cream cheese
1 tbsp. butter

2 cups confectioners' sugar
1 tsp. vanilla

Cream all ingredients until smooth.

Mrs. Herbert Steely, Williamsburg Woman's Club
Mrs. J. C. Wells, Lackey Garrett Wayland Woman's Club

ORANGE GLAZE

2 cups confectioners' sugar
¼ cup margarine

½ cup orange juice

Blend sugar and margarine that has been softened to room temperature. Add orange juice. Spread on cake or use as a topping for waffles.

Mrs. Bessie Kerns, Jackson County Woman's Club

RUM GLAZE

1 cup sugar
¼ cup water

¼ cup light rum
¼ cup butter

Mix in a saucepan and boil 3 minutes. Pour over cake while hot.

Mrs. Melvin Hart, Falmouth Woman's Club

CHOCOLATE GLAZE

1 cup confectioners' sugar
3 tbsp. cocoa
2 tbsp. butter

2 tsp. vanilla
3 tbsp. hot water

Combine all ingredients and mix well.

Mrs. Jimmie Maupin, Clinton County Woman's Club

VANILLA GLAZE

1 cup confectioners' sugar
2 tbsp. milk

½ tsp. butter flavoring
½ tsp. vanilla

Sift sugar into a bowl; moisten with milk to spreading consistency. Add flavoring. Spread.

Mrs. C. W. Gleaves, Lexington Woman's Club

Mrs. Romanza O. Johnson, Bowling Green Woman's Club, substitutes 2 tsp. rum flavoring, and adds 2 tsp. butter and ½ cup chopped nuts to make a rum glaze.

BROWN SUGAR GLAZE

½ cup brown sugar, firmly
   packed
⅓ cup light corn syrup

⅓ cup water
2 tbsp. lemon juice

Combine brown sugar, corn syrup, and water in a saucepan; place over low heat and bring slowly to a boil; boil 2 minutes. Add lemon juice. Use on fruit cakes or rich yeast rolls.

From WOMAN'S HOME COMPANION COOKBOOK (1942)

DRIED APPLE FILLING FOR STACK CAKE

1 lb. tart dried apples
1 cup brown sugar
½ cup white sugar

2 tsp. cinnamon
½ tsp. cloves
½ tsp. allspice

Stew and mash the apples; add sugars and spices, stirring well. Spread between layers and allow to stand several hours before cutting.

Mrs. N. M. Hill, Williamsburg Woman's Club

FIG FILLING

1 cup pressed figs   1 cup water
1 cup sugar

Finely chop figs. Combine with sugar and water. Cook over low heat, stirring constantly, until it becomes a thick paste. Cool before spreading.

Mrs. W. Ed Hamilton, K.F.W.C. President, 1964–1966

ORANGE-LEMON FILLING

2 tbsp. butter
5½ tsp. cornstarch
1 cup orange juice
2 egg yolks

juice and grated rind of 1 large lemon
⅛ tsp. salt

Mix butter and cornstarch until very smooth. Bring orange juice to a boil; pour slowly over cornstarch mixture, stirring constantly. Add well-beaten egg yolks, lemon juice, and salt. Cook slowly, stirring often, until thick. Spread while hot between cooled cake layers.

Mrs. H. R. White, Williamsburg Woman's Club

Pies

PIE CRUST

1½ cups flour   pinch of salt
⅓ cup solid shortening

Blend with a pastry blender; add enough water to handly easily.

Mrs. J. M. Thompson, Horse Cave Woman's Club

Mrs. M. J. Cundiff, Bullitt County Woman's Club, has a simple formula for pie crust: Half as much shortening as flour; half as much water as shortening.

PIE CRUST

4 cups sifted flour   1 egg
1 tbsp. sugar   1 tbsp. vinegar
1½ tsp. salt   ½ cup water
1½ cups lard

Blend flour, sugar, and salt; add shortening and beaten egg. Blend in vinegar and cold water. Makes 4 9-inch crusts.

Martha Kelsch, Heritage Heights Woman's Club, Augusta

SCOTTISH RICE TARTS

One of the "don't miss" events in Central Kentucky is the Harvest Market held on the last Friday in September in even-numbered years at the Little House in Versailles. The market, sponsored by the Woodford County Woman's Club and the Woodford County Garden Club, features the last of the garden vegetables and late fruits, fall flowers and dried arrangements, a Christmas shop, and a country kitchen. The box lunch at noon is superb—chicken salad, country ham with beaten biscuits, an herbed cottage cheese sandwich, and a Scottish rice tart.

¼ cup butter	1 tsp. baking powder
2 tbsp. sugar	1 tsp. vanilla
1 egg	strawberry preserves
4 tbsp. rice flour	12 tart shells

Cream the butter, sugar, and egg. Add rice flour, baking powder, and vanilla. Place 1 tbsp. strawberry preserves in a lightly baked tart shell. Top with 1 tbsp. filling mixture. Bake at 400° until lightly browned. Makes 12.

Mrs. David Silcox, Woodford County Woman's Club

TRANSPARENT PUDDINGS

These seem to be a regional treat, originating around Mason and Fleming counties. The name may be misleading, but it is traditional and they are never called "little tarts" by the local cooks.

1 cup butter	few grains of salt
2 cups minus 2 tbsp. sugar	4 eggs
2 tbsp. white corn syrup	1 tsp. vanilla

In the top of a double boiler, lightly cream the butter, sugar, corn syrup, and salt. Add unbeaten eggs, one at a time, and blend, do not beat. Add vanilla. Place over hot but not boiling water; stir occasionally until sugar is dissolved. Do not cook. Line small shallow tart pans with pastry. Fill each about ⅔ full; place on a cookie sheet and bake in a preheated 400° oven 10 minutes or until filling has a jelly-like consistency. Let cool slightly in pans, then remove carefully and place on wire racks or paper towels to cool completely.

Mrs. A. G. Thomson, Scott County Woman's Club

APPLE DELIGHT

1 cup sugar	2 cups thinly sliced apples
1 tbsp. flour	(preferably Winesap)
1 tsp. nutmeg	2 eggs, beaten
1 tsp. cinnamon	¼ cup butter
¼ tsp. allspice	about 50 inches of ¾-inch
	unbaked pastry strips

Mix sugar, flour, and spices. Add to apples and stir, being careful not to break slices. Add eggs and mix well but carefully. Pour into an unbaked 9-inch pie shell and chip butter over top. Cover with lattice top. Bake at 350° about one hour, or until crust is brown.

Mrs. Marcus C. Yancey, Williamsburg Woman's Club

MACAROON APPLE PIE

4 cups apple chunks	½ cup flour
¼ tsp. cinnamon	½ tsp. soda
1 cup sugar	¼ tsp. salt
2 tbsp. butter	¼ tsp. vanilla
1 egg	½ cup shredded coconut

Peel apples and cut them into large pieces. Mix cinnamon and ½ cup sugar; add apples and stir to coat thoroughly. Place in a buttered 9-inch pie tin. Bake at 375° for 20 minutes. Cover with topping: Cream together butter and remaining ½ cup sugar. Add beaten egg, then sifted dry ingredients. Stir in vanilla and coconut. Return pie to oven and bake 30 minutes longer. Serve warm or cold with ice cream or whipped cream.

Mrs. Robert Livziey, Campbellsville Woman's Club

FRIED APPLE PIES

Family reunions are a common summer activity in Kentucky but none reaches such proportions as that of the Combs family. Since 1960, on the third Sunday in August the Combses, as many as 2,000 of them, have met at Buckhorn State Park. Nor do many families have a special newspaper published to bring the family news. On Thursday before the reunion, Oscar Combs, Hazard newspaper publisher, puts out the "Combs Family News." Profit from the sale of the paper furnishes a nursing scholarship to a Combs or one whose mother or grandmother was a Combs.

"Dinner on the grounds" is spread at noon, with all the old-time goodies and many new recipes. Several dishes are never absent from the menu. Among these are ham or sausage on biscuits (either baking powder or beaten), Granny's pickles (page 298), and the following fried apple pies:

1 lb. dried apples	cinnamon to taste
¾ cup sugar	pastry
small lump of butter	

Soak the apples overnight in water to cover. Drain and add a small amount of fresh water, cover the pan, and cook slowly until tender. Mash the apples. Add sugar, butter, and cinnamon. Let cool.

Make your favorite pie crust, using only half the regular amount of shortening. Roll on a floured board to a medium thinness; cut into 4- to 6-inch circles. Place a generous tablespoonful of filling on one side of each circle. Moisten fingertips, wet the crust edge, fold it over, and press firmly to seal. Fry in about ½-inch of hot lard, turning once. When brown drain on paper towels. While still warm sprinkle with sugar. To serve at a tea or coffee, cut the crusts the size of a silver dollar and proportion filling accordingly.

Mrs. Earle Combs, Woman's Club of Richmond

BROWN SUGAR CRUNCH APPLE PIE

Filling:
6 tart apples
1 tsp. lemon juice
½ cup sugar
½ tsp. nutmeg
1 tbsp. butter

Topping:
⅓ cup butter
¾ cup light brown sugar, firmly packed
¾ cup flour

Peel and slice apples; put into a 9-inch unbaked pie shell. Sprinkle with lemon juice, sugar, and nutmeg. Dot with butter. For topping, cream butter until soft, then blend in brown sugar. Sift flour; measure and mix with butter and sugar until crumbly. Sprinkle over apples. Bake at 425° for 10 minutes; reduce heat to 350° and bake 45 to 50 minutes longer.

Shirley Tucker, Heritage Heights Woman's Club, Augusta

A similar recipe was sent by Mrs. Harley C. Davis, Richmond Younger Woman's Club, who puts the pie in a no. 25 grocery bag and bakes it at 425° for 1 hour.

Even the food experts cannot always agree on the best recipe. Certainly that was true of the late Duncan Hines and his wife Clara. Mr. Hines, a native of Bowling Green, was known throughout the world for his books on cooking and eating. With Mrs. Hines's permission here are their recipes for apple pie:

CLARA HINES APPLE PIE

Crust:

1½ cups sifted flour
pinch of salt
2 tbsp. poultry fat
2 tbsp. butter
3¾ tbsp. ice water

Filling:

¼ lb. butter
1 cup sugar
1 heaping tbsp. sifted flour
6 to 8 Winesap apples

Sift together flour and salt. Cut in poultry fat and butter, add ice water, and mix gently. Roll thin and place in a 9-inch pie tin that has been heavily buttered. Save the leftover pastry to make strips for the top.

For filling, slice half the butter over the crust. Mix together sugar and 1 heaping tbsp. flour; sprinkle half this mixture over the buttered crust. Peel and chop enough apples to fill the pie tin, heaped up. Cover with remaining sugar mixture. Top with strips of pastry and slice remaining butter over the top. Bake at 450° for 10 minutes; lower temperature to 350° and bake 25 to 30 minutes.

DUNCAN HINES APPLE PIE

1 cup sugar
2 tbsp. sifted flour
½ grated nutmeg
½ cup orange juice

⅓ cup melted butter
3 tbsp. light corn syrup
6 to 8 Winesap apples, thinly
    sliced

Combine all ingredients except apples. Add apples and stir gently but thoroughly. Butter a 9-inch pie tin heavily before putting in your pastry. Fill the shell with the apple mixture and place pastry strips over the top. Bake at 400° for 15 minutes; then reduce heat to 250° and bake 35 to 40 minutes longer.

From DUNCAN HINES FOOD ODYSSEY;
used by permission of Mrs. Duncan Hines;
contributed by Mrs. Joseph Mayfield, Bowling Green Woman's Club

APPLE-GOOSEBERRY PIE

1 heaping cup fresh or frozen   ¾ to 1 cup sugar
    gooseberries   butter
2 or 3 medium apples   ¼ cup water
2 tbsp. flour

Place gooseberries in an unbaked 8-inch pie shell. Pare and slice enough apples to finish filling the shell. Mix flour and sugar, sprinkle evenly over fruit. Dot with butter and pour water around the inside edge of the crust. Cut vents in top crust, place on pie, and seal. Bake at 400° for 15 minutes; reduce heat to 350° and continue baking until lightly browned.

Mrs. Homer Rouse, Williamstown Woman's Club

GREEN TOMATO PIE

1 cup sugar   1 quart thinly sliced green
½ cup flour   tomatoes
pinch of salt   1 tbsp. vinegar
2 tbsp. butter

Combine sugar, flour, and salt. Place half the mixture in an unbaked 9-inch pastry shell. Dot with butter, add tomatoes, sprinkle with vinegar, and cover with remaining flour mixture. Cover with a lattice top. Bake at 375° for 50 minutes.

Mrs. Hamilton Render, Beaver Dam Woman's Club

Another recipe sent for green tomato pie listed among its ingredients 4 tbsp. brandy or whiskey, with this story: In the early part of this century churches in small towns could not always afford full-time ministers, so student preachers filled many pulpits on an every-other-week basis. The young men were always invited to take Sunday dinner with a member of the congregation. One who went out from the Louisville Baptist Seminary visited the same church quite often and was always hoping to be invited to Mrs. Pendleton's because she made the best green tomato pie he had ever tasted. Kentucky liquor laws and the staunch Baptist stand on the use of liquor kept him from knowing what made the pie so deliciously different. The family certainly did enjoy their secret, though.

BLACKBERRY PIE

3 cups fresh blackberries   2 tbsp. lemon juice
1 cup honey   ⅛ tsp. salt
2 tbsp. quick-cooking tapioca   1 tbsp. butter

Mix all ingredients except butter. Pour into a 9-inch unbaked crust, dot with butter, and cover with a vented top crust. Bake at 450° for 10 minutes; reduce heat to 350° and bake 25 to 30 minutes longer.

Mrs. James Anderson, Carlisle Junior Woman's Club

RAISIN PIE

1 cup sugar   1 tbsp. butter
1 tbsp. flour   dash of salt
1 cup raisins   1½ cups boiling water
1 tbsp. vinegar

Mix first six ingredients; pour boiling water over them and mix well. Set aside while preparing pastry for 2 8-inch crusts. Pour filling into lower crust and cover with a top crust. Bake at 400° for 10 minutes; reduce heat to 300° and bake until crust is brown.

Mrs. Robert E. Vick, Greenville Woman's Club

Butter Pie: Omit raisins and vinegar. Mix flour and sugar; stir in boiling water. Pour into an 8-inch unbaked pastry shell. Dot with ½ cup butter and sprinkle with nutmeg. No top crust. Bake at 275° for 45 minutes.

Mrs. Mattie Young, Beaver Dam Woman's Club

SOUR CREAM RAISIN PIE

2 eggs   1 cup seedless raisins
1 cup sugar   1 cup sour cream
½ tsp. cinnamon   ⅛ tsp. salt
½ tsp. cloves   2 tbsp. vinegar

Beat the eggs well; add sugar and spices that have been blended. Stir in remaining ingredients; beat well. Pour into an unbaked 9-inch pie shell. Cover with top crust. Bake at 350° for 15 minutes; reduce heat to 300° and bake 30 minutes longer.

Mrs. Homer B. Davis, Williamsburg Woman's Club

RHUBARB PIE

Filling:
3 cups diced rhubarb
1 cup sugar
3 tbsp. flour

Topping:
1 cup rolled oats
½ cup flour
½ cup sugar
½ tsp. cinnamon
¼ tsp. salt
⅓ cup melted butter

Combine rhubarb, sugar, and flour; mix well and spoon into a 9-inch unbaked pie shell. Combine topping ingredients; blend well with a pastry blender. Sprinkle over rhubarb. Bake at 375° for 35 to 40 minutes.

Mrs. Edgar VanHoose, Louisa Woman's Club

PUMPKIN PIE

¾ cup sugar
2 tbsp. butter, melted
2 eggs, beaten
1 tbsp. flour
¾ cup cream

1 cup mashed pumpkin
½ tsp. allspice
½ tsp. cinnamon
½ tsp. nutmeg
½ tsp. ginger

Mix in order given; stir until smooth. Pour into an unbaked 8-inch pie shell. Bake at 350° for 15 minutes, reduce heat to 250°, and bake 45 minutes longer or until set.

Mrs. Robert Hocker, Jr., Arlington Woman's Club

Mrs. Stephen McCoy, Beechmont Woman's Club, doubles the amount of pumpkin and uses ½ cup brown sugar and ½ cup white sugar. Bake at 450° for 15 minutes; reduce heat to 350°, and bake 35 to 45 minutes longer.

Sherry Lynn Ketteler, Erlanger Junior Woman's Club, increases the butter to ½ cup, sugar to 1½ cups, pumpkin to 2½ cups. She omits cream and adds 3 tbsp. whiskey. Bake as Mrs. McCoy does.

Sweet Potato Pie: Substitute 1½ cups mashed sweet potatoes for pumpkin; use brown sugar instead of white; and omit all spices except 1 tsp. nutmeg; add 1 tbsp. lemon juice.

Mrs. William Markesbery, Florence Woman's Club

Persimmon Pie: Substitute 1¼ cups persimmon pulp; omit spices except cinnamon; increase cream to 2 cups; add 1 tsp. lemon juice.

Miss Lena Porter, Pikeville Woman's Club

BUTTERSCOTCH PIE

1 tbsp. butter, measured	1½ cups top milk
generously	3 eggs, separated
1 tbsp. flour	6 tbsp. white sugar
1 cup brown sugar	

Brown the butter; add flour, brown sugar, milk, and beaten egg yolks. Mix well. Cook over low heat until thick. Pour into a 9-inch unbaked pie shell. Bake in a hot oven (375° to 400°) until the crust is browned. Remove from oven and cover with meringue made with stiffly beaten egg whites and white sugar. Return to oven for a few minutes to lightly brown the meringue.

Recipe of Mrs. John Gifford;
contributed by Miss Chloe Gifford, K.F.W.C. President, 1946–1948;
G.F.W.C. President, 1958–1960

BUTTERSCOTCH PIE

1 cup brown sugar	2 eggs, separated
¼ cup flour	4 tbsp. butter
1 cup milk	½ tsp. vanilla extract

Combine sugar and flour in the top of a double boiler; stir in milk slowly. Cook over boiling water, stirring constantly, until thick. Stir a small amount of the hot mixture into the slightly beaten egg yolks; add to mixture remaining in the double boiler and cook 3 minutes over hot water, stirring constantly. Remove from heat and add butter. Cool, then add vanilla. Pour into a graham cracker crumb crust in a 9-inch pie pan. Beat egg whites until frothy, gradually add 4 tbsp. sugar. Continue beating until stiff. Spread over filling. Bake at 375° until brown.

Mrs. Homer Bryant, Sr., Pleasure Ridge Woman's Club

In the early 1930s a crust of graham cracker or vanilla wafer crumbs was a new innovation in cooking. Such a crust was a "quick" food and a boon to the non-pastry cook. Mrs. Bryant sent this recipe not only because the filling is excellent but because it was used when she tasted her first graham cracker crust in 1935.

OLD FASHIONED CUSTARD PIE

3 eggs, separated
½ cup sugar
1 tbsp. flour
pinch of salt

¼ tsp. nutmeg
2 cups milk
1 tsp. butter

Place egg yolks in the top of a double boiler. Mix sugar and flour; add to eggs. Add salt and nutmeg and beat well with a fork. In another pan heat milk until very warm; slowly stir into egg mixture. Cook over boiling water, stirring constantly, until mixture begins to thicken. Stir in butter. Pour into a 9-inch unbaked pie shell. Bake at 450° for 10 minutes; reduce heat to 350° and bake 35 minutes longer. Cover with meringue and sprinkle with nutmeg. Brown in the oven.

Mrs. George Reed, Stanford Woman's Club

This recipe was handed down from Mrs. Reed's great-grandmother, who came from England and was a first cousin of Charles Dickens. She and her husband, James Chelf, owned and operated an inn at Dawson Springs before and during the Civil War.

FRENCH SILK CHOCOLATE PIE

Shell:
2 egg whites
⅛ tsp. salt
½ tsp. cream of tartar
½ cup sugar
½ cup finely chopped nuts
½ tsp. vanilla

Filling:
½ cup butter
¾ cup sugar
1½ squares unsweetened
    chocolate, melted
1 tsp. vanilla
2 eggs
2 egg yolks

Add cream of tartar and salt to egg whites and beat until stiff. Gradually add sifted sugar and continue beating until mixture peaks. Fold in nuts and vanilla. Spread in a lightly greased 8-inch pie tin, building up sides. Bake at 300° for 50 to 55 minutes.

Thoroughly cream butter and sugar; blend in melted chocolate and vanilla. Add eggs, 1 whole egg and 1 yolk at a time, beating 5 minutes after each addition. Pour into cooled pie shell. Garnish with shaved chocolate or nuts.

Mrs. Ruth Scott, Eddyville Woman's Club

IRON SKILLET CHOCOLATE PIE

1½ cups sugar	3 eggs, separated
3 rounded tbsp. flour	1½ cups milk
2 rounded tbsp. cocoa	2 tsp. vanilla
4 tbsp. butter	

Mix sugar, flour, and cocoa. Melt butter in an iron skillet; add dry ingredients and mix lightly. Combine beaten egg yolks with milk; add to mixture in the skillet. Cook over low heat, stirring constantly, until thick. Add vanilla and pour into a baked 9-inch pie shell. Cover with meringue made from the 3 egg whites. Brown at 350°.

Mrs. Carl Johnston, Nortonville Woman's Club

Mrs. J. M. Thompson, Horse Cave Woman's Club, omits the flour and substitutes 1 small can evaporated milk for the milk and 2 whole eggs for the egg yolks. Mix well and pour into an unbaked pie shell. (Use no meringue.) Bake at 325° for 40 minutes.

LEMON PIE

Heat until boiling 1½ cups water with butter size of an egg [¼ cup], mix together thoroughly 2 mixing spoons corn starch, 1 cup sugar, 1 teaspoon cream of tartar. Separate 2 eggs, beating the yolks, adding 1 tablespoon lemon extract. Cook slowly in a double boiler. Pour into baked crust and use whites of eggs beaten with a tablespoon of sugar on top of pie, brown slightly in oven. Let cool.

Mrs. Albert Thomas, Maysville Woman's Club

This recipe is over 100 years old.

SHAKER LEMON PIE

2 large lemons	4 eggs, well beaten
2 cups sugar	

Slice unpeeled lemons paper thin. Remove seeds, add sugar, and mix well. Let stand 2 hours or longer, stirring occasionally. Thoroughly blend eggs into the lemon mixture. Turn into an unbaked 9-inch pie shell, arranging lemon slices evenly. Cover with a vented top crust. Bake at 450° for 15 minutes; reduce heat to 375° and bake 20 minutes longer or until a silver knife inserted near the edge comes out clean. Cool before serving.

Contributed by Mrs. Kellis Chilton, Harrodsburg Woman's Club

OLD FASHIONED LEMON PIE

2 large lemons	4 tbsp. flour
3 cups sugar	2 cups water
4 eggs, separated	

Grate rind and squeeze juice from lemons; add sugar, beaten egg yolks, flour, and water. Fold in stiffly beaten egg whites. Pour into a 9-inch unbaked pastry shell. Bake at 350° for 30 minutes or until set.

Mary Richardson, Munfordville Woman's Club

Mrs. Ruth Pohl, Horse Cave Woman's Club, makes a similar pie using boiling water, but cooks the filling 5 minutes before baking. She uses the egg whites, ½ cup sugar, and ½ tsp. baking powder to make meringue. Pour into a baked pie shell and brown the meringue at 350° for 10 to 15 minutes.

Mrs. Leslie B. Hoover III, Woman's Club of Madisonville, uses 2 cups milk instead of water. She bakes it as Mrs. Pohl does.

CHESS PIE

1 cup butter	1 tsp. vanilla
3 cups sugar	2 tbsp. vinegar
6 eggs	pinch of salt

Cream the butter and sugar. Add well beaten eggs, vanilla, vinegar, and salt. Pour into 2 unbaked 9-inch pie shells. Bake at 300° for 10 minutes; then increase temperature to 350° and bake 35 minutes longer.

Mrs. Minnie M. Payton

LEMON CHESS PIE

4 eggs	1 tbsp. white cornmeal
1½ cups sugar	1 tbsp. flour
1 tbsp. grated lemon rind	¼ cup milk
¼ cup lemon juice	pinch of salt
¼ cup butter, melted	

Beat eggs; gradually add sugar. Stir in remaining ingredients. Pour into an unbaked 9-inch pie shell. Bake at 350° for 40 minutes or until brown. Do not overbake.

Shirley W. Allen, Woman's Club of Elizabethtown

OLD KENTUCKY CHESS PIE

1½ cups sugar	1 tsp. vanilla
½ cup butter	pinch of salt
4 eggs, separated	2 tbsp. cinnamon
2 tbsp. cornstarch	1 tbsp. nutmeg
1 cup milk	

Combine all ingredients except egg whites, cinnamon, and nutmeg; beat well. Pour into an unbaked 9-inch pie shell and sprinkle with mixed spices. Bake at 350° for 40 minutes. Remove from oven. Cover with meringue made from the 4 egg whites; return to oven until meringue is brown.

Mrs. Hazel Stephenson, Cumberland County Woman's Club

Cornmeal Pie: Omit milk, cornstarch, and spices; use 2 whole eggs instead of 4 yolks; add 2 tbsp. cornmeal. Cook over low heat until smooth and slightly thickened before pouring into an unbaked 9-inch pie shell. This pie has no meringue.

Mrs. Thomas Byrum, Arlington Woman's Club

TALBOTT TAVERN PIE

Old Talbott Tavern in Bardstown has been open for business since 1779. It was originally known as the Stone Inn. Cooking was done in two fireplaces at the rear of the main room, and the upstairs loft was divided into two sleeping rooms, one for men, the other for women. By the end of the eighteenth century it was the western end of the stagecoach route from Virginia. The list of well known guests includes an exiled king, several United States presidents, and many senators and explorers. Some chef in the long history of the tavern concocted a pie which he called Talbott Tavern Pie, not as well known as chess pie but very good.

¾ cup sugar	*Meringue:*
½ cup flour	2 egg whites
¼ tsp. salt	½ cup sugar
1¼ cups water	2 tbsp. water
2 egg yolks	dash of salt
½ cup orange juice	
1 tbsp. grated orange rind	1 navel orange
2 tbsp. lemon juice	grated coconut

Combine sugar, flour, and salt in the top of a double boiler. Stir in water, keeping mixture free from lumps. Cook, stirring constantly, over direct heat for 5 minutes. Stir a little of the hot mixture into slightly beaten egg yolks; add to remaining mixture in pan. Cook 5 minutes longer over rapidly boiling water, stirring constantly. Remove from heat, add orange juice, orange rind, and lemon juice. Chill thoroughly. Pour into a baked 9-inch pie shell.

Make meringue by putting egg whites, sugar, water, and salt in the top of a double boiler. Beat with a rotary beater until thoroughly mixed. Place over rapidly boiling water; beat 1 minute. Remove from heat and continue beating until mixture will stand in peaks. Pile lightly on filling. Peel a navel orange; separate into sections; remove membrane and arrange on top of meringue. Sprinkle with coconut.

Bardstown Woman's Club

PECAN PIE

2 tbsp. butter	¼ tsp. salt
½ cup sugar	1 tsp. vanilla
2 eggs, beaten	1 cup light corn syrup
2 tbsp. flour	1½ cups chopped pecans

Combine ingredients in order given; beat well. Pour into an unbaked 9-inch pie shell. Bake at 375° for 10 minutes; reduce heat to 350° and bake 30 to 45 minutes longer.

Mrs. Lois Zook, Somerset Literary Club

Mrs. Robert Jeter, Campbellsville Woman's Club, omits the flour and adds 2 tbsp. more butter and 1 egg, and substitutes dark for light corn syrup.

Mrs. Harry Faulkner, Stanford Woman's Club, doubles both eggs and sugar, and increases the butter to ½ cup. She reduces the oven temperature to 300°.

BURNT SUGAR PIE

2 cups sugar
3 eggs, separated
1 tbsp. flour

2 tbsp. butter
1½ cups milk

Caramelize the sugar in an iron skillet. Be very careful, as it will burn quickly. In a saucepan combine egg yolks, flour, butter, and milk. Heat and pour slowly into browned sugar. Cook until well blended. Pour into a baked 8-inch pie shell. Top with meringue made with the 3 egg whites. Bake at 350° until meringue is light brown.

Mrs. A. Baxter Riley, LaCenter Woman's Club

KENTUCKY ████████ PIE

½ cup margarine, melted
1 cup sugar
½ cup flour
2 eggs, slightly beaten

1 tsp. vanilla
¾ cup English walnuts
¾ cup chocolate chips

Mix in order given; pour into an unbaked 9-inch pie shell. Bake at 350° for 30 minutes.

Mrs. Kenneth Evans, Danville Woman's Club

Mrs. Marow Cox, Ossoli Woman's Club, substitutes ¼ cup brown sugar for part of the white sugar.

AMBER PIE

1 cup sugar
1 tbsp. flour
1 cup blackberry jam

1 cup sour cream
½ cup butter, melted
3 eggs, separated

Blend sugar and flour; add jam, sour cream, melted butter, and beaten egg yolks. Mix well. Pour into an unbaked 9-inch pie shell. Bake at 350° for 45 minutes. Cover with sweetened meringue made from the 3 egg whites; brown lightly.

Mrs. Bryan Houchens, Glasgow Woman's Club

Jam Pie: Reduce butter to 1 tbsp. and sugar and jam to ½ cup each; substitute ½ cup milk for sour cream; add 1 tsp. allspice. Use 4 whole eggs in the filling; the pie has no meringue.

Mrs. T. C. Carroll, K.F.W.C. President, 1938–1940

SORGHUM PIE

Like the country ham, sorghum has its promoters in Eastern and Western Kentucky. Each October, Hawesville in Hancock County and West Liberty in Morgan County hold a three-day Sorghum Festival. Local crafts are displayed, demonstrated, and sold. Lunch stands provide a choice of favorite Kentucky foods—country ham on biscuits, soup beans and cornbread, and fried pies. At the country store you can purchase dried apples, stack cakes, home-canned foods, and country ham. At the gristmill you can buy freshly ground cornmeal. The highlight of the exhibits is the sorghum stir-off area, where you can watch the mule make thousands of turns to crush the cane that is fed into the grinder one stalk at a time. The juice trickles down the spout into the cooking pans, where it is constantly stirred and skimmed as it flows from one pan to the next. When it reaches the right color and thickness it is caught in a barrel. Tasting is allowed—all you need do is cut a piece of cane, dip it in the foam or syrup, and lick.

Sorghum Pie is one of the favorites of the festival.

3 eggs, separated	½ tsp. salt
1½ cups sorghum	1 tbsp. flour
2 tbsp. butter, melted	1 tbsp. cornstarch
¾ cup brown sugar	pecans
½ tsp. nutmeg	white sugar
½ tsp. cinnamon	

Beat egg yolks until thick; add sorghum and butter. Combine brown sugar, spices, salt, flour, and cornstarch; add to egg mixture and mix thoroughly. Fold in stiffly beaten egg whites. Pour into an unbaked 9-inch pastry shell. Bake at 425° for 15 minutes. Cover filling with a layer of broken pecans, sprinkle with sugar, and continue baking for 15 minutes.

Pamelia P. Walter, Morgan County Woman's Club

BUTTERMILK PIE

Take 3 eggs, 2 cups sugar, ½ cup butter, 3 tablespoons flour or 2½ tablespoons corn starch (not both), 1 cup buttermilk. If the milk is not very acid put in ½ juice of one lemon. Season with nutmeg and vanilla. Bake in single crusts. Makes 2 pies.

From HOME AND FARM MAGAZINE (1882);
contributed by Mrs. Lorena Brown, Beaver Dam Woman's Club

VINEGAR PIE

1 cup sugar	½ tsp. cloves
⅓ cup flour	2 cups water
¼ tsp. salt	¼ cup cider vinegar
1 tsp. cinnamon	2 eggs
1 tsp. nutmeg	2 tbsp. butter
1 tsp. allspice	

In a heavy pan combine sugar, flour, salt, and spices; mix thoroughly. Add water, vinegar, and eggs; beat vigorously with a rotary beater for a few minutes. Cook, stirring constantly, until thick. Remove from heat; stir in butter. Pour into a baked 9-inch pie shell. Cool. Serve plain or with whipped cream.

Mrs. C. R. Puckett, Falmouth Woman's Club

STACK PIE

6 8-inch pastry shells	2 cups whipping cream
6 egg yolks	2 tbsp. butter, melted
1½ cups sugar	

Mix by hand egg yolks, sugar, cream, and butter. Divide evenly into the 6 shells. Bake 2 at a time at 375° for 30 minutes. Allow pies to cool before stacking. Stack, using caramel icing between the layers and on top.

Mrs. Don Long, Harrodsburg Woman's Club

Mrs. Charles Judge, Carlisle Junior Woman's Club, makes Blackberry Stack Pie by rolling and cutting 1 recipe of biscuit dough into 8-inch rounds. When baked they are split and stacked with stewed fresh blackberries and a pat of butter between the layers.

FRESH STRAWBERRY PIE

1 qt. strawberries	1 3-oz. pkg. cream cheese
1 cup sugar	1 cup whipping cream
3 tsp. cornstarch	

Wash and hull berries. Mash and strain 2 cups berries. Combine juice, sugar, and cornstarch; boil slowly for 10 minutes, stirring constantly. Remove from heat and allow to cool. Soften cream cheese with a small amount of cream and spread in the bottom of a baked 9-inch pie shell. Put 2 cups hulled berries on top of cheese. Pour glaze over. Chill. Just before serving spread sweetened whipped cream over the top. Serves 8.

Miss Carol Roark, Greenville Woman's Club

FLUFFY LIME PIE

¼ cup flour	1½ cups boiling water
¼ cup cornstarch	3 eggs, separated
1 cup plus 2 tbsp. sugar	⅓ cup lime juice
dash of salt	2 tbsp. butter

Mix flour, cornstarch, ½ cup sugar, and salt; slowly add boiling water. Cook in the top of a double boiler, stirring constantly, until thick. Beat egg yolks with ½ cup sugar and the lime juice until thick. Stir a little of the hot mixture into egg yolks; add to remaining mixture in pan and cook 2 minutes longer, stirring constantly. Remove from heat; stir in butter and allow to cool. Beat 1 egg white with 2 tbsp. sugar; fold into lime mixture. Pour into a baked 9-inch pie shell. Top with meringue made with remaining egg whites. Brown in a 350° oven.

Mrs. Beuford Stanley, Williamstown Woman's Club

Mrs. Charles M. Summers, Campbellsville Woman's Club, makes her Key Lime Pie the easy way: she combines 1 can condensed milk, 4 egg yolks, and ¼ cup lime juice, then folds in 1 beaten egg white. The remaining egg whites are used for meringue.

MOUNTAIN TOP PIE

1 cup sweetened condensed milk	1 5-oz. can crushed pineapple, drained
1 9-oz. carton prepared whipped topping	½ cup grated coconut
juice of 2 lemons	½ cup chopped nuts
	¼ cup maraschino cherries, cut up

Combine in order given; pour into a baked 9-inch pie shell. Refrigerate for several hours.

Mrs. W. E. Burgin, Stanford Woman's Club

Candy and Cookies

CANDY

To candy lovers in Kentucky, a "colonel" is neither a goateed gentleman nor the holder of a commission from the governor. It's a candy unique to Kentucky. The original Kentucky colonel begins with a fondant center with a generous allotment of bourbon, encased in pecan halves and dipped in thin dark chocolate. The allotment of bourbon is so generous that the postal authorities will not let the candy be sent through the mail. The originator was the late Mrs. Ruth Booe of Frankfort, co-owner of Rebecca-Ruth Candy, Inc., where many other candies are made that can be shipped anywhere. Rum and creme de menthe colonels are among them. The Kentucky creams for which we are giving the recipe were probably her next most famous confection. Mrs. Booe died in 1973 but her son still keeps the candy kettles boiling, and if you are in Frankfort you are invited to visit the kitchen.

CREAM CANDY

2 cups sugar
½ cup whole milk
¼ cup heavy cream

½ tsp. vanilla
⅛ tsp. salt

Bring sugar, milk, and cream slowly to a boil, stirring constantly to make sure the sugar is thoroughly dissolved before the mixture boils. Cook, without stirring, to 250°. Pour onto a well-buttered marble-top table. Let cool. Do not overly cool or it will harden. When the candy is cool, add vanilla and salt and start pulling. Pull until candy is white, fluffy, and feels like it is about to cream. Pull into a long rope about the size of your wrist and cut into pieces with cold scissors. Place the pieces on a buttered slab until thoroughly creamed.

Melt bitter chocolate (about ½ pound) in the top of a double boiler. The water in the bottom should be hot but must not boil. When chocolate is melted, remove pan from water and beat chocolate until it is cool to the upper lip. Dip each piece with a fork and place on waxed paper to dry. Yield: About 1 pound.

Used by permission of Rebecca-Ruth Candy, Inc.

A similar recipe, using 4 cups sugar, 1 cup cream, and ½ cup water, was sent by Mrs. Scott Wicker, Eddyville Woman's Club.

CREAM CANDY

3 cups sugar
1 cup boiling water
1 pinch salt

1 pinch soda
1 cup light cream
¼ cup butter

Put sugar and water in a large kettle; stir until sugar is dissolved. Bring to a boil over low heat and continue cooking without stirring to very firm ball stage (250°). Put salt and soda into cream. Add 1 tbsp. of cream at a time to the syrup—do not let boiling stop. Add butter and cook to hard ball stage (265°). Pour candy onto a lightly buttered marble slab. When cool enough to handle without burning your hands, start pulling and continue pulling until candy is firm enough to cut with scissors.

Sandra Wood, Brooksville Town and Country Woman's Club
Mrs. J. C. Hager, Louisa Woman's Club

DIVINITY

2½ cups sugar
3 tbsp. light corn syrup
½ cup water

2 egg whites
pinch of cream of tartar
nuts (optional)

Place sugar, syrup, and water in a saucepan. Cook and stir until sugar is dissolved. Cook without stirring until it will spin a thread (232°). Meanwhile in a large bowl beat the egg whites and cream of tartar until stiff enough to form peaks. Gradually pour about one-third of syrup over egg whites, beating them constantly from this point. Return remaining syrup to heat and boil until it reaches the firm ball stage (246°). Slowly pour half of syrup into egg white mixture. Again return syrup to heat and boil until light crack stage (265°) is reached. Add slowly to beaten mixture. Add flavoring to taste, and stir in chopped nuts, if desired. When mixture is quite firm and will hold its shape, drop from a teaspoon onto a cookie sheet covered with waxed paper. Cool and store in a tightly covered container. Makes 40 to 50 candies.

Mrs. James Austin, Lone Oak Woman's Club

OPERA FUDGE

7 cups sugar
1 qt. whipping cream
½ tsp. cream of tartar
2 tsp. vanilla

½ cup candied cherries, halved
½ cup English walnuts, broken coarsely
red or green food coloring

Mix sugar and cream in a large kettle. Stir over medium heat until it begins to boil. Add cream of tartar. Continue to stir while cooking to 238°. Be sure to stir under the thermometer to prevent scorching. Pour gently onto a marble slab that has been moistened with cold water. Do not scrape the kettle. When candy is cool to the touch, it is ready to be worked with fondant paddles. (This process will require two people.) Scrape candy from marble with a circular motion until it begins to cream. Scrape paddles frequently to prevent graininess. When candy has become a firm mass, cover with a damp cloth and let rest for 10 to 15 minutes before kneading. Knead, add vanilla, and knead again. Divide into two portions. Color one half red or green and add nuts. Mix cherries into other half. Press into a 9-inch square pan, colored half on the bottom, white on top. Cool until firm. Cut in squares. Store in a tightly covered container.

Mrs. Sturgeon Riley, Carrollton Woman's Club

CANDY PUDDING

Fondant:
2 cups sugar
½ cup water
⅛ tsp. cream of tartar
2 tbsp. butter
pinch of salt

1 tsp. vanilla
Pudding:
¾ cup Angel Flake coconut
½ cup broken pecans
1 3-oz. pkg. candied cherries
unsweetened chocolate

To make fondant, combine all ingredients except vanilla in a 3-qt. saucepan. Cook over medium heat until mixture begins to boil. Cover and cook for 3 minutes to dissolve crystals. *Do not stir!* Remove the lid and place a heated candy thermometer in the pan; when it reads 236° remove from heat. *Do not stir or scrape the pan!* Pour onto a large buttered platter. Let cool until lukewarm. Add vanilla and beat until it turns milky white. Knead, shape into a ball, and store in an airtight container for 24 hours or longer, until you are ready to make the pudding.

To make pudding, mix coconut, nuts, and cherries into the fondant. You may need to use your hands. Shape into a loaf and refrigerate until firm. Cover with melted unsweetened chocolate. When chocolate has hardened store in the refrigerator. Slice to serve.

Mrs. John Morgan, Lexington Woman's Club

CHOCOLATE FUDGE

4 squares unsweetened
   chocolate
½ cup water
3 cups sugar
¼ cup cream

¾ cup milk
3 tbsp. butter
1 tsp. vanilla
nuts, if desired

Combine chocolate and water in a saucepan; melt slowly. Add sugar, cream, and milk. Cook to soft ball stage (234°). Remove from heat; add butter and vanilla. Cool 5 minutes. Beat until thick and creamy. Add nuts. Pour into a buttered pan and cut into squares.

Mrs. A. W. Fullerton, Jr., Florence Woman's Club

FUDGE

2 cups sugar   1 cup milk
1 tbsp. cocoa   nut meats, if desired

Mix all ingredients. Cook over medium heat, stirring constantly, until a small amount will form a soft ball when dropped in cold tap water (234° to 240°). Remove from heat. Beat until creamy. Pour onto a buttered plate. Cut into squares.

Mrs. Ethel Squires, Somerset Literary Club

LEMON DROPS

1 cup powdered sugar   lemon juice

Pour enough lemon juice into the sugar to dissolve it. Boil to hard crack stage. Drop onto buttered baking sheets to cool and harden. This recipe dates from 1855.

Mrs. William Major, Madisonville Woman's Club

MOLASSES CANDY

1   cup dark molasses   1   tbsp. vinegar
½ cup sugar   2   tbsp. butter

Boil together all ingredients until syrup will form a hard ball in cold water (265°). Pour into a buttered flat pan. Cool until it can be handled easily. Grease hands with butter and pull candy, beginning with a small amount and gradually adding to it. Pull until it becomes a light golden color. Stretch and twist into a rope about ¾ inch around. Cut with greased scissors into bite-size pieces.

Mrs. Monroe Riehlman, Fern Creek Woman's Club

SORGHUM MOLASSES CANDY

4   cups sorghum molasses   ¼ tsp. soda

Cook sorghum over medium heat until it spins a thread (232°). Remove from heat. Add soda and beat until thick. Pour into a buttered pan. Let stand until cool. Pull in long strings like taffy. When hard, cut into pieces with buttered scissors.

Mrs. Shelby McBrayer, Lewisport Woman's Club

BOURBON BALLS

½ cup chopped pecans
5 tbsp. bourbon
1 lb. confectioners' sugar
¼ lb. butter

Coating:
6 oz. dipping chocolate
1 finger of paraffin

Soak pecans in bourbon for several hours or overnight. Blend sugar into softened butter. Add nuts and bourbon. Refrigerate until firm enough to shape into balls. Chill balls overnight. Melt chocolate and paraffin in the top of a double boiler. Dip balls in chocolate and place on waxed paper to dry.

Bardstown Woman's Club

BOURBON BALLS

1 cup vanilla wafer crumbs
1 cup pecans, chopped
1 cup confectioners' sugar

2 tbsp. cocoa
2 jiggers bourbon
1½ tbsp. light corn syrup

Mix crumbs, pecans, confectioners' sugar, and cocoa. In a separate dish, mix bourbon and corn syrup; add to crumb mixture. Form into small balls and roll in confectioners' sugar. Store in an airtight container in a cool place until ready to serve.

Mrs. Victor Sams, Somerset Woman's Club

TROUFFLES CANDY

½ cup butter
1 egg yolk, beaten
1 lb. confectioners' sugar
2 oz. unsweetened chocolate, melted

¼ cup cream
1 tbsp. coffee
1 tbsp. vanilla
chocolate shot or pecan halves

Cream butter; add egg yolk and a small amount of the sugar. Add other ingredients alternately with remaining sugar. Mixture will be fairly soft. Make into small balls. Roll in chocolate shot or ground pecans. For a more decorative candy, press a pecan half into each ball.

Mrs. Zach L. Church, Jr., Frankfort Woman's Club

DATE CONFECTIONS

4 or 8 marshmallows   16 pecan halves
1   8-oz. box pitted dates   granulated sugar

Cut marshmallows into halves or quarters. Press a piece of marshmallow into each open date. Put pecan half on top of marshmallow, cover with a second date, pressing firmly. Roll in granulated sugar. Wrap separately or put in an airtight container. Refrigerate if desired.

Barbara M. Davis, Elizabethtown Junior Woman's Club

COCONUT BALLS

1   can sweetened condensed milk
2   lb. confectioners' sugar
1   cup butter
2   cups nuts

2   cups flaked coconut
2   tsp. vanilla
Coating:
1   lb. semisweet chocolate
¾-inch bar of paraffin

Mix all except coating ingredients in order given. Make into balls; chill overnight. Melt chocolate and paraffin in the top of a double boiler over hot water. Dip balls in chocolate and lay on waxed paper to dry. Makes about 100 balls.

Mrs. Jimmie Maupin, Clinton County Woman's Club

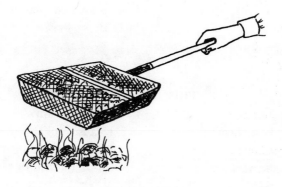

POPCORN

In the mid-1930s, Calloway County claimed the title of Popcorn Capital of the World. Its farmers produced 30 million pounds of popcorn a year. All the major popcorn distributors encouraged them by providing seed and guaranteeing the price.

Popcorn has always been the hallmark of a good time. Before the days of the electric machine that produces a fresh batch every five minutes at fairs, ball games, and such, it was popped at home, either as a treat for the family or for guests. In those days it was popped on top of the stove in an iron kettle or skillet with a lid, or in a long-handled wire basket over the open fire.

Today, Dr. J. Matt Sparkman of Murray prefers a pressure cooker to the automatic electric popper. Here are his instructions:

In a 4-quart pressure cooker put 2 tbsp. corn oil seasoned with black pepper. Heat the oil until a grain of corn will pop immediately. Add ½ cup popcorn and shake the pan so all grains are saturated with the oil. Place the lid on the cooker, but without the pressure gauge, and shake frequently to prevent scorching. When popping ceases, remove lid, pour popcorn into a bowl, and add salt and melted butter to taste.

And here's what Mrs. Sparkman does with his freshly popped corn:

SUGARED POPCORN

1½ cups sugar	1 tsp. salt
1 cup water	2 qt. popcorn, freshly popped

Cook sugar, water, and salt until the candy thermometer registers 238°. Remove from heat. Beat until creamy. Add popcorn and stir quickly to coat each kernel. Put on a greased platter and separate the kernels.

Mrs. J. Matt Sparkman, Murray Woman's Club

CANDIED APPLES

1 doz. apples	¼ tsp. cream of tartar
3 cups sugar	red food coloring
⅔ cup water	

Wash and dry the apples and push sticks into the cores. Combine sugar, water, and cream of tartar. Cook over medium heat until mixture will form a hard ball when tested in cold water (265°). Add a few drops of red coloring. Mix well. Dip apples in syrup and turn until surface is completely coated. Dip in cold water to set.

Mrs. William Blair, Paintsville Woman's Club

COOKIES

ANGEL COOKIES

1 cup shortening	1 tsp. vanilla
½ cup white sugar	2 cups flour
½ cup brown sugar	1 tsp. soda
1 egg	1 tsp. cream of tartar

Cream shortening and sugars until light and fluffy. Add egg and vanilla; beat well. Sift together flour, soda, and cream of tartar; add to creamed mixture. Roll into small balls. Dip in water and roll top half of ball in sugar. Place sugar side up on a greased cookie sheet. Bake at 375° for 10 to 12 minutes. Yield: 4 to 6 dozen cookies.

Mrs. John McCubbin, Campbellsville Woman's Club

APPLESAUCE COOKIES

½ cup shortening	½ tsp. soda
1 cup brown sugar, firmly packed	½ tsp. nutmeg
	2 tsp. baking powder
1 egg	1 tsp. cinnamon
2 cups cake flour	½ cup applesauce
½ tsp. salt	1 cup seedless raisins

Cream together shortening and sugar. Add egg and beat well. Mix dry ingredients with applesauce; stir into creamed mixture. Add raisins. Drop by teaspoonfuls onto a greased cookie sheet. Bake at 400° for 12 to 15 minutes. Yield: 4 dozen cookies.

Mrs. Mary King Glass, Arlington Woman's Club

BLACK WALNUT COOKIES

1 cup butter	1 tsp. soda
1½ cups brown sugar	1 cup raisins
3 eggs, well beaten	1 cup black walnuts
2½ cups flour	¼ tsp. salt

Cream butter and sugar; add eggs and mix well. Sift flour with soda; add to creamed mixture. Stir in raisins and salted walnuts. Drop by teaspoonfuls onto a greased cookie sheet. Bake in a moderate oven (375° to 400°) 10 to 12 minutes. Yield: 70 to 80 cookies.

Ruby Scott Fouts, Woman's Club of Elizabethtown

PECAN QUICKIES

1 egg white	1 tbsp. flour
1 cup brown sugar	1 cup pecans, finely chopped
pinch of salt	

Beat egg white to a stiff froth. Gradually add sugar, salt, and flour. Fold in nuts. Drop from a teaspoon onto a greased cookie sheet, placing far apart. Bake at 300° for 15 minutes. Remove from cookie sheet when slightly cooled. Yield: 24 cookies.

Mrs. Betty Durrett, Woman's Club of Elizabethtown

PRALINE COOKIES

3 tbsp. butter	¼ cup flour
1 cup brown sugar	1 tsp. vanilla
1 egg, well beaten	1 cup pecan halves

Preheat oven to 350°. Grease a cookie sheet and coat well with flour or powdered sugar. Melt butter and stir in brown sugar. Add egg, flour, vanilla, and nuts. Drop from a teaspoon onto the cookie sheet, placing well apart. Bake 8 to 10 minutes. Let cool for a minute or two before removing from cookie sheet. Yield: 2½ dozen cookies.

Virginia Harris, Woman's Club of Elizabethtown

PERSIMMON COOKIES

2 cups sifted flour	1 cup sugar
1 tsp. soda	1 large egg
¼ tsp. salt	1 tsp. vanilla
1 tsp. cinnamon	1 cup persimmon pulp
½ tsp. nutmeg	1 cup raisins
½ cup butter	1 cup chopped nuts

Sift flour with soda, salt, and spices. Cream butter with sugar until light. Add egg and vanilla; blend well. Stir in persimmon pulp, sifted dry ingredients, raisins, and nuts. Blend thoroughly. Drop by spoonfuls onto a greased cookie sheet. Bake at 350° for 20 minutes. (Instead of making drop cookies you can spread the batter in 2 greased 8-inch square pans.) Yield: 3 to 4 dozen cookies.

Miss Lena Porter, Pikeville Woman's Club

ANIS COOKIES

3   large eggs
1   cup plus 2 tbsp. sugar

2   cups flour (about)
¼   tsp. anis oil

Beat eggs and sugar for 30 minutes. They will be very thick and creamy. Add 1½ cups sifted flour and oil. Add last ½ cup of flour a little at a time, stopping when batter is stiff enough to hold its shape. Drop from teaspoon onto a greased cookie sheet. Let stand at room temperature for several hours, preferably overnight. A crust will form on the tops of the cookies. Bake at 325° approximately 15 minutes. Bottoms should be golden. Store in a tightly covered container. Yield: 6 dozen cookies.

Mrs. Calvin Kummer, Covington Art Club

This recipe was brought to Kentucky in 1882 by Mrs. Kummer's grandparents, who had previously run a bake shop in Bern, Switzerland. These cookies are a Christmas tradition with them, and although many recipes have more ingredients, the Kummers find these four ingredients make a delicious and pleasing cookie.

ICEBOX COOKIES

1   cup butter
2   cups brown sugar
2   eggs, beaten
1   tsp. soda

4   cups flour
1   cup nuts or candied cherries
    (or both, mixed), chopped

Mix ingredients in order given, blending well after each addition. Shape into a roll and wrap in waxed paper. Chill for 24 hours. Slice very thin; place on an ungreased cookie sheet. Bake at 350° for 10 to 12 minutes. Yield: 4 dozen cookies.

Pam Hamilton, Cumberland County Woman's Club

ORANGE-PECAN REFRIGERATOR COOKIES

1 cup shortening	1 tbsp. grated orange rind
½ cup white sugar	2¾ cups flour
½ cup brown sugar	¼ tsp. soda
1 egg, well beaten	¼ tsp. salt
½ tsp. vanilla	½ cup pecans, chopped
2 tbsp. orange juice	

Cream shortening; add sugars, egg, vanilla, orange juice, and rind. Beat until well blended. Sift flour; measure and sift again with soda and salt. Add to creamed mixture. Stir in pecans. Shape into a roll about 1½ inches in diameter. Chill. Cut in thin slices, place on an ungreased cookie sheet, and bake at 350° for 10 minutes. Yield: 5 dozen cookies.

Mrs. W. B. Frazier, K.F.W.C. President, 1958–1960

ICEBOX FUDGE BAR

First layer:

½ cup butter
¼ cup sugar
5 tbsp. cocoa
1 tsp. vanilla
1 egg
2 cups graham cracker crumbs
1 cup coconut
½ cup chopped nuts

Second layer:

¼ cup butter
3 tbsp. milk
½ cup vanilla pudding mix
2 cups confectioners' sugar
4 sticks peppermint candy (optional)
mint flavoring (optional)

Third layer:

4 squares semisweet chocolate
1 tbsp. butter

For the first layer, combine butter, sugar, cocoa, vanilla, and egg in a bowl. Set over boiling water and mix well. Stir in crumbs, coconut, and nuts. When well mixed, pack into a 9-inch square pan.

For the second layer, cream butter and add milk and dry pudding mix. Blend in confectioners' sugar. Spread over first mixture. This layer may be varied by adding crushed peppermint candy and pink food color, or mint flavoring and green food color.

For the third layer, melt chocolate with butter. Spread quickly over second layer. Refrigerate until ready to serve, then cut into squares.

Mrs. Bill G. Sewell, Cumberland County Woman's Club

BROWNIES

2 oz. unsweetened chocolate	1 tsp. vanilla
⅓ cup shortening	¾ cup flour
1 cup plus 1 tbsp. brown	½ tsp. baking powder
sugar, firmly packed	½ tsp. salt
2 eggs, well beaten	½ cup chopped pecans

Melt chocolate and shortening over hot water. Blend in sugar and eggs. Add vanilla. Sift flour, baking powder, and salt together into chocolate mixture. Mix well but do not beat. Add pecans. Pour into a greased 8-inch square pan. Bake at 350° for 30 minutes. Cool and cut into squares.

Mrs. B. B. Stone, Stamping Ground Woman's Club

BROWN SUGAR BROWNIES

⅔ cup shortening	1 tsp. salt
2¼ cups brown sugar	1 cup walnuts or pecans,
3 eggs	coarsely chopped
2⅔ cups flour	1 6-oz. pkg. semisweet
2 tsp. baking powder	chocolate bits

Preheat oven at 350°. Grease and flour a 10- by 15-inch baking pan. Melt shortening in a saucepan; stir in brown sugar. Cool slightly, then beat in eggs, one at a time. Sift together flour, baking powder, and salt; stir into brown sugar mixture. Add nuts and chocolate bits. Pour into prepared pan. Bake 25 minutes. When almost cool cut into bars.

Mrs. W. K. Freeland, Woman's Club of Elizabethtown

Mrs. Gerald McKenney, Nicholasville Younger Woman's Club, adds 1 can Angel Flake coconut to the same recipe and calls them Congo Bars.

CARAMEL CAKES

1 lb. brown sugar	1 tsp. salt
½ cup butter	1½ tsp. vanilla
1 cup flour	4 eggs
1 tsp. baking powder	1 cup nuts, chopped

Cream sugar and butter; add flour, baking powder, and salt. Mix well. Add vanilla and eggs. Fold in nuts. Pour into a greased 13- by 9-inch pan and bake at 375° for 30 minutes. Cool and cut into squares.

Mrs. Mamie Haycraft, Mrs. Dorothy Ritz,
Brandenburg Woman's Civic Club

DATE SQUARES

¾ cup margarine	1½ cups quick-cooking oats
1 cup brown sugar	½ cup water
½ tsp. soda	½ cup sugar
1 tsp. vanilla	1 pkg. dates, chopped
1½ cups flour	

With a pastry blender mix margarine, brown sugar, soda, and vanilla. Add flour, then oats. Blend together until crumbly. Cook water, sugar, and dates until slightly thick. Pat half the crumbs in the bottom of an 8-inch square pan. Cover with date mixture. Sprinkle remaining crumbs on top; pat lightly. Bake at 375° for 30 minutes. While still warm cut into squares.

Julia R. O'Neal, Ghent Woman's Club

GINGERBREAD MEN

¼ cup butter	½ tsp. salt
½ cup sugar, brown or white	½ tsp. cloves
½ cup sorghum	½ tsp. cinnamon
3½ cups flour	1 tsp. ginger
1 tsp. soda	

Cream butter and sugar; beat in sorghum. Sift flour; add soda, salt, and spices; sift again. Add to creamed mixture, kneading when dough becomes too stiff to stir with a spoon. Grease a cookie sheet and roll dough directly onto it. With a floured cookie cutter, cut out men. Remove excess dough. Bake at 350° about 8 minutes or longer, according to thickness. Remove from pan at once and place on a wire rack. When cool, decorate with confectioners' sugar icing. Yield: about 6 gingerbread men.

Mrs. Martha Wells, Morgan County Woman's Club

ALMA'S MELTAWAYS

1 cup butter	*Frosting:*
½ cup confectioners' sugar	2 tbsp. butter
¾ cup cornstarch	1 cup confectioners' sugar
1 cup flour	1 tbsp. lemon extract

Cream butter with sifted dry ingredients. Chill for 1 hour. Shape into balls; place 1 inch apart on an ungreased baking sheet. Bake at 350° for 15 minutes. Combine frosting ingredients, mix well, and spread on cooled cookies. Yield: 4 dozen cookies.

Mrs. John Berry, Lexington Woman's Club

DATE FINGERS

1 8-oz. pkg. dates	1 cup nuts
½ cup margarine	½ cup coconut
1 cup brown sugar	confectioners' sugar
2 cups Rice Krispies	

Put dates, margarine, and brown sugar in a saucepan. Cook on medium heat until margarine is melted. Remove from heat. Fold in Rice Krispies, nuts, and coconut. Allow to cool. Form into fingers and roll in confectioners' sugar. Yield: 3 to 4 dozen cookies.

Mrs. Dyer Lockwood, Highland Woman's Club, Louisville

JUMBLES

1¼ cups lard	1 tsp. vanilla
2 cups sugar	5 cups flour
1 tsp. soda	1 tsp. baking powder
½ cup sour milk	1 tsp. nutmeg
3 eggs	

Cream lard and sugar. Dissolve soda in milk; add beaten eggs and vanilla. Stir into creamed mixture. Add flour that has been sifted with baking powder and nutmeg. Mix well. Chill overnight. Next day, divide dough for easier handling and roll half of it on a floured board to ⅛-inch thickness. Cut with a 2-inch or 2½-inch cookie cutter. Bake on an ungreased cookie sheet at 375° for 10 to 12 minutes.

To make filled cookies, cut a small hole in the center of half the cookies. Place 1 tbsp. filling (below) on an uncut cookie, cover with a cutout cookie, and press edges to seal.

Date filling:
1½ cups chopped dates
¾ cup sugar

¾ cup water
1½ heaping tsp. flour

Combine ingredients and bring to the boiling point; cover and simmer 5 minutes. Yield: 6 dozen plain or 3 dozen filled cookies.

Mrs. R. W. Ellington, Brooksville Town and Country Woman's Club

SPRINGERLE

Mrs. Cruse's grandmother, Margaret Zeitz, came to America on a sailing vessel in 1843 as a girl of fifteen. She had come to live with relatives and become an American citizen. Because there was little space on the ship, she was allowed to bring only six personal articles with her. One of these was a springerle board made by her father from the wood of a special tree that grew only in the Black Forest in Germany. Since the pictures on the board were carved by hand it was necessary to use the proper wood. With the mold she brought her springerle recipe, which has been passed down through the family. The mold, used for many years, remains in perfect condition and is one of Mrs. Cruse's cherished possessions.

4 large eggs
1 lb. confectioners' sugar
4 drops anise oil

1 tsp. baking powder
6 cups cake flour

Beat eggs in a large mixing bowl for 20 to 30 minutes. Do not cheat on time. Slowly mix in sugar. Add anise oil and baking powder. Work into this mixture small amounts of unsifted flour. You will have to use your hands to knead the dough when it becomes very stiff. Divide dough into portions; while working with one part cover remaining dough to prevent drying out. Roll dough on a floured board to about ½-inch thickness. Lay smooth dough on your springerle roller or mold. Press firmly with thumb or palm so as to get all details of pictures imprinted in the dough. Cut apart, put on trays, and set in a cool place overnight. Bake in a moderate oven, 325° to 350°, for 15 to 20 minutes. Springerle is best when made 4 to 6 weeks before using. Store cooled cookies in a covered container to ripen. Yield: 4 to 5 dozen cookies.

Mrs. W. C. Cruse, Jr., K.F.W.C. President, 1956–1958

CHRISTMAS LIZZIES

½ cup bourbon	½ cup margarine
3 cups seedless raisins	1 cup brown sugar, firmly
3 cups flour	packed
3 tsp. soda	4 eggs
3 tsp. cinnamon	1 lb. pecan halves
1 tsp. nutmeg	½ lb. citron, chopped
1 tsp. cloves	1 lb. candied cherries, whole

Pour bourbon over raisins; let stand for 1 hour. Sift together flour and spices; set aside. Cream margarine and brown sugar; add eggs, beating well. Blend in dry ingredients. Stir in raisins, pecans, citron, and cherries. Drop by spoonfuls onto a greased baking sheet. Bake at 325° for 15 minutes. Yield: 8 dozen cookies.

Mrs. James Robertson, Blue Grass Junior Woman's Club

TEA CAKES

2 cups sugar	3½ tsp. ammonium carbonate
¾ cup butter	flour
6 eggs	

Cream butter and sugar well. Add eggs, 3 at a time, beating well after each addition. Dissolve the ammonium carbonate in a small amount of boiling water. Add it and enough flour to make a soft dough. Roll as thin as possible. Cut, place on a cookie sheet, and sprinkle with sugar. Bake at 400° until lightly browned. These cookies will keep indefinitely in a tightly covered container.

Mrs. Elizabeth Nickell, Georgetown Woman's Club

[*Note:* Ammonium carbonate was a leavening agent available 75 years ago. It is no longer sold.]

TEA CAKES

2½ cups flour	½ cup butter
¼ tsp. salt	2 eggs, beaten
2 tsp. baking powder	3 tbsp. milk
1 cup sugar	¼ tsp. vanilla or lemon extract

Sift together flour, salt, baking powder, and sugar. Add butter and beaten eggs. Mix well. Add milk and flavoring. Turn onto a floured board. Roll thin, cut, and place on an ungreased cookie sheet. Sprinkle with sugar. Bake at 400° for 10 to 12 minutes or until lightly browned. Yield: 4 dozen cookies.

Mrs. Orman Cannon, Eddyville Woman's Club

In Mrs. Cannon's mother's kitchen, flour was kept in a barrel that was covered by a wooden board. When making tea cakes she sifted the dry ingredients onto the board, made a hollow in the center, poured in the other ingredients, mixed the dough and rolled it, with all the work being done on the board.

A similar recipe was sent by Mrs. Katie Bodkin, Bardwell Woman's Club, who doubles all the ingredients except the eggs and uses ½ tsp. soda instead of baking powder.

SUGAR COOKIES

½ cup butter	1 tsp. soda
1 cup sugar	2 tsp. cream of tartar
2½ cups flour	⅔ cup milk

Cream butter and sugar. Sift together flour, soda, and cream of tartar. Add to creamed mixture alternately with milk. Roll ⅛-inch thick; cut into desired shapes. Sprinkle with sugar, place on a greased cookie sheet, and bake at 400° for 6 minutes. Yield: 4 dozen cookies.

Mrs. John Acree, Stringtown Woman's Club

MARGUERITES

1 cup sugar	¼ tsp. vanilla
½ cup water	½ cup English walnuts,
5 marshmallows, diced	finely chopped
2 egg whites	24 saltines
2 tbsp. shredded coconut	

Boil sugar and water until syrup will spin a thread (232°); remove from heat. Add marshmallows and stir until melted. Beat egg whites until stiff; continue beating while gradually adding hot syrup. Stir in coconut, vanilla, and nuts. Spread on crackers and bake in a hot oven until delicate brown.

Mrs. Walter Quinn, Woman's Club of Henderson

Preserving Foods

Kentucky's pioneer women were expert in devising methods for preserving foods. They had to be, for their families' survival depended on a plentiful supply of food to see them through the winter months when gardens were dormant and even wild game was often unavailable. They accepted as their responsibility the role of keeping the table amply supplied. Even today many women proudly tell of using the foods "put up" three or more years earlier, and boast that they "haven't used one jar canned in the last three years." They are keenly aware that there have been, through the ages, "seven years of plenty and seven years of famine." They feel the need for canning all the blackberries, for example, because "Next year there might not be a good crop," or even "Next year is locust year and of course we won't be able to use the berries then." Such statements are widespread and are carefully adhered to in planning for home food preservation in some areas of Kentucky.

The Indians called Kentucky "the happy hunting ground." Great numbers of wild animals roamed the area, partly drawn by the presence of numerous salt licks. By trailing animals which were instinctively guided to the source of this health-giving mineral, the early explorers discovered many of these salt licks. To the pioneer settlers, salt was vitally important for preserving food for winter. Meat and game were salted and cured for use during the period when wild animals were in hibernation. Freshly killed meat must be thoroughly cooled. Often the carcass was cut into "sides" or halves, spread on tables or wooden horses, or hung. When thoroughly cooled, the sides were cut into pieces for convenient handling, then covered with salt, and packed into large boxes or troughs "to take the salt." The length of time required for salting depended upon the size and thickness of the meat and the weather during this period. Meat took the salt slowly if frozen, so freezing weather was avoided if possible. After salting, the meat was hung to dry. It was at this time that smoking was done. Smoking not only added flavor but also helped to cure and dry the surface of the meat.

Salt was also indispensable in making the winter supply of sauerkraut. Nutritionists credit sauerkraut as the major source of Vitamin C for the pioneer settlers. Cabbage would be finely shredded, mixed with coarse salt, and pounded with a wooden pestle in a large barrel or crock until juice rose to cover the cabbage. Lactic acid fermentation began within a few days. The scum was skimmed from the brine daily until fermentation was completed. The time required for this process depended upon the weather and the size of the container. Sauerkraut was usually made in the late fall when nights were becoming cool, so it was desirable to have a good supply of fall cabbage.

Salt was also an essential ingredient in pickling. Many vegetables, including green beans, corn, beets, and especially cucumbers, were pickled. Wild fruits and berries provided the juices which were fermented into vinegar for pickling. Apples and wild crab apples were the favorite fruits for vinegar but other fruit and berry juices were also used. Pickles were much prized for the variety of flavor they could contribute to the somewhat limited diet of the winter months. Brining and pickling made it possible to preserve more mature vegetables than could otherwise be preserved with the facilities available at that time.

Drying was another widely used method of preserving foods, particularly vegetables and fruits. Peas, butter beans, pole beans, bunch beans, black-eyed peas, and corn, could be used as dried seeds. The pods were allowed to dry and then were shelled. Ears of corn were shelled after the shucks had dried. The prudent housewife carefully put aside those dried seeds needed for the next year's planting before she counted on the remaining seed for winter food. Green beans were strung on slender canes or string (if it was available) and allowed to air dry. Such beans were known as "shucky beans" or "leather britches." They required long soaking and then long slow cooking. This could easily be done by cooking in a Dutch oven in the coals of the big fireplace, or in a pot hung on a crane over the open fire.

Dried corn was made into whole grain hominy by soaking it in lye which was made from the wood ashes. Care was taken to soak only until the hard hull could be removed. Lye was also an essential ingredient of soap, which was made from the fats saved in cooking meats. A fat 'possum or racoon was valued for its "soap fat" as well as for its meat.

Pumpkins and squash could be kept for many weeks by covering them with corn fodder in the corn shocks. But to be sure of having pumpkin and squash for pies in late winter, it was wise to dry some. This was done by cutting the squash or pumpkin into narrow bands or belts, hanging these over poles for sun drying in the late fall, and then hanging them over the rafters of the kitchen, where the heat from the open fire would complete the drying process.

Fruits, especially apples and crab apples, were dried for sauce, for fried apple pies, and for stack cakes and pies. Drying was usually accomplished by spreading a single layer of the sliced fruits on a cloth exposed to full sunshine throughout the day. In the late afternoon, before the evening dew, the corners of the cloth were brought together to form a bag and the fruit was carried into the house. Next morning after the dew evaporated, the fruit was again taken outside and spread in a single layer to dry. It was not long before someone discovered that sulfur could be secured by evaporating the water from the many sulfur springs in the area. Exposing fruit which was to be dried to the fumes of burning sulfur not only tended to repell insects but also helped to retain the original color of the fresh fruit. Soon, too, it was discovered that apples exposed to sulfur fumes and stored in crocks or earthern jars would keep for many weeks without drying and without losing the bright color which enhanced their appeal. Cooks quickly learned that cooking sulfured apples in an uncovered vessel would permit the sulfur flavor to dissipate in steam. To complete the cooking process, the lid would be replaced on the pot.

Ingenious methods were developed for the safe sulfuring of fruit. Probably the most frequent method was to stretch a loosely woven cloth over the top of a large barrel from which both ends had been removed. This barrel was placed on rocks which held it a few inches above the ground. The sulfur, wrapped in paper or cloth, was burned on the ground and the fumes would rise to penetrate the sliced fruit suspended above. Various lids were devised to cover the top of the barrel. Sometimes a wooden top was made to slip over all, or a metal tub might be the cover. Many people made a loosely woven basket of thinly split green wood with a handle that could be placed on a pole across the barrel or box to let the fruit come nearer the sulfur fumes. Others made wooden racks, stretching the cloth over them. Several racks could be sulfured at the same time by stacking them. A large box was constructed to fit over all and keep in the fumes.

Instead of being dried, late pears and apples were sometimes stored in a root cellar, dug in the hillside, which also held potatoes, carrots, turnips, winter squash, and pumpkins.

After becoming well established on the frontier, a family frequently built three structures which helped in preserving the family food supply: a springhouse, an icehouse, and a smokehouse.

The springhouse, often constructed in a hillside beside a spring, provided a storage place to keep dairy products cool and fresh, to chill watermelons for Sunday afternoon feasts, and to store pickled fruits and preserves for winter.

The icehouse was somewhat later in construction than the springhouse. After ice became four to six inches thick on ponds and lakes, it was harvested in large blocks, put into the pit of the icehouse, and carefully covered with a heavy layer of straw to insulate it from the summer heat. The ice was used for kitchen iceboxes and to make ice cream, which was featured at church and community socials, as well as at home, throughout the summer. Mild winters caused understandable concern. Several records report that "ice didn't freeze for filling the icehouse until early in March. Families had almost despaired of putting up ice." The icehouse also provided extra storage space for thorough cooling of pails of fresh milk and buttermilk. This involved a hazard, however. Often the lids of the milk pails were inadvertently pierced by the pitchfork prongs as the straw was probed to locate the ice blocks and the milk buckets!

Springhouses and icehouses are seldom functional today, replaced by electric refrigeration. Only the smokehouse survives, and even that is little used today compared with yesteryear. Before freezer-locker plants and "deep freeze" equipment made it possible to preserve fresh meats, most people smoked and cured their bacon, pork shoulders, and of course hams. Sometimes the tenderloin strip was also smoked and cured for later consumption rather than immediate enjoyment. In recent years the curing of pork has been restricted almost entirely to hams, and this has evolved into a very specialized industry. Kentucky-cured hams are famous for their hickory-smoked flavor. Smoking requires special skill to achieve the unique flavor and color in the ham, and many Kentucky men are indefatigable in their efforts to perfect this skill. In recent years competition has been encouraged through the Kentucky Ham Breakfast at the state fair. The honor of producing the champion cured ham may yet become as great as the honor of owning the winner of the Kentucky Derby!

In the mid-nineteenth century, county fairs developed into big agricultural and social institutions in which all members of the family participated. The rivalry within a community or county to exhibit prize-winning farm products stimulated variety as well as excellence in home-produced foods, the goal being the largest and most nearly perfect product of the garden or field.

With the increase in the varieties of home-produced vegetables and fruits, new ways of pickling and preserving developed. Recipes for apple butter, marmalades, jams, chili sauces, and pickled vegetables burgeoned and were shared with relatives and friends. The use of glass jars was a great stimulus to this county fair competition. To be able to see the product resulted in fancy packs, use of artificial colors, combinations of foods, and much experimentation in food preservation.

The glass jar was patented in 1858, although the person who developed the "glass bottle" and wrote the first treatise on *Food Preservation in the Glass Bottle* was not the individual who patented the glass jar. In 1795, when Napoleon Bonaparte was waging his war of conquest for all of Europe, he bemoaned the fact that his soldiers were dying from lack of adequate food while on the march. He offered a reward of 12,000 francs to anyone who could devise a way to provide fresh food to his armies. A little confection shop owner, Nicolas Appert, immediately began research in an effort to win the reward. He developed a wide-mouth glass bottle into which he could put large pieces of food, and cork covers which excluded the air. Then, through much trial and error, he established the length of time the foods must be cooked in the bottles. At last in 1810 he was awarded the prize.

It is interesting to note that food preservation by canning began in an effort to feed an army of conquest. Succeeding wars have stimulated research in dehydration and freeze-drying, methods of preservation which greatly reduce the shipping weights of food and make possible preservation without refrigeration, desirable factors in providing rations for armies stationed around the earth and on the seas.

Canning in tin came along not long after the glass bottle. An Englishman about 1805 had a tinsmith fashion a tin cannister after the English tea cannister. This container was introduced into America by the Underwood Canning Company when they began canning oysters in tin in 1820. The name of the container was shortened to "can" by the accountant of that company, according to legend. During the Civil War the urgent need for food in army camps stimulated the commercial canning industry.

After the Civil War the Cooperative Extension Service of the Department of Agriculture was one of the agencies that helped accelerate and improve the home canning of foods. In 1913, Farmers Bulletin 521 was printed, an event that marked the entry of youth clubs into a community program of home canning. The products of the youth clubs were, and still are, featured in county and state fairs.

Canning has progressed from the open-kettle method to the water-bath method, in which food is cooked and sealed in the can or jar, and more recently to the processing of low-acid foods in pressure canners at a temperature much higher than that of boiling water. Each new method has made home-canned foods safer and more palatable.

Progress in temperature control has been an important factor in improving food preservation. This progress is well illustrated by the evolution from iceboxes to refrigerators to refrigerator-freezer combinations. During the decades from 1830 to 1910 little change occurred in the icebox with the drip-pan that had to be emptied daily. Early catalogs picture iceboxes of different sizes and with slight variations in the materials used for lining the food storage compartment and for shelving. For the most part, this lining and shelving material was wood, which absorbed moisture and food odors as well as retaining its natural wood odor.

The Sears Roebuck and Company Catalogue for fall 1900 pictures seven models of their "Michigan Ash Refrigerators." The models were available in different sizes with ice capacities varying from 34 to 100 pounds. One model had a porcelain-lined water cooler and faucet, and the catalog indicated that this feature reduced the 100-pound ice capacity to 47 pounds. One notation of special interest states: "We do not have any condensation on exposed metal plates, but carry the air directly to the ice, which is the greatest purifier known to modern science!" The insulation used was charcoal sheathing, which is odorless and tasteless and a perfect nonconductor, according to the ads. Some iceboxes of that period had porcelain and galvanized zinc linings and some had slate shelves, although this type of shelf was not a predominant feature.

By 1910 refrigerators cooled by electricity and capable of freezing ice were in general use in areas where electricity was available. Shortly thereafter, oil-burning refrigerators were introduced in rural areas. In the latter, the refrigerant was controlled by oil burners which were periodically ignited, usually at twenty-four-hour intervals. During the late 1930s the development of the Tennessee Valley Authority and the rural electric cooperatives brought electricity to fairly remote areas, and the oil-burning refrigerators were replaced by electric refrigerators and refrigerator-freezer combinations. The "deep freeze" now became the miracle piece of equipment in many homes. Some homes boasted two freezers, one reserved solely for corn-on-the-cob!

Strawberry shortcake in January soon became commonplace. Freezers permitted families to convert a fruit that had been available in fresh form for only a few weeks into a year-round luxury. The ease with which vegetables, fruits, and meats could be frozen greatly stimulated family production and preservation of food. Freezing replaced canning and drying of many products, especially berries and meats, though some families continued to can beans, tomatoes, and peaches in preference to freezing them.

The change within four or five generations from whole-grain lye hominy to a freezer filled with corn-on-the-cob evidences the remarkable progress that has occurred in the preservation of home-produced food.

World War I created tremendous interest in home-grown and home-canned foods, as did the Great Depression of the 1930s. World War II, with its "victory garden" slogans, continued to encourage families to produce and preserve much of their own food. During the last decade the ecology movement, the energy crisis, the inflated economy, and the resulting need to stretch the food dollar have contributed to a revival of interest in older methods of food production and preservation.

Two hundred years ago Kentucky pioneers could secure wild game, fish, nuts, fruits, and herbs by hunting or merely by finding and gathering. Today, although lakes and streams continue to supply fish, and wild blackberry bushes still supply berries for jams, cakes, and even an occasional batch of blackberry "shrub," most Kentuckians don't have to produce their own food. They can easily satisfy their food needs at the supermarkets now readily available to almost every family in the Commonwealth. In a comparatively short time span we have observed incredible changes in methods of food production, marketing, storage, and cooking. Yet many Kentuckians continue to enjoy and take pride in producing at least some of their own foods and in preserving them for use during the months when fresh local produce is unavailable. They find that home-preserved fruits and vegetables, pickles, jams, and jellies have a special flavor not found in commercial products.

Throughout the continual changes of the past two hundred years, Kentucky men and women have shown their resourcefulness and adaptability to new situations, new equipment, and new methods. Nevertheless, the spirit of hospitable friendly exchange still flourishes. Family reunions and community festivals continue to offer occasions for sharing recipes and homemade products created either by time-honored methods or by newer methods more attuned to today's fast-paced life.

"We'll take a jar of the new pickles to Cousin Jane. Be sure to copy the recipe for her. She'll want it, I know." "We'll make a jam cake but use the spice cake mix instead of making it from scratch. I wonder if anyone will recognize the difference?" Such comments illustrate the spirit which has prevailed throughout our history. They also suggest that Kentuckians are willing and eager to accept the innovation of convenience foods, prepared mixes, and the many canned, frozen, and dehydrated products so easily accessible, and are adapting them to their individual family life-styles. Having weathered a two-hundred-year continuum of change, the salt of the "happy hunting ground," Kentucky hospitality, has not lost its well-famed savor.

Elizabeth Helton

PEAR HONEY

4 cups pears   3 cups sugar
3 cups crushed pineapple

Wash, peel, and grate the pears. Add pineapple and sugar. Cook over medium heat about 1 hour, stirring frequently. When mixture is the desired thickness, remove from heat and pour into sterilized jars. When cool, cover with paraffin.

Mrs. William Major, Woman's Club of Madisonville

APPLE BUTTER

The Johnson County Apple Festival began in 1963 as a one-day event. Now it is difficult to crowd all the activities into the three days that comprise the festival on the first weekend in October. The booths that line the streets of Paintsville sell apple products and other things. Bushels of apples are auctioned on the courthouse steps. Visitors come from all around to see the parade, the Apple King, Queen, Prince, Princess, and Baby, and Miss Apple Blossom. An Apple Bake-Off contest brings a prize to the winner and provides some of the best recipes for apple dishes that you will find anywhere.

One of the high spots is always the apple butter cooked on the street in copper-lined kettles, by the following recipe:

7 bushels Rome Beauty or	100 lb. sugar
Grimes Golden apples	liquid cinnamon to taste
2 gal. water	

Wash, peel, core, and slice the apples. Keep them in airtight bags until ready to cook. Wash a 30-gallon copper kettle with salt and vinegar just before using. Put the kettle over a rousing open wood fire and add 1 gallon of water and 4 gallons of apples. Cook until apples are soft, stirring constantly with a long handled wooden paddle. Add more apples and water until all have been used. When the apples are mushy, begin adding sugar, ten pounds at a time, stirring constantly. The cooking time will be 8 to 10 hours or until the apple butter thickens and turns dark red. Add liquid cinnamon and stir well just before pouring into sterilized jars. Seal at once.

Mrs. William D. Blair, Paintsville Woman's Club

ORANGE MARMALADE

4 oranges	3 qt. water
2 lemons	4 lb. sugar

Slice oranges and lemons, removing seeds. Put pulp and peel through a food chopper, using the coarse blade. Cover with the water and let stand 24 hours. Next day, bring to a boil and allow to simmer 1 hour. Just before removing from the stove stir in sugar. Let stand another 24 hours, then return to the stove and boil slowly until thick. Pour into small sterilized jars and cover with paraffin.

Mrs. William G. Woods, Jessamine Woman's Club

APRICOT MARMALADE

1 lb. dried apricots   1 20-oz. can crushed pineapple
1 qt. water   1 lemon
4 lb. sugar

Wash apricots, add water, and soak overnight. Next morning remove apricots. To water in which apricots were soaked add sugar, and juice drained from pineapple. Bring to a boil. Grind apricots and lemon and add to syrup, along with pineapple. Cook until thick, about 30 minutes. Pour into hot sterilized jars. Cool and cover with paraffin.

Mrs. J. K. Johnson, Midway Woman's Club

STRAWBERRY PRESERVES

1   qt. strawberries   3½ cups sugar
boiling water   1   tbsp. vinegar

Cap strawberries and wash them, taking care not to leave them in the water. Cover with boiling water. Let stand a few minutes; drain well. Add 1½ cups sugar and bring to a boil. When boiling rapidly add remaining sugar and vinegar. Boil rapidly 20 minutes. Remove from heat. Set aside until the next day, stirring frequently. Pack in hot sterilized jars. Cover with paraffin and seal. Do not try to make a larger quantity at a time.

Mrs. Mabel Hay, Clinton County Woman's Club

TOMATO PRESERVES

5 lb. firm ripe tomatoes   1 orange, thinly sliced
8 cups sugar   1 lemon, thinly sliced

Peel and quarter tomatoes, cover with sugar, and allow to stand overnight. Drain off syrup; heat to the boiling point and cook until the syrup will spin a long thread (232°). Add tomatoes and orange and lemon slices. Cook over low heat until tomatoes are transparent. Seal in hot sterilized jars. Makes 12 6-oz. glasses.

Mrs. Robert Haggerty, Maysville Woman's Club

BRANDIED PEACHES

9 lb. peaches

9 lb. sugar

1 qt. water

2 sticks cinnamon

2 tbsp. whole cloves with heads removed

3 cups brandy

Select ripe cling peaches. Peel and weigh them. Boil together sugar and water, with the spices tied in a bag, until clear. Drop whole peaches, a few at a time, into boiling syrup. Cook until tender but not soft. Place fruit on a platter to cool and drain. Repeat until all are cooked. Measure out 3 cups of the syrup and allow to cool. Add to it 3 cups brandy. Put the fruit in a stoneware crock or in sterilized jars. Pour brandied syrup over peaches and seal. Peaches done in the summer will be ready for use at Thanksgiving.

Mrs. Scott W. Moore, Glasgow Woman's Club

The syrup left after the peaches have been eaten may be used to glaze hams, mixed with mayonnaise for a sweet salad dressing, added to mincemeat pie filling, or served as a sauce.

PEACH PICKLES

6 lb. cling peaches

whole cloves

4 lb. sugar

1 pt. vinegar

stick cinnamon

Peel peaches and stick 2 or 3 cloves in each. Make a syrup of sugar, vinegar, and stick cinnamon by boiling together a few minutes. Cook peaches in syrup until tender. Put in a large jar or crock and leave overnight. On each of the next three days, pour the syrup into a pan and bring it to a boil. Pour back over peaches. On the third day put the peaches in sterilized jars, cover with syrup, and seal.

Mrs. Ralph Tessineer, Florence Woman's Club

ICE CUBE PICKLES

1 gal. cucumbers	*Pickling syrup:*
8 small onions	5 cups sugar
2 green peppers	5 cups vinegar
½ cup salt	1½ tsp. turmeric
1 qt. ice cubes	½ tsp. ground cloves
	1 tsp. celery seed
	2 tbsp. mustard seed

Wash cucumbers but do not peel; slice crosswise. Peel and slice onions. Wash, seed, and cut peppers into small pieces. Put vegetables in a glass or enamel container; add salt and ice cubes. Refrigerate at least 3 hours; drain thoroughly. In a kettle combine ingredients for the pickling syrup. Add vegetables and heat to the boiling point but do not boil. Pack into hot sterilized jars and seal at once.

Mrs. J. Chester Porter, Woman's Club of Elizabethtown

GREEN TOMATO PICKLES

1 peck (8 qt.) green tomatoes	¾ cup salt
12 medium onions	2 qt. vinegar
2 heads cauliflower	4 cups sugar
3 green peppers	⅔ cup pickling spices
1 bunch celery	

Wash and slice tomatoes; peel and slice onions. Separate cauliflower into small flowerets. Remove seeds from green peppers, and chop. Wash and dice celery. In a large kettle place vegetables in layers, sprinkling salt on each layer. Let stand overnight. Next morning drain. Add 1 quart of the vinegar and 2 quarts of water. Bring to a boil and cook 15 minutes. Drain again. Make a syrup by boiling together the remaining quart of vinegar, the sugar, and the spices tied in a cheesecloth bag. Boil syrup 15 minutes, then add vegetables. Bring to a boil again and pour immediately into hot sterilized jars.

Mrs. Raymond Stone, Woman's Club of Greenville

Mrs. Stone's mother, Mrs. W. O. Milliken, Kuttawa, won first prize with this recipe in a *Courier-Journal* pickling contest in 1940.

LIME PICKLES

8 lb. cucumbers

2 cups lime

2 gal. water

2 qt. vinegar

9 cups sugar

1 tsp. salt

2 tbsp. pickling spices

Wash and slice cucumbers; put them in a solution made by mixing lime and water. Soak for 24 hours. Drain and rinse well with cold water. Place in fresh cold water and leave from 3 to 12 hours. Rinse again. Put cucumbers in a large kettle. Add vinegar, sugar, salt, and spices (in a tea-ball or cheesecloth bag). Bring to a boil and simmer 30 minutes. Pack in hot sterilized jars and seal.

Mrs. Shelley Caulder, Buechel Woman's Club

CANDIED DILL PICKLES

½ gal. commercially packed
    dill pickles

1 box pickling spices

3⅜ cups sugar

¼ cup tarragon vinegar

Drain pickles and slice thickly or cut into chunks. Place in ice water for 30 minutes. Drain well. Tie spices in a cheesecloth bag. Layer pickles and sugar in the jar, with the spice bag as near the center as possible. Pour vinegar over the pickles. Seal tightly and turn the jar upside down several times to dissolve the sugar. Refrigerate at least 3 days before using. Remove spice bag when vinegar begins to darken.

Mrs. Mark Sharff, Lexington Woman's Club

GRANNY'S PICKLES

Slice small-to-medium cucumbers and cover with 1 gallon of boiling water to which 1 cup of pickling (coarse) salt has been added. Place a saucer or plate over the cucumbers in the brine to hold the slices under. Let remain overnight. The next day drain and rinse. Heat to boiling equal parts of vinegar and sugar. After washing and draining the slices, put them in the boiling vinegar-sugar solution. Add only enough slices to fill the size jar you are using. Allow them to come back to a boil but do not let them cook. Immediately pack them in hot sterilized jars. Cover with vinegar-sugar solution and seal.

Mrs. Earle Combs, Woman's Club of Richmond

GRANNY'S CORN RELISH

12	ears sweet white corn	1	bunch celery
6	green peppers	2	lb. sugar
4	sweet red peppers	1	qt. vinegar
2	hot red peppers	4½	tsp. salt
6	cucumbers	1	tbsp. white mustard seed
6	onions	1	tbsp. celery seed

Wash vegetables thoroughly. Cut corn from the cob. Cut peppers in half; remove seeds and white membranes. Peel cucumbers and onions. Remove celery tops. Coarsely grind all vegetables except corn. Combine sugar, vinegar, salt, mustard seed, and celery seed in a large kettle; add vegetables. Place over medium heat, bring to a boil, and cook slowly for 20 minutes, stirring frequently. Pack in hot sterilized jars. Seal immediately.

Mrs. H. E. Raymond, Beechmont Woman's Club

PEPPER RELISH

6	green peppers	1½	cups vinegar
6	sweet red peppers	1	cup brown sugar
6	onions	1½	tsp. salt

Chop peppers and onions coarsely. Mix vinegar with sugar and salt; add vegetables. Bring to a boil and cook 20 minutes. Seal in hot sterilized jars.

Mrs. Luther Ambrose, Berea Woman's Club

AUNT NAN'S CHILI SAUCE

1	peck (8 qt.) tomatoes	3	scant tbsp. salt
6	medium onions	2	cups brown sugar
1	heaping tsp. whole cloves	1¾	cups vinegar
5	sticks cinnamon, broken	¼	cup water
1	small red pepper		

Wash, peel, and dice tomatoes. Peel and chop onions. Tie cloves, cinnamon, and red pepper in a muslin bag. Combine all ingredients and cook slowly about 3 hours, stirring occasionally as it thickens. Remove spice bag. Pour into sterilized jars and seal.

Mrs. Charles Parks, Carlisle Junior Woman's Club

CHILI SAUCE

1 gal. tomatoes	3 medium red mangoes,
1½ cups vinegar	chopped
2 cups white sugar	3 medium green mangoes,
1 cup brown sugar	chopped
3 tbsp. coarse salt	1 tbsp. whole allspice
2 cups chopped onions	1 tbsp. whole cloves
	1 stick cinnamon

Scald and peel tomatoes, cut in quarters, and measure a heaping gallon. Cook 1 hour. Add vinegar, sugars, salt, onions, and mangoes. Tie spices in a cheesecloth bag, add bag to pan, and cook all ingredients until thick. Pour into sterilized jars and seal while boiling hot. Makes 7 pints.

Mrs. R. L. Mullins, Williamstown Woman's Club

RIPE TOMATO CATSUP

½ bushel ripe tomatoes	1 tbsp. black pepper
10 large onions	1 tbsp. ground allspice
10 sweet red peppers	1 tbsp. salt
2 cups sugar	1 tbsp. chili powder
2 cups cider vinegar	1 pod red pepper or 1 tsp.
1 tbsp. ground cinnamon	cayenne
1 tbsp. ground cloves	

Chop tomatoes, onions, and peppers. Cook until thick; put through a colander. Measure 5 pints of the pulp. Add remaining ingredients, bring to a boil, reduce heat, and simmer until thick, stirring occasionally. Put into sterilized bottles or jars and seal immediately.

Mrs. James N. Farris, Bullitt County Woman's Club

TO PICKLE WHITE WALNUTS

Pare them, until the white appears, then simmer for ten minutes in salted water, drain, and put them into the bottles with a little mace and sliced nutmeg; lastly, pour on the vinegar (hot) and cork immediately. Use soft young walnuts before the shell has begun to set.

Mrs. Richard McClure, Crescent Hill Woman's Club

ARNOLD FAMILY "RECT" FOR CURING BEEF

Cut up quarters of beef. To each hundred weight take—
½ peck coarse salt
¼ lb. saltpetre

¼ lb. saleratus [bicarbonate of soda]
1 qt. molasses or 2 lb. brown sugar

Sprinkle some of the coarse salt in the bottom of a wooden barrel. Put in a layer of beef, a layer of salt, until all the beef and salt are used. Let stand overnight. Next day dissolve the saleratus and saltpetre in a little warm water, add to the molasses or brown sugar, and pour over the meat. Add enough water to cover the meat. Lay a weighted board on top to keep the meat under the brine. The meat will be ready to use in 10 days.

Mrs. Harold Gaines, Maysville Woman's Club

SHUCKY BEANS

Before glass jars were available in abundance, the resourceful housewife having to preserve her excess green beans for winter eating would dry them. The beans were strung and broken in the same manner as for cooking, then spread thinly on a sheet and placed in the sun. Each day before the dew fell the sheet was brought in, then taken back out each morning after the sun rose. It usually took from 7 to 10 days to dry them properly. After they were thoroughly dried they were placed in covered containers and stored in the cellar.

Mrs. Oscar C. Sowards, K.F.W.C. President, 1968–1970

To cook shucky beans, see page 148.

CANNED GREEN BEANS

½ gal. fresh green beans
½ cup vinegar
1 tbsp. salt

2 tbsp. sugar
1 qt. water

Prepare beans as for table use, either whole or broken. Mix remaining ingredients in a large pan and heat. Add beans and boil for 20 minutes. Place in sterilized jars and seal. Before using, pour off liquid and put beans in fresh water. Season with a piece of bacon or ham bone. Boil until tender, about 20 minutes.

Mrs. Homer Bryant, Sr., Pleasure Ridge Woman's Club, Louisville

Illustrations

Contributors

JAY ANDERSON is director of the Colonial Pennsylvania Plantation. He is a well-known authority on American foodways.

R. GERALD ALVEY is professor of folklore at the University of Kentucky and a specialist in Appalachian folk culture.

OTIS K. RICE is chairman of the History Department and the Division of Humanities at West Virginia Institute of Technology. His most recent book is *Frontier Kentucky*.

MARCIA CEBULSKA has taught a course in folk food traditions at Indiana University. She has studied the foodways of South America and Europe as well as the United States.

MARY McCLINTON CLAY is the field representative in Kentucky for the Museum of Early Southern Decorative Arts, Old Salem, Winston-Salem, North Carolina.

ELIZABETH C. KREMER is food director at Shakertown at Pleasant Hill. A graduate of the University of Kentucky, she has also managed restaurants in New York, Louisville, and Cincinnati.

BURTON MILWARD is a former editor of the *Lexington Leader* and author of numerous articles and several books on Kentucky history. He is now assistant editor of the Henry Clay Papers.

MARIE CAMPBELL is emeritus professor of English at the University of Massachusetts. She is best known for her many books on regional folk cultures, especially those of Kentucky.

SHIRLEY SNARR is associate professor of nutrition at Eastern Kentucky University. She has traveled widely in Europe and the Far East and has maintained a lifelong interest in regional foods.

ELIZABETH HELTON retired in 1974 as state specialist in foods and nutrition with the Cooperative Extension Service of the University of Kentucky. She has conducted many workshops on food preservation in the state.

DOROTHEA C. COOPER is a member of the Kentucky Federation of Women's Clubs and a collector of cookbooks which are more often read than used. Editing this book for the Federation was a challenge that she could not resist.

MIRIAM WOOLFOLK, a member of the Kentucky Federation of Women's Clubs and past president of the Lexington Art League, has had works selected for both Kentucky's and the nation's Bicentennial exhibitions.

Index of Recipes

Among the most interesting features of old cookbooks were the household hints—recipes for everything from laundry soap to hand lotion to mustard plasters. We regret that space did not permit us to include several such items that were submitted. We wish to thank the following women, who contributed them: Mrs. R. L. Blevins, Covington Art Club; Mrs. John W. Eaves, Greenville Woman's Club; Mrs. Leon Gresham, Eddyville Woman's Club; Mrs. A. M. Howell, Somerset Literary Club; Ms. Mildred C. Moore, Brooksville Town and Country Club; Mrs. Ella Nunn, Clinton County Woman's Club; and Mrs. William Peniston, Danville Woman's Club.